Big Skies & Bygone Days

Wild Tales from Powder River Country

Shane Dunning

ISBN 978-1-59152-329-1

Design by Steph Lehmann

Cover, top left: Walter Shirlaw's sketch "Nearing the End."
ORIGINALLY PUBLISHED IN *THE CENTURY MAGAZINE*, VOLUME XLVII, NO. 6 (NOVEMBER 1893). PUBLIC DOMAIN.

Cover, bottom left (and title page): "Fort Howes Defenders."
PHOTOGRAPH COURTESY OF THE AMERICAN HERITAGE CENTER, LEVI S. HOWES PAPERS, COLLECTION 4430, BOX 1

Cover, bottom right: Grant Dunning, his cowboys, the Moncreiffe Brothers, and horses intended for use by the British Empire in the Boer War at Bovino, February/March 1902.
PHOTOGRAPH COURTESY OF THE CHARLIE DUNNING FAMILY.

For more information or to order extra copies of this book call
Farcountry Press toll free at (800) 821-3874 or visit www.farcountrypress.com

sweetgrassbooks
an imprint of Farcountry Press

Produced by Sweetgrass Books
PO Box 5630, Helena, MT 59604; (800) 821-3874; www.sweetgrassbooks.com

Produced and printed in the United States of America.

29 28 27 26 25 2 3 4 5 6

CONTENTS

Introduction

This is meant to be a casual history book, if such a thing exists. While I address some serious topics and apply appropriate standards, this book is not the product of a single intellectual endeavor. This is a collection of mostly short newspaper columns from the *Powder River Examiner* in Broadus, Montana.

Here's the thing about local history columns in small-town rags: they are less formal than academic history journals or university press books. Happily, this lack of formality allows me to communicate history to a (mostly) working-class audience that appreciates the local nature of what I'm writing about. In the *PRE,* I'm allowed to explore more entertaining subjects, where the sourcing is less than rigorous, so long as it's under 1,500 words. There is limited citing of sources, no footnotes, and no peer review. If I adequately inform my audience about any reliability issues and make no sweeping, unsupported conclusions, I feel I can discuss topics that would otherwise only be discussed across a barroom table, never to be recorded. But this is also why so much local history is lost. Stories heard are not written down, and after a few generations, they are forgotten or so distorted they are of no use to the historical record.

Included in this collection are a few items that meet a higher standard. Two and a half articles from *Montana, the Magazine of Western History* take their place in this tome with the kind permission of its editors. *MMWH* is the official journal of the Montana Historical Society. Articles in its magazine are peer reviewed and go through extensive editing by the Magazine's knowledgeable staff. Theirs is a collaborative process between author and editors, and I am most appreciative of their assistance in making these articles the strong manuscripts they are. They certainly did not start out that way.

So, when I identify this as a casual history book, I hope you take my meaning. The collection's primary purpose is to provide an initial record of the local history I have been able to research. Its secondary purpose is to entertain and provide the impetus for people to share their own history, particularly with me.

Therefore, this casual history book will forgo the usual five-page acknowledgment section required in more serious academic-style manuscripts. When I write my own formal history books (as I intend to do), I will be sure to list the dozens of people who have assisted me. For now, I will give my sincere thanks to four groups of people: my family, my publishers, my sources, and my readers.

I could not do what I do without the support of my mother and father, Susan and Forest Dunning. Also included in this group are my extended Dunning, Moreland, and Tucker families.

The people at the *Powder River Examiner* in Broadus took a chance on a nobody who had never published anything in his life. This collection is a testament to their patience and unwavering support. Thank you, Billy Stuver!

I also need to thank the staff at *Montana, the Magazine of Western History,* especially Diana Di Stefano and Jeff Bartos. Included in this thanks are the many staff members behind the scenes who make *MMWH* the beautiful and powerful publication it is.

Most, if not all, of the stories in this collection required the cooperation of sources. Libraries and university archives throughout the West were accessed in support of these columns. Special thanks go to those neighbors and friends who have shared their memories, their family history, and their photographs. One of the reasons I created this collection was to be able to credit some of these people. That, and to answer the question I'm most often asked: Where the hell did you get that [piece of information]?

The last group I need to thank is my readers. Some enjoy my stuff in the *Powder River Examiner,* while others read my work through my website, www.redshalerelections.com. Their support and feedback have been invaluable. Columns published after the publication of this book will take their place among their colleagues. You can subscribe to my email notifications to be alerted to new content as I update things.

Which brings me to my last point. You might wonder, if most of these pieces are freely available on your website, why have you put together this collection and sold it to the public? That is a good question, one I will address directly.

This collection includes some content that is NOT available on my website. Specifically, the website cannot feature the *Montana* magazine articles. The editors have allowed me to reprint them in this form, and I am most grateful. If you don't have the specific issues of the magazine, the only way to access these articles is through this book collection. I'm very proud of these pieces, and unfortunately, many of my readers are not members of the Montana Historical Society.

At the end of each chapter is a "Notes" section. This is where I discuss some of my sources and other key material that went into the production of each particular piece. This information is also not available on the website versions. I have also been able to include photographs that could not be published in the original because they were too graphic or did not have sufficient space.

Two *PRE* columns available on my website are not included in this collection. In 2021, I published two articles in the *Examiner* regarding the Winnie Brown murder and the Geddes trials. Later on, in 2022, I published a much more detailed version of the same story in *Montana, the Magazine of Western History.* These articles (a main article and a sidebar) are included in this collection. Since the two *PRE* stories had no information that was not included in the *MMWH* articles, I decided not to make you read the same story twice. If you want to read the original *PRE* articles, they are available on my website.

Finally, I'll tell you that some of these stories have been edited since their original publication. I have not changed any facts or statements. Most of the changes are to the earliest columns when, to be frank, my writing wasn't as crisp as it later became. I cringe reading over some of these early columns. The majority of the changes are grammatical and better clarify my intended point. In a few cases, I have corrected errors in the original publication. All error corrections in this collection are acknowledged and discussed in the "Notes" section.

I hope you have as much fun reading these as I had producing them!

— ***Shane Dunning***
Birney, MT

This collection is dedicated to the memory of my friend

RON LANGMACHER

1937–2024

A wonderful man who left this world at the tender age of 39. . . .

Horton S. Boal, son-in-law of Buffalo Bill Cody. PHOTOGRAPH COURTESY OF THE AMERICAN HERITAGE CENTER, LARAMIE, WY. GEORGE T. BECK PAPERS, IDENTIFIER AH00059_05454

1

Buffalo Bill's Sad Legacy on Hanging Woman Creek (Part 1)

For many people, the name Buffalo Bill sparks thoughts of the quintessential American West. Those of us who live in these western states know "The Honorable William F. Cody" as a flamboyant and controversial showman, an Army scout, and a hunter. In this area specifically, Cody's more famous exploits are an essential aspect of our local history. What is less known are the multiple tragedies that plagued his family life and how much of that played out here in Southeastern Montana and Northern Wyoming.

Buffalo Bill and his seven siblings lost their father at the age of eleven, an event partially blamed on Issac Cody's virulent antislavery activities in pre-Civil War Kansas. William was the only male sibling to survive to adulthood. Cody married Louisa Frederici at age 20 in 1866. They called each other "Willie" and "Lulu." They would have four children in all. Their eldest child, Arta Lucille, was born in 1866, followed by their son, Kit Carson, in 1870 and daughter, Orra Maude, in 1872. The family eventually settled in the North Platte, Nebraska, area in the 1870s and established the famous Scout's Rest Ranch in 1886. Cody's youngest daughter, Irma Louise, was born in 1883.

Buffalo Bill and his wife, Louisa, may very well claim the credit for having America's first tabloid marriage. Throughout Cody's showman years, Louisa heard near-constant infidelity rumors while she stayed home with the children. Bill Cody acutely wished to avoid the social stigma of divorce. The family was strained by their son, Kit Carson's, death from scarlet fever in 1876 at age five. Tragedy struck again when Orra Maude died in 1883 at age nine, although the death may have also reconciled Cody's marriage for a short while.

In North Platte, his eldest daughter, Arta Lucille, met and suddenly married a young Chicagoan from a wealthy family named Horton Sinclair Boal. Buffalo Bill was away with his Wild West Show at the time of the marriage.

His first grandchild, Arta Clara Boal, was born in 1890. Prior to 1892, the Scout's Rest Ranch in North Platte had been ably managed by Cody's sister, Julia, and her husband, Al Goodman. Lulu and Arta began pressuring Bill to make Horton Boal manager against his better judgment. Boal lacked the ability and experience to manage the ranch, Cody felt. "Boal is no man to run it," Cody wrote to his brother-in-law, Al Goodman.

In 1892, Boal was made manager, creating tension between Cody and the Goodmans. This was the state of the family when Bill Cody began his business interests in Northern Wyoming. He had been in the area in the 1870s as a scout in Crook's Army. In 1894, he arrives in Sheridan and first steps on the porch of the Historic Sheridan Inn. He partnered with George Canfield, and the Sheridan Inn quickly became the social center of the area for hundreds of miles. The charm and showmanship of Buffalo Bill and his beautiful daughter, Arta, contributed mightily to the social and financial success of Sheridan.

Arta and her husband, Horton Boal, moved to Sheridan County in 1894 after an unsuccessful stint running Cody's North Platte ranch. Arta reigned as hostess at the Sheridan Inn and Horton established the 3X Bar ranch in the community of Slack, with range in northern Sheridan County and the Crow Reservation in Montana. In 1896, their son, William Cody Boal, was born.

The 3XBar Ranch Headquarters on Hanging Woman Creek. PHOTOGRAPH BY L.A. HUFFMAN, COURTESY OF THE MONTANA HISTORICAL SOCIETY, L.A. HUFFMAN COLLECTION, 981-307.

Another view of Horton Boal's 3XBar Cabin on Hanging Woman Creek. The cabin was purportedly a wedding gift from Boal's father-in-law, Buffalo Bill Cody. PHOTOGRAPH BY L.A. HUFFMAN, COURTESY OF THE MONTANA HISTORICAL SOCIETY, L.A. HUFFMAN COLLECTION, 981-308.

In 1900, Arta and Horton purchased land in the rapidly growing Tongue River Valley in the cattle country near Birney in what was then Custer County, Montana. The property had been initially settled by William and Mary Linville. In the summer of 1900, the 3X Bar relocated to the East Fork of Hanging Woman Creek. Buffalo Bill gifted the couple a fancy cabin that was erected on a spring at the head of the creek.

Arta's social success in Sheridan was replicated in Birney. They became friends with local ranch owners like John B. Kendrick (of the OW Ranch) and George Brewster (of the Quarter Circle U). Birney resident Letha Ebaugh Salveson reported in her memoirs that Arta threw a grand housewarming party, including ice cream. The cabin, she recalls, was decorated with statues of Buffalo Bill and a life-size portrait of the man himself. She found herself sitting on the porch:

> *On a large arm chair upholstered in red velvet and I saw a brass plate on the back. I looked closer and saw what was engraved there: "The King of England Sat Here." I noticed there were other chairs like mine and read the different names on them. One was the chair the Shah of Persia sat in; another was the chair the Czar of Russia sat in; another was where Franz Josef of Austria-Hungary sat. Of course, these chairs were from the Buffalo Bill Wild West Show, which played before all the crowned heads of Europe.*

Horton's lack of success running the Scout's Rest Ranch followed him to the East Fork of Hanging Woman. His employee, John Hudson "Shorty" Caddel, recalled of Boal, "he was a good man. A regular stranger to livestock, but he was a good man."

Despite appearances, Arta and Horton seemed to be having issues. Letha Salveson recalled Arta "stayed all summer at her ranch and spent the winter in Sheridan, then came out again next summer." Merton Edwards, in the book *Faded Hoofprint, Bygone Dreams,* recalled that Buffalo Bill: "had a relative, some said a son-in-law, that was a cattleman over near the Otter Creek, that I knew fairly well. Lived there alone and run a bunch of cattle. Alone, I say he always seemed alone any chance I ever chanced that way. A quiet, morose sort of fellow."

On December 28, 1900, Horton Boal, along with his hired hand Shorty Caddel, were two of the eleven cattlemen who slaughtered 2,000 head of sheep at the head of Otter Creek. The raid, led by future Governor and US Senator John B. Kendrick, targeted a partnership of John Daut and R.R. Selway and is detailed in a book written by my father, Forest Dunning, called *Slaughter on the Otter.* During the days of the sheep raid, Arta was in Sheridan, putting on a play called "That Box of Cigarettes" at the Cady Theatre.

NOTES ON CHAPTER 1:

- This article was originally published in the *Powder River Examiner* on October 3, 2019.
- The 3X Bar cabin remained on Hanging Woman until the 1970s. In the 1950s, my grandfather briefly attempted to turn the ranch into a dude ranch. He was unsuccessful, but I have pictures of my infant father in the Boal cabin. Later, the cabin was moved about twenty miles south near Barber Draw.
- Itinerant Birney author Ned Randolph intended to write a newspaper story about the Boal cabin at the 3X Bar. His papers at the American Heritage Center contain some of his notes and a few black-and-white pictures of the cabin and other parts of the property in the 1960s.

Arta Cody Boal, Buffalo Bill's daughter, is pictured here with William Cody Boal. PHOTOGRAPH COURTESY OF THE AMERICAN HERITAGE CENTER, JOHN B. KENDRICK PAPERS.

2

Buffalo Bill's Sad Legacy on Hanging Woman Creek (Part 2)

It is not known with certainty what were the tensions between Horton and Arta. While Horton's family apparently had money, there were rumors that his ranch was heavily in debt. Arta clearly adored her father, and Horton seemed to chafe under his father-in-law's shadow. Their daughter, Clara, was in a girl's school in Denver. William Cody Boal was often with his grandmother, Lulu, in North Platte. Nellie Yost's book, *Buffalo Bill: His Family, Friends, Fame, Failures and Fortunes,* mentions rumors surrounding Arta and Dr. Charles Thorp when the Boals resided in North Platte. In September 1902, the North Platte Telegraph reported that "Mrs. H.S. Boal will go to Kansas City Thursday, where she will make her home."

On October 28, 1902, Horton Boal was staying at the Sheridan Inn. That morning he had a drink at the bar with Al Johnson. When their conversation was over, he bought a bottle of brandy to take to his room, where Johnson recalled he intended to write some letters. At 3:00 A.M., he was missed, as recalled in the book *Reflections of the Inn* by Patti Atkins:

> *. . . someone went to his room and knocked on the door. The smell of chloroform was apparent, and the door was forced open. Boal was found on his bed with a shoe, in which he had placed the chloroform, held to his face."*

He had left a note for his wife and another to the Inn's manager:

> *Friend Howard—*
> *Excuse this trouble I am about to make in your hotel, but I will have to make use of your hospitality in this way for the last time; would rather be close to friends in a thing of this sort than among strangers.*
> *—H.S. Boal*

Patti Atkins' book states that in the note to Arta, Horton "would have used a gun but the only one he had belonged to her, and since he did not want to use hers, he decided to use the chloroform instead. He also asked that his saddle horse follow the hearse to the cemetery and be shot over his grave." It was said to have been the largest funeral in Sheridan at the time. Boal's horse indeed led the procession, but thankfully the animal was spared his owner's intentions by the authorities.

Arta spent the next year resolving Horton's estate. The 3X Bar was purchased by John B. Kendrick. Sometime later while in Denver, Arta began to feel ill with stomach issues while she became re-acquainted with Dr. Charles Thorp. Less than two years after Horton Boal's death, on January 1, 1904, Arta married Dr. Thorp with her father in attendance. A month later she was dead from those stomach issues. She was buried alongside her younger brother and sister. Her daughter Clara was raised by Horton Boal's family in Chicago, while William Cody Boal went to live with his grandmother, Louisa.

Arta's death was one of the final straws in Buffalo Bill and Lulu's rocky marriage. Bill had initiated the divorce proceeding, and Louisa (who did not want the divorce) made a threat to denounce Cody at Arta's funeral. Arta had apparently written a harsh letter to her father in her final weeks regarding the divorce, and Louisa accused Bill of breaking Arta's heart. Thus began the final tragedy of Buffalo Bill that occurred in this area, for the infamous divorce proceeding would be taken to trial in Sheridan, Wyoming.

Under the divorce laws of Wyoming, grounds for divorce included "making the marriage relation intolerable." For this reason, Bill initiated the divorce in Wyoming instead of Nebraska. During the divorce, sensational charges and counter-charges were made by both sides. Bill accused Louisa of trying to poison him, and of being a generally uncooperative nag. Louisa, for her part, provided ample evidence of Bill's infidelity and inability to manage money.

Several witnesses were deposed and testified before Judge R.H. Scott. Much of this made it to the newspapers. In the end, Buffalo Bill was refused his divorce petition. Thus ended the significant activity of Buffalo Bill in this area. The Honorable William F. Cody and his family continued their activities in the Big Horn Basin and other areas in the West, but they have little in the way of local flavor. Nonetheless, it cannot be denied that Northeastern Wyoming and Southeastern Montana will be forever tied to the family legacy of Buffalo Bill Cody.

Alternate view of Horton S. Boal, from the same photo shoot as the previous image. PHOTOGRAPH COURTESY OF THE AMERICAN HERITAGE CENTER, LARAMIE, WY. GEORGE T. BECK PAPERS, IDENTIFIER AH00059_05456.

NOTES ON CHAPTER 2:

- This article was originally published in the *Powder River Examiner* on October 10, 2019.
- The 3X Bard cabin was notable for cutting the interior portions of the logs so that they had smooth, perpendicular walls. This was done so that Arta could attractively hang all of her portraits.
- The original 3X Bar property eventually became part of the Bones Brothers Ranch of Birney.

Walter Shirlaw's sketch *Nearing the End* shows Head Chief, in full war bonnet, riding down a hill in Lame Deer toward waiting soldiers. ORIGINALLY PUBLISHED IN *THE CENTURY MAGAZINE*, VOLUME XLVII, NO. 6 (NOVEMBER 1893). PUBLIC DOMAIN.

3

An Artist's Firsthand View of the Old West in Action

An underappreciated aspect of Western history has been the contribution of artists. Cassilly Adams' *Custer's Last Fight,* reprinted by the Anheuser Busch company and distributed to saloons and bars all over the country, represents one of the most iconic and recognized images of that historic fight. Artists have also impacted our understanding of "ordinary" Western life by depicting those who lived it. Charles M. Russell, Frederick Remington, and Bill Gollings are revered in our area and worldwide for their works. However, these artists were rarely actual eyewitnesses to history. An extraordinary and relatively unrecognized exception was Walter Shirlaw's involvement in the suicide-by-soldier deaths of Head Chief and Young Mule at Lame Deer on September 13, 1890.

Walter Shirlaw was born in Scotland in 1838. His family emigrated to America when he was three. Earning enough money during his younger years to pay for art education in Europe, he developed his style and quickly became highly regarded, especially with his painting *The Tuning of the Bell.* Perhaps his most important work, *Sheep Shearing on the Bavarian Highlands,* was completed in 1876. Shirlaw returned to America to continue his career and was made a member of the National Academy in 1887.

During the Census of 1890, the American government sent out special agents to enumerate the number and conditions of Native Americans then under Federal jurisdiction. Among these agents were several artists, including Julian Scott, Peter Moran, and Walter Shirlaw. They were charged with providing enumerative figures and "illustrative material" for assigned tribes that eventually were presented in the report *Indians Taxed and Not Taxed for the Eleventh Census of the United States.* Shirlaw was dispatched to report on the Crow and Northern Cheyenne Tribes of Montana. In addition to his report, he contributed two full-color paintings, *The Race* (Crow) and *Omaha Dance* (Cheyenne) to that historic document.

Walter Shirlaw's sketch entitled *The Challenge* is shown above. THIS SKETCH ACCOMPANIES SHIRLAW'S ARTICLE PUBLISHED IN *THE CENTURY MAGAZINE,* VOLUME XLVII, NO. 6 (NOVEMBER 1893). PUBLIC DOMAIN.

This was the reason a world-renowned artist was in Lame Deer, Montana, that September 13, when Head Chief and Young Mule made their way down Squaw Hill.

For those unfamiliar with that story, in 1890 the Northern Cheyenne were suffering mightily from starvation due to inadequate rations that were the responsibility of the federal government. Because of these deprivations and a lack of game, some Cheyenne would go off their reservation and kill the cattle of ranchers who lived nearby. This caused considerable tension among the Northern Cheyenne, the federal government, and the local White population. In the fall of 1890, a teenager named Hugh Boyle was killed when he came upon a cow being butchered by Indians. The body was hidden. A search was organized by the ranchers after Boyle went missing, and the body was soon discovered in a ravine on a tall hill.

Eventually, the Cheyenne chief American Horse discovered that his daughter's boyfriend, Head Chief, had done the deed. Head Chief was a known hothead who had been too young to fight during the Indian wars and acutely felt a need to prove his warrior prowess. He was around twenty-five years old and had a teenaged devotee named Young Mule, who idolized him and followed him everywhere. Both had apparently been involved in Boyle's killing. Head Chief admitted to the killing but refused to be turned over to the Whites and be "hung like a dog." American Horse told the Indian Agent, J.C. Cooper, that Head Chief would meet his soldiers on ration day.

This solution was deemed acceptable by the Indian agent. On ration day, a detachment of U.S. Army Cavalry under the command of Lt. S.C. Robertson deployed along a ridge under a large, commanding hill. Shirlaw observed what happened next in the company of the Indian Agent Cooper, a doctor and Lt. Robertson. He reported his observations in the magazine *The Century* in November 1893. Along with his article, "Artist's Adventures: The Rush To Death," Shirlaw included three sketches of the incident. The artist had also provided another sketch to accompany an article detailing this event written by his fellow eyewitness Lt. Robertson in *Harpers' Weekly* (October 18, 1890).

Shirlaw's short article describes how the local geography created an ominous location for an assembly of the tribe to witness the events that followed:

> *In an instant the young bucks who had fringed the outer space of the agency mounted their ponies, and from camp to camp conveyed the word of challenge. Then in haste they sought the rounded edges of the hills bordering the western bank of the Lame Deer, seeking reserved seats in the natural amphitheater. Following them went the squaws old and young, with their papooses and their household effects.*
>
> *The military and Indian police took their initial positions, and around 2:00 pm, two Cheyenne braves on horseback appeared on a rocky point. Head Chief wore full regalia including war-paint and a large feather head-dress. They moved with great rapidity from point to point, shouting their battle-cry and firing, while showers of bullets plowed the ground about them. For one full hour this natural fortress was held by them, when, taken in the rear by a troop of cavalry, they were compelled to seek shelter on the plains or wooded hills beyond. Head Chief, still mounted, acted the hero, knowing that in the legends of the witnessing tribe his name would be celebrated as one who died a true brave. Unseen, he crossed the plain, taking flight for the opposite hills, where without warning he met a detachment of troops. The challenge was "to kill and be killed." So it was. Head Chief bit the dust ten feet from the point of encounter. Four bullets had done their work, and the Indian was laid low.*

A Rush to Death by Shirlaw was published in a different article than the artist's own (published three years later in *The Century*). THIS IMAGE WAS PRINTED IN HARPER'S WEEKLY (OCTOBER 18, 1890) ACCOMPANYING LT. S.C. ROBERTSON'S "A RUSH TO DEATH: TWO CHEYENNES FIGHT THREE TROOPS OF CAVALRY." PUBLIC DOMAIN.

Young Mule was unmounted (his pony had been shot under him) and sought shelter in a dry run. He kept firing at the troops until his ammunition ran out and was shot dead, probably by the Indian Police.

> *The tragedy over, the multitude, eight hundred strong, came down the hills pell-mell, with colors and dust flying, the young bucks leading the van, sweeping the plain like a whirlwind; the squaws coming on with shrill shouts, chanting their dirges, which mingled with the howling of the dogs—a scene never to be forgotten.*

There are several, more detailed eye-witness accounts of Head Chief's and Young Mule's end, both from White and Indian perspectives, and some details of Shirlaw's article should certainly be scrutinized. John Stands-in-Timber eloquently paints the story from the Cheyenne side, as does Patty Hardground's and Fannie Standing Elk's documented eye-witness accounts. Lt. Robertson told his version to both *Harper's Weekly* and the *St. Paul Pioneer Press* in better detail.

Shirlaw's sketch entitled *Sweeping the Plain Like a Whirlwind.* THE *CENTURY MAGAZINE*, VOLUME XLVII, NO. 6 (NOVEMBER 1893). PUBLIC DOMAIN.

Both Shirlaw's article and his US census reports reflected the prevailing paternalistic attitudes of many white men towards Native Americans at the time. Perhaps the most important contribution that Walter Shirlaw brings to this key moment in Western History, however, are his sketches, the rarest combination when the artist met the moment.

NOTES ON CHAPTER 3:

- The *Powder River Examiner* first published this article on October 24, 2019.
- John Stands-In-Timber's recollections are available in the book with Margot Liberty, *Cheyenne Memories.* More is included in Liberty's *A Cheyenne Voice: The John Stands-In-Timber Interviews.*
- My father, Forest Dunning, wrote a novel of historical fiction called *Death at Lame Deer* that features the Head Chief-Young Mule Incident.

A Ute woman curing meat at a camp on the Powder River circa 1906. PHOTOGRAPH COURTESY OF THE WYOMING STATE ARCHIVES, P2000-15.

4

The Utes Come to Powder River Country

The history of this area and its native inhabitants has, for the past hundred and fifty years, primarily been the story of the Crow, the Sioux, and the Cheyenne. This is naturally the result of those tribes' residence in the Powder River valley as white settlement intruded. Casual students of local history can perhaps be forgiven for being unaware of the tragic story of the Northern Utes when they came to this country in 1906.

The White River Band of Utes in 1905 resided in the Uintah Reservation in northeastern Utah. They were one of several bands of Utes who once ranged throughout the middle Rocky Mountain region. The 1870s had been a difficult decade for the White River Utes. Their initial reservation and hunting ground in western Colorado were opened to white settlement. State and federal agencies were pressured to force the Utes into smaller and more desolate areas in Utah. A religious zealot was made agent-in-charge of the Uintah Reservation and he quickly antagonized the White River Utes to the point of anticipated violence. The agent, Nathan Meeker, called for federal troops to restore order despite attempts by more peaceable Ute leaders to calm the situation. As the troops descended on the reservation, a violent faction of the Utes murdered Meeker, killed several of his white workers, and kidnapped Meeker's wife along with two other women. After order was restored, the guilty parties were executed, and the Utes settled into their considerably smaller, desolate reservation in Utah.

In 1902, however, powerful mining interests arranged for the Ute reservation to be opened ONCE AGAIN to white settlement. Congress passed an act releasing the Uintah Reservation to white settlement. After a USGS survey (which took years to complete), an allotment of land in severalty was distributed to the Utes without a new treaty. The remaining land was opened to settlers. Ute Sub-Chiefs Appah and Red Hat resisted this effort to little effect. By 1905, they were completely disillusioned and conceived of an extraordinary meeting of several Native American tribes to bring attention to their grievances and find better lands to hunt. Apparently, some Sioux visitors years before had impressed them with stories of grand hunting grounds near the Black Hills.

Appah decided to abandon their desolate reservation in favor of seeking an alliance with the Sioux. To that end, over 300 Utes began a slow sojourn through the state of Wyoming on their way to South Dakota. They made their journey in small bands, traveling by horse and travois. They were heavily armed and sullen, hunting game along the way according to their traditions. The lands they traveled over were much better than the reservation lands they had left, and by late August 1906, most of the Utes had gathered near Douglas, Wyoming.

As can be imagined, this caused considerable angst among the local ranchers. Wyoming's governor, B.B. Brooks, demanded action from the Indian Bureau. The Indian agent in charge of the Utes unsuccessfully tried to convince them to return. With regard to Governor Brooks' demand for action, the Indian commissioner refused to do anything more substantial than persuasion, claiming the Indians were a case "for the local authorities rather than this department."

Ute Indians camped at Belle Fourche, Capt. Johnson of the Sixth Cavalry addressing them. PHOTOGRAPH COURTESY OF THE LIBRARY OF CONGRESS. LOT 7779, LC-USZ62-51800.

This reluctance was due to the Indian Affairs' understanding that, by allotting land to Utes and doing so without using a treaty, Congress may very well have conferred U.S. citizenship on them (Native Americans weren't granted U.S. citizenship until 1924). Unfortunately for the federal and Wyoming governments, this legal distinction was lost on the Utes, who rejected the very idea of the allotment plan as a violation of previous agreements with an untrustworthy party. Let the white man have the worthless land in Utah, they felt. They had a right to hunt game and graze their herds. Governor Brooks feared imminent violence and began clamoring for federal troops to force the Utes back. Special Indian Agent James McLaughlin was dispatched to renew the negotiations. He caught up with the Utes near Newcastle, Wyoming, as breathless reports of violence filled newspapers across the United States. Almost all these reports turned about to be false, but they still had the practical effect of increasing local tensions almost to the breaking point.

McLaughlin recalled his council with Red Cap, Appah, and Soccioff in his book *My Friend The Indian:*

> *Each one closed with the declaration that he would die rather than return to Utah, and Soccioff was independent and defiant to the point of more than hinting at his willingness to make trouble. The council closed without any advantage to the government . . .*

With McLaughlin's failure, President Theodore Roosevelt approved using military forces, and the U.S. Army converged on the Utes from three directions. Two troops of U.S. Cavalry from Fort Robinson in Nebraska were transported to Wyoming via rail and made initial contact with the Utes along the Powder River fifty miles north of Gillette. The commander wisely determined he did not have enough troops to make the Indians stop, so he waited for reinforcements. Fearing that the Utes may attempt to join with the Cheyennes (who had threatened their own outbreak less than ten years before), another two units of cavalry were dispatched from Ft. Keogh in Miles City to flank the Utes from the north and west. A final group of troops was sent from Ft. Meade in South Dakota, should the Utes attempt to make for the Black Hills. Since negotiation had failed, the army intended to impress the potential hostiles with overwhelming numbers.

The return of the Sixth Cavalry bringing the Ute Indians with them through Belle Fourche, SD, 1906.
PHOTOGRAPH BY LOUIS G. BILLINGS, COURTESY LIBRARY OF CONGRESS. LOT 7779, LC-USZ62-99286.

Locally, this was the state of things in early November 1906, when the Utes crossed the Montana border following the Powder River. In the Powder River history book, *Echoing Footsteps,* my great-grandmother, Beatrice Tucker Dunning, reported that the troops from Ft. Robinson included African American Buffalo Soldiers. As she recalled, this caused considerable excitement:

> *The Cavalry from Fort Keogh came to Ashland to protect the white people and the Cavalry from Fort Robinson came to meet the Utes. This was a colored unit and many school children saw Negroes for the first time.*

Local wolfer Charlie Flory reported meeting the Ft. Keogh cavalry on the Tongue River with Captain Joe T. Brown of the Three Circle Ranch. He recalled Captain Brown treating the officers to a turkey dinner at his ranch. George Linville reported being hired as a scout by the Ft. Keogh Cavalry. Violet Traub Bull and Francis Traub recalled:

> *The Utes went into camp on the 3 Bar Creek near the head of Bay Horse Creek. Some of these Indians came to the ranch (of George Traub) giving Mother quite a scare. They did not bother any of the settlers or their stock but depleted the deer and antelope considerable. A company of Cavalry from Fort Robinson, Nebraska, came in and the Indians (after much pow-pow) agreed to be moved to a reservation in South Dakota.*

The Utes marched under escort to Fort Meade and later to the Cheyenne River Agency temporarily while the government agreed for the Ute leadership to meet with President Roosevelt in Washington. This ended the "last outbreak" of the reservation period. Unfortunately for the Utes, the Sioux did not welcome them, as they mightily struggled on their reservations. The Utes were settled in the Thunder Basin area of the Cheyenne River reservation for two years before they agreed to return to Utah. For all the excitement their odyssey had caused, the Utes had violated no laws except for gaming laws (and perhaps some stock depredation), and no Indian or white casualties had occurred. Now, this sad aspect of local history is all but forgotten, with no monuments and few history books to mark its passing.

NOTES ON CHAPTER 4:

- This article was first published in the *Powder River Examiner* on November 21, 2019.
- Much of the scholarship regarding this period of Ute history was accomplished by Utah historian Floyd O'Neal. He published several excellent pieces in mostly Utah-related journals.
- The Meeker massacre and its associated events make up a chapter in Dee Brown's *Bury My Heart at Wounded Knee.*
- Charley Flory's account of the area's reaction to the Ute odyssey is found in his interview with Charles Helvey. A transcript is available in Helvey's papers located at the American Heritage Center in Laramie.

An example of the anti-German propaganda put out by the U.S. government during WWI. ILLUSTRATION BY HARRY R. HOPPS, PHOTOGRAPH COURTESY OF THE LIBRARY OF CONGRESS, POS-WWI-US, NO. 457A.

5

How an Otter Creek Homesteader's Big Mouth Shook the State and the Nation

To say being German in Montana in 1917 was complicated would be an understatement. The United States had, at long last, abandoned neutrality and entered World War One on the Allied side. Along with the declaration and its build-up came a wave of anti-German hysteria that was particularly virulent in Montana. Sauerkraut was renamed "Liberty Cabbage" and Daschunds were called "Liberty Hounds." On a much more serious front, the politics of the war in Montana became mixed with the toxicity surrounding labor unions (particularly the International Workers of the World) and the Anaconda Copper Mining Company. In Butte in 1918, IWW agitator Frank Miller was lynched for his supposedly "pro-German" political views.

On June 18, 1917, President Woodrow Wilson signed the Espionage Act of 1917. This law ostensibly made it illegal to utter false statements interfering with the operation or success of military operations while the United States was at war. However, anti-German hysteria around the country caused the arrest of pacifists and other simple war critics under the new law. At the time, there was not a significant amount of free-speech case law, and the constitutionality of these type of laws was an open question. A legal confrontation was imminent.

The focus of all these forces ultimately came down upon, of all things, a well-known Otter Creek homesteader and cattleman named Ves Hall. In 1900, Hall was working for John B. Kendrick's OW Ranch. He and Ves Newell had a cattle and horse operation (Hall and Newell) on Otter Creek just south of Ashland before the Newells sold out to run the Ashland Inn. In 1916, his ranch was bought by the Gentrys.

In January 1918, Hall lived in Ashland and expressed some decidedly anti-war views. He was indicted in federal court in Butte on four counts for spreading false reports and statements calculated to defeat the military and naval forces of the U.S. and for causing and attempting to cause insubordination, disloyalty, mutiny, and refusal of duty by defaming President Woodrow Wilson. Among Hall's statements testified to were:

- That Germany would whip the United States, and he hoped it would be so.
- President Wilson was a British tool.
- That President Wilson was the crookedest son-of-a-bitch to ever be president and was the richest man in the United States.
- That Germany had a right to sink ships such as the *Lusitania* and kill Americans without warning.
- That the U.S. was fighting for Wall Street millionaires and to protect J.P. Morgan's interests in England.

The U.S. Attorney in Montana was Burton K. Wheeler, a future U.S. Senator. He considered prosecution of the Espionage Act very problematic and quickly gained a reputation for being less than aggressive in such cases. However, he was away in Washington when Hall and Ashland banker A.J. Just were arrested. In his stead, F.F. Haynes, a strongly pro-war Rosebud County prosecutor was placed in charge of the case. He ordered Hall and Just to remain in Ashland while out on bail. Hall sought the advice of Rosebud County Judge Charles Crumm. Crumm recommended Hall and Just talk to Wheeler, who had just returned to Butte, and they immediately left on a train.

When Haynes learned Hall had left Ashland, he wired the sheriff in Butte and had them arrested as soon as they stepped off the train. Wheeler's return from Washington found the press loudly supporting Hall's prosecution. Federal Judge George Bourquin was sympathetic to Wheeler's skepticism on the Espionage Act and told the U.S. Attorney he (Bourquin) was in a better position to deal with the issues presented by the new law.

The *Great Falls Tribune* stated that:

> *Witnesses for the defendant testified today that Hall had subscribed for $3,000 worth of Liberty bonds, and attended a food conservation meeting, and that he had referred with pride to the fact that his father had fought in*

the Civil War and that his brother had been killed at the battle of San Juan Hill in the Spanish-American War.

In their opening statement, his attorneys insisted that many of Hall's remarks were made jocularly and that he was not in earnest when he remarked to a woman at the Newell hotel that he would go to Mexico before he would fight.

Bourquin's opinion in *United States vs. Ves Hall* dismissed the case that eventually became a landmark in free speech case law. His directed verdict specifically authored his opinion "because of the grave issues and the necessity for interpretation of the Espionage Act, to the end that a precedent be established. . . ." Hall and Just were free men.

Bourquin did not question whether Hall made the "unspeakable" comments that caused the case:

Having in mind the rule applicable to this motion for a directed verdict, the evidence would justify a finding that defendant did so make the declarations charged. But it would not support a verdict of guilty of any of the crimes charged. It appears the declarations were made at a Montana village of some 60 people, 60 miles from the railway, and none of the armies or navies within hundreds of miles, so far as appears. The declarations were oral; some in badinage with the landlady in a hotel kitchen, some at a picnic, some on the street, some in hot and furious saloon argument.

The opinion's immediate effects were many and significant. Hall and Just were released. Rosebud County Judge C.L. Crumm, who had testified as a character witness for Hall, went to the State Attorney General S.C. Ford's office to discuss the implications of the Hall case. As he entered Ford's office, he found his nemesis Haynes already there, visiting the attorney general. Haynes stated to Crumm as he entered the room: "I came to get General Ford's opinion on the dicta in the decision. Since nothing can be done under United States law, it is absolutely necessary that something be done under state laws with the pro-German element of Rosebud county."

Judge Crumm replied, "I don't believe there are any pro-Germans in Rosebud County." Haynes responded that he believed Judge Crumm himself was pro-German. Crumm then pulled an automatic pistol and aimed it at Haynes, shouting:

> *God damn you, I'll kill you like a dog. You have published me in eastern Montana as a traitor and I'll kill you like a dog!*

Judge Crumm quickly backed down. Before the *Ves Hall* case, Crumm possessed a sterling reputation. This incident at the attorney general's office caused him to be the first judge impeached by the State of Montana. The legislature was so determined to impeach him that it continued its proceedings even after Crumm resigned his office.

The effort to do something in state law to curb the plague of sedition in Montana eventually bore fruit in the special session of 1918. Montana passed its own sedition law and eventually seventy-nine Montanans were jailed in 1918 and 1919, some sentenced to over twenty years. Montana's law was used as a template for stronger anti-sedition legislation on the federal level. Eventually, anti-German hysteria died down. In 2006, Governor Schwietzer posthumously pardoned those jailed on the state charges. Judge Crumm was exonerated in 1991 by a 46 to 0 vote of the Montana Senate.

U.S. Attorney Wheeler eventually became a U.S. Senator for Montana, where he played a critical role in stopping FDR's attempt to pack the U.S. Supreme Court. In his autobiography, he cites the *Hall* case and the anti-German hysteria for his decision to support so strongly the independence of the federal court.

Ves Hall returned home briefly but quickly left the state for Alaska, passing away in 1954. In my research, I could find no picture of the man whose words caused such a commotion. If anyone has a picture in their family photos, I would appreciate being able to get a good copy of it. He virtually disappears from local history books and none mention this unfortunate moment in Montana history.

NOTES ON CHAPTER 5:

- This article was originally published in the *Powder River Examiner* on January 24, 2020.
- As of this collection's publication, I still have not found a photograph of Ves Hall.
- Ves Hall plays a small part in another story, "The Unsolved Murder of John L. Tucker," in this collection.

For information regarding the Ves Hall trial and its consequences, see *Darkest Before Dawn: Sedition and Free Speech in the American West,* by Clemens Work.

A portrait of George Mitchell, circa 1909, not long before he was killed by Ray Tarbell. PHOTOGRAPH COURTESY OF THE MITCHELL FAMILY.

6

THE PRELIMINARY TRIAL OF RAY TARBELL (TARBELL PART 1)

In 1909, newspapers such as *The Sheridan Post* called it "the question of the range." It was a euphemism for the political, economic, and cultural conflicts that resulted from the decades-old federal land policy usually referred to as "open range." In Powder River country, that question of the range often turned violent in ways the local legal systems seemed unable (or unwilling) to address. In 1900, sheepmen John Daut and R.R. Selway had over 2,000 head of ewe lambs clubbed to death in a single night by eleven masked vigilantes. Selway's later attempt to bring those he felt responsible to justice through the law failed miserably. In 1901, Hank Greenway found a whitecap message saying he would "need a coffin" if he brought his sheep to Powder River.

Events such as these demonstrated that any small livestock operation in the Yellowstone Valley that depended on open range could not rely on the legal system to protect their rights from an extra-legal threat. In practical terms, small operators could only ally themselves with other outfits (big or small) for mutual cooperation and security. In some cases, these extra-legal factions actually served to escalate any private tensions that occasionally resulted in tragedy. Such a case occurred on September 8, 1909, with the killing of cattleman George Mitchell by Ray Tarbell.

Tarbell had quickly surrendered himself to Custer County officials, with bail being secured by his friend and local sheepman Link Wilson. A preliminary hearing occurred on September 27th. The purpose of the preliminary hearing was to determine if the state had cause to put Tarbell on trial for murder, and the atmosphere was very tense. The prosecution was led by County D.A. Sharpless Walker. Ray Tarbell's defense counsel consisted of Judge Charles H. Loud (perhaps the most distinguished lawyer in eastern Montana) and his partner Donald Campbell. Justice of the Peace John Gibb presided over the proceedings.

It is the nature of preliminary hearings that the defense counsel does not present a full-throated defense unless the evidence is overwhelming enough in favor of their client to result in a dismissal. In this case, Loud and Campbell clearly understood that their client was going to full trial and used the preliminary hearing to put the state's witnesses on the record and only hinted at the defense they would use later at the full trial: that Ray Tarbell shot George Mitchell in self-defense. The preliminary hearing was covered closely by the local press, resulting in a tale strongly suggesting that George Mitchell had been murdered in cold blood.

The star witness of the preliminary hearing was Ray Mitchell, the son of the deceased. He was riding next to his father during much of the dispute. Also testifying for the state was Scott Mitchell, the deceased's nephew, and four others.

On the morning of September 8th, George Mitchell and his son Ray, along with his friend Henry Jackson, rode into the sanctioned roundup then being run by the UA outfit at the mouth of Sheep Creek. This location was about a mile away from the Selway post office on Pumpkin Creek (near the present-day community of Sonnette). As they rode up, 300 to 400 cattle had been collected by around a dozen cowboys. Some of these cowboys were keeping the cattle collected while others were off their horses, relaxing and waiting for the next group to be driven into the roundup. Eighteen-year-old Ray Mitchell observed what he believed to be some of his father's cattle among the herd.

The last group to move cattle to the roundup arrived within an hour after the Mitchells' arrival. This group was driven by Ray Tarbell, William Eubanks, and John Woodley, among others. Woodley and Tarbell were running the roundup on behalf of the UA outfit and were known associates of local pioneer rancher Link Wilson. As soon as George Mitchell was spotted, Tarbell and Woodley loped their horses aggressively in his direction. Eubanks also headed toward the group along the other side of the roundup herd. The three arrived together in front of Mitchell. Woodley was in the lead, and as soon as he got within arms distance of Mitchell, they exchanged words about Mitchell's intentions. Woodley suddenly pulled out a six-shooter and tried to strike Mitchell physically with it. He missed, and Henry Jackson rode his horse between his friend and his attacker to separate them. Then the shooting began.

By all accounts at the preliminary hearing, the only people to successfully pull out their pistols and fire during this first fight were Tarbell, Jackson,

Eubank, and Woodley. Tarbell apparently shot first at Jackson, possibly hitting Jackson's horse in the leg. The horse bucked his rider off, and Jackson returned fire while on the ground, running to a flat near where he landed. Around twenty shots were fired between the four of them, with no apparent casualties. During a lull in the fighting when Tarbell, Woodley, and Eubanks apparently reloaded their weapons, George Mitchell rode to Jackson's location and, significantly, took up Jackson's gun. He then rode back to his son and stated, "Come on and let's go home." With that, both Mitchells turned and started away from the roundup toward their ranch.

Ray Tarbell, finished reloading, rode to catch up with the Mitchells and hollered:

"Hold on, I don't want to have to shoot you in the back!"

George and Ray Mitchell turned their horses and faced Tarbell.

"You have made your boasts," Tarbell accused George Mitchell, who responded,

"I have made no boasts."

"You have, and I can prove it."

They continued arguing while Eubanks and Ray Wilson (the son of Link Wilson) rode up.

What happened next varied from witness to witness. Some say only one shot rang out. Others said they heard two shots. When it was over, George Mitchell fell off his horse, shot once through the left side of his chest, tearing his aorta and killing him almost instantly.

Ray Tarbell turned to George Mitchell's son and ordered him to drop his gun, which he did. He then told the deceased's son "Ray, you go on or I will kill you." Ray Mitchell refused to leave his father, and Tarbell rode off for the moment. Tarbell then ordered the roundup to continue moving, allowing Ray Mitchell and Lehman Wilkes to stay with George Mitchell's body. After some confusion, a buggy from Mitchell's ranch came and picked up the body.

Most of these details were provided by Ray Mitchell. Fourteen-year-old Scott Mitchell, who had been working the roundup for several days, testified that Woodley and Tarbell would not allow him to cut his uncle, George Mitchell's, cattle (Scott was repping for his father, Henry Mitchell), but gave no reason for the exclusion. Three other eyewitnesses, Lehman Wilkes, John Wethers, and H.W. "Bummy" Schubert, offered limited and sometimes conflicting testimony, as they were some distance from confrontation. Coroner A.R. Varco testified on the nature of Mitchell's wound.

Tarbell did not take the stand in his own defense at this hearing. His counsel focused on the final confrontation and whether both men fired at each other at approximately the same time. They also inquired if the state's witnesses were aware of any threats George Mitchell had made to kill Tarbell or Woodley if they came on his range, a charge the witnesses largely denied any knowledge of. No defense witnesses were called, and Justice Gibb ordered Ray Tarbell bound for trial on a charge of first-degree murder.

This ended the preliminary hearing of Ray Tarbell, charged with killing George Mitchell. The press coverage of the one-sided nature of the preliminary hearing seemed to put Tarbell in a desperate situation. The full trial would take place that December, and the results again called into question the usefulness of the legal system in an era of faction and intimidation.

Friends of George Mitchell and cattlemen seemed convinced of Tarbell's guilt and Mitchell's innocence. Tarbell and Woodley's allies, associated with Link Wilson and those who ran sheep as well as cattle, seemed to rally to his cause. George Mitchell, they whispered, was a dangerous and quarrelsome man who had previously threatened both Tarbell and Woodley.

After two trials, Ray Tarbell was eventually acquitted of all charges, with witnesses on both sides completely contradicting one other, seemingly dependent on which faction they allied. The resulting bitterness was strongly felt in the area for decades. The story of the full trial and its aftermath will be told in a future article.

Author's note: In researching this story, the files of the Custer County Court were found to be incomplete. I was only able to obtain the transcript of the preliminary hearing and some minor documents that relate to the two full trials of Ray Tarbell. During last year's centennial, I visited with several people on many subjects, some who claimed they had a full transcript of the Ray Tarbell trial. Unfortunately, I did not write down their names and only later learned the courthouse records were incomplete. If anyone has a copy of the trial transcript, other than the preliminary hearing, I would appreciate being able to obtain a copy of it for the historical record of this fascinating event. Another note, in this article I have spelled his name as Tarbell, with two L's. It should be noted that historically his name was spelled as "Tarbell" and "Tarbel."

NOTES ON CHAPTER 6:

- This article was first published in the *Powder River Examiner* on March 26, 2020.
- This is the first article in a series of four on the George Mitchell-Ray Tarbell incident.
- While I discovered several more documents regarding the legal case against Ray Tarbell, a complete transcript of the two criminal trials remains elusive.

Ray Tarbell (right) seated next to Fred Orschel, taken some years after the George Mitchell trial.
PHOTOGRAPH COURTESY OF BRUCE KEIL AND FAMILY.

7

The Trial of Ray Tarbell (Tarbell Part 2)

On September 28, 1909, the preliminary trial of Ray Tarbell for the killing of George Mitchell earlier that month ended. Justice of the Peace John Gibb ruled there was enough evidence to charge the thirty-five-year-old cattleman with first-degree murder. The local newspapers covered the hearing extensively and were reprinted throughout Montana and Wyoming. Attorneys for the defense did not call a single witness and seemingly focused on getting the state's witnesses on the record, holding their fire for the criminal trial. The result was a tale that presented Ray Tarbell as the cold-blooded killer of an innocent father of eight children and a wife pregnant with twins.

The criminal trial would commence in December of that year. Before the trial began, the defense prepared an aggressive argument to counter the state's case: that Ray Tarbell had shot George Mitchell in self-defense. Such a defense would surely escalate already existing tensions. The general cattleman-sheepman tension that seemingly precipitated the conflict in the first place had been exacerbated by the results of the gunfight itself and the preliminary trial. As the defense gathered possible witnesses, fears for their safety resulted in many witnesses being secured in the protective custody of the Custer County Jail. Roy Garber recalled to his family that his skill at checkers was developed during his time in the facility.

Judge Sidney Sanner began the criminal trial in Miles City on December 15, 1909, with District Attorney Sharpless Walker representing the state. The defense team was led by perhaps the best lawyer in eastern Montana, Judge Charles H. Loud. Loud was a former cattleman and had been a member of Montana's Constitutional Convention.

The state's case closely followed that of the preliminary hearing. The testimony of that proceeding was discussed in a previous article and will only be summarized here. The key state witness was Ray Mitchell, the eighteen-year-old son of the deceased, who was on his horse beside his father when the killing happened. Also testifying for the state were Scott Mitchell, the deceased's fourteen-year-old nephew, and two employees of George Mitchell.

The state's testimony consistently claimed that an initial shootout during a roundup between Ray Tarbell, John Woodley, William Eubanks, and Henry Jackson (all on horseback) had been started by Tarbell. No one was shot, but Jackson was thrown from his horse. During a pause in the shooting to reload, George Mitchell rode to his friend Jackson and picked up his gun. He returned to his son, Ray's, location, and they attempted to withdraw but were recalled by Tarbell. As the two faced each other and exchanged words, Ray Tarbell shot George Mitchell dead with one shot through the aorta. Some of the state witnesses claimed that Mitchell had not fired at Tarbell, while others could not specifically confirm this due to their blocked view of the final confrontation.

The defense called eyewitnesses William Eubanks, Roy Garber, Art Yarger, Sven Swenson, Sam Hoaglund, Beecher Warner, Bummie Schubert (recalled from the preliminary hearing), and Ray Wilson. Most importantly, Ray Tarbell took the stand in his own defense. Together, these witnesses described an event quite different from the state witnesses. Eubanks explained how, on an earlier visit to Mitchell's ranch, George Mitchell had threatened to kill Tarbell or Woodley if they came on his range. Two witnesses claimed that Henry Jackson was the first to shoot and that Ray Mitchell had also participated in the general shootout. Wilson, Garber, and others described how Ray Mitchell and Henry Jackson had come armed to the roundup the previous day.

Ray Tarbell testified that he had been warned that Ray Mitchell had come armed to the roundup and of the threats made by his father. Because the previous day's roundup had proceeded without incident, the Mitchells returned the next day (when the shooting occurred). However, both Tarbell and Woodley brought their six-shooters, something they had not done regularly before. When George Mitchell was sighted at the roundup, he claimed he sent Woodley over to Mitchell to determine his intentions. After some arguing, Henry Jackson fired the first shot. After the initial shootout, Mitchell obtained Jackson's gun and was confronted by Tarbell:

> *I rode towards him and asked him what about threats. He said he had made no threats against me but had threatened Woodley, and he still intended*

> *to do so. Just then Ray Wilson rode in between us and began talking. Ray Mitchell also said something. I told Ray Mitchell I wanted to have no words with him nor trouble with him.*
>
> *Mr. George Mitchell told Wilson to shut up. Then he told me to shut up and fired at me and I then immediately shot and killed him. I thought I had to kill him or he would kill me.*

Six other defense witnesses testified that George Mitchell's "reputation for peace and quietness was bad." Six subsequent state witnesses were sworn and testified that "as to the reputation of George Mitchell for peace and quietness, all admitting that it was good, but that a good many considered him quarrelsome."

Tarbell's testimony also reveals that the jury had at least some knowledge of critical information. Ray Tarbell also shot and killed a man in self-defense in Bridgeport, Nebraska, in 1903. Tarbell had been exonerated by the coroner's jury, with no charges filed. During the final arguments, the *Miles City Independent* stated that "the crowd of spectators was so large that standing room was at a premium."

After an initial deliberation, the jury informed Judge Sanner that they could not agree on a verdict. The judge declined to accept this and sent them back for more deliberation. Later that day, being notified by the jury that a judgment was again impossible, Sanner terminated the trial, with the jury being ten for acquittal and two for conviction of some degree of homicide. A second trial took place six months later, in June 1910.

The testimony for the second trial reflected that of the first. This time, however, the jury returned a verdict of acquittal. The reaction of the populace, mirroring the testimony, was conflicted. Friends of the defendant were understandably pleased, while those of the victim were decidedly not. The legal system in Custer County seemed to be another unintentional victim. The *Miles City Independent* reported the verdict with an unexpected social commentary:

> *There was not a Miles City man on the jury, contrary to the general belief, which asserted that Miles City people have turned loose every man from the county charged with a crime.*

Tarbell and his friends naturally were elated with the result of the verdict.

Because of the verdict in the *Tarbell* case, assault charges against Woodley, Jackson, and Eubanks were dropped by the district attorney. The dismissal of these charges gave Judge Sanner the opportunity to lambaste the factionalism of the Powder River country and its practice of carrying guns:

> *The jury in the last case [Tarbell's] either concluded that there was ground for reasonable doubt or adopted the defendant's contention as to who was at fault in this most regrettable affair. But it seems to me the whole thing could have been avoided. . . .*
>
> *I want to impress upon these two factions existing on Powder River this fact: There have been three homicides in that section on the country within a short space of time. In one of them it was ascertained the principle was insane; one was the result of accident; of the other the investigation has just closed. Not any of these homicides would have occurred had there not been the habit of the indiscriminate use of firearms, where none were necessary at all.*
>
> *The time was when men got into controversies and lost their temper they were content with the weapons nature gave them, but it seems in these times and in that particular locality it is customary to carry firearms and sometimes to use them without any conception of what the consequences may be. I suggest to those factions on Powder River that this is an excellent time to eliminate this indiscriminate firearm business and try to do away with this rashness and ill-feeling.*

The conflicting testimony will be examined in a forthcoming third article in this series, and the drama will be placed in context. As an aside, in my first article, I described the difficulty of obtaining a transcript of either of the full trials. Despite several optimistic possible leads, the transcripts remain elusive. This article was prepared using newspaper accounts of the trial testimony. I am grateful for the assistance of the Tarbell, Mitchell, Garber, and Wilson family members for their help in researching this event. If anyone knows where a copy of either trial transcript can be found, I would appreciate them contacting me.

NOTES ON CHAPTER 7:

- This article was originally published in the *Powder River Examiner* on April 30, 2020.
- This is the second article in four series on the George Mitchell-Ray Tarbell incident.
- The snippet about Roy Garber learning to play checkers in the Custer County Jail was described to me by Vic Garber, Roy's grandson.
- In retrospect, my description of Charles Loud's legal reputation in the Tarbell articles is somewhat simplistic. Charles Loud was the district judge for two of the most controversial incidents in this area, the *Little Whirlwind* and the *Geddes* trials. I discuss the *Geddes* trials at length later in this collection. At the time of the *Tarbell* trial, Loud had returned to private practice. His experience as a judge clearly improved his performance as a lawyer. Two *Geddes* convictions and the *Little Whirlwind* cases were overturned by the Montana Supreme Court. In his later years, Loud became involved in financial scandal regarding a Forsyth bank. Nonetheless, at the time of the *Tarbell* trial his services were in demand, and they were not cheap. Link Wilson was said to be the financial backer of the defense.

Hole in the sandstone that functioned as the cabin's only entrance or exit. PHOTOGRAPH BY SHANE DUNNING.

8

How Deadman's Gulch Got its Name

In southern Rosebud County, on private land just off the east side of the Tongue River (near Birney), is an isolated ravine with the ominous name "Deadman's Gulch." The origin of that name has been lost to anything resembling "official" history, but thankfully the story still exists in the rich oral history of the area.

Back in the 1880s, the area was very sparsely populated by white settlers. The first cattle herds from Texas were beginning to enter the Tongue River valley, and the area was a crossroads for the various local Native American tribes. Some of the first white settlers of eastern Montana were, in fact, engaged in fur trapping and trading, not cattle. Two such trappers had established a home in an isolated draw just off the Tongue River, miles from the nearest white settlement.

Their isolation required extraordinary measures for security, and the trappers made clever use of a unique geological formation deep in the gulch. Among several sandstone cliffs jutting the valley was a large sandstone on flat ground, approximately ten feet high, fourteen feet wide, and six feet deep. In the direct center across the width of the stone, about a foot off the ground, was a hole that an average-sized man could fit through. Several pictures of this rock are included with this story.

The trappers built their simple one-room cabin on the flat ground snugly behind this rock and cleverly made it so the cabin's only entrance was through the hole in the rock. The cabin had no windows and (like most residences of the time) a dirt floor. They built a fireplace at the opposite end of the place for warmth and cooking. Entering the cabin through the hole took not insignificant effort and several seconds to accomplish.

As mentioned before, this part of southeastern Montana was historically used as a crossroads for various Native American tribes in the region. One day

Another view of the sandstone rock. PHOTOGRAPH BY SHANE DUNNING.

the cabin was occupied by only one trapper, as his partner was away for several days and not expected back anytime soon. To his surprise, he was visited by a group of four Native Americans of an unknown tribe. The trapper, rifle in hand, warned the party to move on. Eventually, the angry visitors left to continue their journey, and the trapper breathed a sigh of relief.

A short time later the trapper, sitting comfortably in the cabin, was alarmed to discover that at least one of the Natives Americans had returned and was making his way through the entrance. Alone and fearing for his life, he took an axe and struck the intruder behind the head as he peeked through the cabin side of the rock's hole. The intruder was dead, but the trapper could not be sure that his companions would not come back searching for him. It was even possible they were outside the cabin at that very moment. As his partner would not be back for several days, he could only think of one solution. He pulled the dead man inside the cabin and buried him in the dirt floor until his partner returned.

Luckily, the trapper remained unmolested until the arrival of his partner. Together they dug the body out of the cabin floor and re-buried the corpse in the sand rock cliffs on the opposite side of the gulch. As more settlers entered the area in a few years, the ravine was named Deadman's Gulch for this extraordinary incident. The cabin was eventually abandoned as cattle replaced the fur trade. The story does not end there, however.

The Brown Cattle Company bought the large 4D Ranch a few miles away from the site under the management of Albert G. Brown, Sr. Among the cowboys then working for Brown in the 1920s was Allen "Big Bones" Alderson. Alderson would later help establish the "Bones Brothers" dude ranch on Hanging Woman Creek with his two brothers. Knowing the story of the trapper's cabin, Big Bones searched the sand rock cliffs opposite the cabin and eventually found the body of the Native American intruder. Morbidly, Alderson brought the corpse's skull as a trophy to his employer, Albert Brown, who placed it on the mantel in his library. It remained there for decades, even after Albert G. "Buster" Brown, Jr. took over the 4D. My father worked for the 4D as a young man and remembered the skull in the library. He also clearly recalls the refusal of Buster Brown's Cheyenne housemaids to clean that room.

The location of the skull is unknown today. It is possibly the only remaining evidence of the trapper's cabin and the tale of Deadman's Gulch. All that remains today is an unusual rock formation with fire pit rocks tucked away in an obscure valley with an enduring name. Most importantly, these are the stories we lose daily as oral histories from our older generation remain unrecorded and their value unrecognized. The history of this area can only be preserved if efforts are made to protect them.

NOTES ON CHAPTER 8:

- This article was first published in the *Powder River Examiner* on April 2, 2020.

- The previously published version of this article incorrectly identified "Big Bones" Alderson as Irv Alderson. This is incorrect. "Big Bones" was the name of Irv's brother Allen Alderson. Allen was the man who discovered the body and brought the skull to Albert Brown. Irv was known as "Little Bones" and had no significance to this story. I have corrected the error on the website and this collection. I apologize for the error.

Ray Tarbell (left), Bert Newcomb (center), and John Morris (right) at Miles City in 1916. PHOTOGRAPH COURTESY OF OF BRUCE KEIL AND FAMILY.

9

The Incomprehensible Trials of Ray Tarbell (Tarbell Part 3)

Reconciling all the conflicting testimony in the criminal case against Ray Tarbell is an exercise in futility. Perhaps the only thing that was not disputed was that Ray Tarbell killed George Mitchell on September 8, 1909, at a roundup near the present-day community of Sonnette. Two previous articles have related the testimony of the preliminary hearing and the two criminal trials. In the end, the jury in the second trial acquitted Tarbell of all charges. That simple sentence, however, belies the difficulty of the Custer County legal system handling this affair.

Nearly every significant item of any relevance to the guilt or innocence of Ray Tarbell was directly contradicted by other testimony of seemingly similar weight. These contradictions were almost total, so much so that it became impossible to genuinely accept either the prosecution's or the defense's case without also accepting that the opposing presentation had been a brazenly dishonest attempt to deceive the jurors.

A key point of considerable disagreement was the identity of the man who first initiated physical hostilities. After an initial confrontation, a general shootout had occurred between at least four, possibly five men, and at least a dozen shots were fired. According to the state's case, directly testified to by Ray Mitchell (the deceased's son), Lehman Wilkes, and four others (including some defense witnesses), John Woodley rode up to George Mitchell and, after exchanging some heated words, took out his pistol and tried to club the elder Mitchell with it. As Mitchell ducked from Woodley's blow, Henry Jackson rode his horse between them, apparently causing Ray Tarbell to fire the first shot of the incident at Jackson. Jackson, Woodley, Tarbell, and W.E. Eubanks then engaged in a literal shooting match. George Mitchell was unarmed and did not participate in the initial shooting. This testimony seemed to establish that both the first physical blow and the first shot of the initial encounter had been perpetrated by the Tarbell faction. The state thus presented Tarbell and Woodley as the conflict's aggressors, at least concerning physical violence.

Such a straightforward chain of events was refuted, just as straightforwardly, by the defense. Woodley, Tarbell, and Eubanks all testified that Mitchell had attempted to strike Woodley with his quirt after the two had words. Woodley striking at Mitchell with his pistol had been retaliatory, they stated. They claimed Jackson had fired the first shot to complete the total contradiction of the state's case. Several other defense witnesses corroborated the assertion that Jackson had fired first.

The participation of Ray Mitchell in this initial round of gunplay was also disputed. In the preliminary hearing (in September) and throughout both trials, Ray Mitchell maintained that, while he had a pistol on his person at the time, he did not fire a shot. His non-shooting status was confirmed by Jackson and the testimony of at least two others. Ray Mitchell's pistol was a 32 Colt automatic and had a distinctive sound as the only automatic in the fight. Woodley, Eubanks, and two others claimed to have seen Ray Mitchell firing or heard his pistol's unique report. The previous day, Ray Mitchell and Henry Jackson had come armed to the roundup, a vital assertion of the defense's self-defense claim.

While Tarbell, Woodley, and Eubanks stopped firing to reload their guns, George Mitchell rode to Jackson and retrieved his weapon. The elder Mitchell and his son then started to ride away from the conflict when they turned around (the reason for this is also disputed) back toward the roundup herd and Ray Tarbell. With Jackson's pistol in his hand, George Mitchell had a few more words with Tarbell when (according to the prosecution) a single shot was fired by Tarbell, killing Mitchell instantly.

Not only was this version of the killing blow disputed by the defense, but they presented another mutually exclusive set of alternate facts. According to the defense, Mitchell had fired first, with Tarbell shooting back almost instantaneously. Interestingly, in attempting to paint Mitchell as the aggressor, Tarbell claimed he had made this instantaneous and deadly single shot while initially looking away from Mitchell when the deceased pulled his trigger.

Presenting mutually exclusive facts on crucial aspects of the trial was not limited to the defense. In presenting their case that Tarbell had shot Mitchell in self-defense, the defense counsel used the testimony of Eubanks and

J.C. Gardner to state that George Mitchell had, that August, made specific threats to kill Woodley and Tarbell if they rounded up on his range. Other members of the roundup were also called to testify that they had heard of Mitchell's threats. This, combined with Ray Mitchell and Jackson coming armed to the roundup the previous day, laid the key predicate for Tarbell to believe Mitchell posed a credible threat to his life.

On redirect in the second trial, the state refuted this threat with the testimony of Mitchell's widow, Eva, Joe Hannan, and Hans Peterson. All three affirmed that they were also present during the conversation when George Mitchell "threatened" Woodley and Tarbell. They firmly denied that Mitchell had made any such statement to Eubanks.

Given the ferocity of this back-and-forth, it is perhaps understandable how the first jury could not render a unanimous verdict. Even the reports of the first jury's final vote were contradictory. The newspapers reported a split of ten for acquittal and two for conviction while printing a total correction (ten for conviction, two for acquittal) on the very same page. It is reasonable that, given such contradictory testimony, the presumption of innocence would sway the second jury towards an acquittal. Both juries had to decide between two versions of events, the logical extension of which was alarming to the rule of law in Custer County. If you believed the prosecution, a cabal of wealthy sheep interests had shamelessly concocted a self-defense story and purchased the perjured testimony of nearly a dozen cowboys. The defense lawyers benefitted from the preliminary trial testimony and three months to form a workable story. If the defendant's case was to be taken at face value, the state had (for unknown reasons) actively prosecuted an honorable man who had done too good a job protecting himself from a known and dangerous crank. In doing so, the state had deliberately ignored most eyewitnesses in favor of the biased testimony of the deceased's extensive family and friends.

Today, the reliability of eyewitness testimony is under serious scrutiny, and the jury system of Custer County at the time was under considerable disregard. In this analysis, I have relied on the newspaper accounts of the first and second criminal trials. I continue to search for the transcripts of either the first (December 1909) trial or the second (June 1910). While the newspapers report the substance of the testimony, they do not describe in detail how specific witnesses responded to cross-examination of opposing counsel. These crucial details remain unavailable, so finding the trial transcripts is important.

Given all this, I believe the truth lies somewhere between the two extremes and that the factionalism that prevailed in the community at the time drove its legal system to a breaking point. What actually happened the morning of September 8, 1909? While I welcome more evidence and would reconsider any opinion, I will lay out my view of the most likely scenario in a fourth and final article.

NOTES ON CHAPTER 9:

- This article was first published in the *Powder River Examiner* on July 9, 2020.
- This is the third article of four series on the George Mitchell-Ray Tarbell incident.
- One of the most curious aspect of writing (and reading) about this incident is the maddeningly frequent presence of a participant with the first name "Ray." In addition to this story's main protagonist, Ray Tarbell, we also have Ray Mitchell (the deceased's son) and Ray Wilson, the son of Link Wilson (Tarbell's financial partner). Throw in for good measure the similar-sounding witness Roy Garber, and you can be forgiven for any difficulty in keeping the facts of this incident straight.

George Mitchell and his thoroughbred horse "Diamond Dick," circa 1907. THIS PHOTOGRAPH IS PURPORTED TO BE BY L.A. HUFFMAN (BUT UNCONFIRMED). COURTESY OF THE MITCHELL FAMILY.

10

WHAT REALLY HAPPENED TO GEORGE MITCHELL (TARBELL PART 4)

George Mitchell was, by even the accounts of his friends, an argumentative and possessive man. That being said, he was also a well-known cattle and horseman in his community, devoted to his large family. He did not like sheep and believed that Link Wilson's ovine interests were a serious threat to his livestock's water and his livelihood.

According to John Daut, Mitchell had a gentleman's agreement with the local sheep magnate Robert R. Selway regarding delineations of range that the elder Selway honored for several years. However, R.R. Selway moved to Sheridan in 1900 and placed his Pumpkin Creek operation in the control of his brother Delos. Delos was not considered as strong as his brother, and I speculate that Link Wilson, Selway's longtime partner in sheep operations, did not honor this pre-existing agreement in the same manner as Bob Selway. This caused the boisterous Mitchell to run his mouth, possibly to the extreme of the death threats testified to. How serious these threats were considered is a matter of debate. It should be stressed that Wilson was not legally bound by this agreement, and that Wilson was at the time transitioning to an expanded cattle operation. By any measure, however, the enmity between the two factions was well established as the month of September began.

The UA Roundup was run by Woodley and Tarbell but was a sanctioned event. Even the contradicting testimony at the trials revealed that Tarbell specifically prevented members of the Mitchell family from working George's cattle. Several head of Mitchell's cattle were in the herd that day, and George Mitchell had more than enough reason and standing to collect his own cattle. If Tarbell seriously felt Mitchell was such a danger, he seemingly had plenty of alternatives available to prevent George Mitchell's physical presence at the roundup. Specifically, he could have allowed Scott Mitchell, George's nephew, who had worked the roundup for at least a week, to cut out his uncle's cattle. Indeed, Scott testified that he was willing to do so but was prevented by Tarbell.

Perhaps the most compelling evidence of George Mitchell's lack of deadly intention that day was the fact that he came to the roundup unarmed. If the elder Mitchell had come to the roundup with some intent other than gathering his own cattle at a roundup being run by his enemies, he was about to poke a grizzly bear with a very short stick. Given his long-established history of being a successful trail boss for the Newman Brothers' N Bar outfit, it is difficult to believe that Mitchell was given to such recklessness.

The testimony establishes that Tarbell, along with Woodley, Eubanks, and several others, brought in the last bunch of cattle that day shortly before the incident. When they did so, they observed the Mitchell party and moved aggressively to confront them. According to his own testimony, Tarbell sent Woodley ahead to find out Mitchell's "intentions." Given Mitchell's threatening statements, an action of this type seems reasonable. What is not reasonable, however, is sending Woodley to make this determination when several obviously less provocative alternatives were immediately available. The whole theory of the defense was predicated on the serious threats Mitchell had supposedly directed specifically toward Tarbell and Woodley. Sending Woodley, of all the available people, to determine Mitchell's intentions was a provocative act and undercuts the defense theory of the case.

That being said, several (but not all) witnesses indicate that Jackson fired the first shot. The fact that both Jackson and Ray Mitchell had come to the roundup armed two days in a row is also revealing. It displays a level of tension that could naturally result in a gunfight. George Mitchell took the specific action to get Jackson's gun and turn for home, telling his son "let's get out of here."

By all accounts, Jackson's gun was in Mitchell's left hand when he turned around to face Tarbell. He and his son Ray did so because Tarbell had hailed them, supposedly with the infamous line, "Hold on, I don't want to have to shoot you in the back." In his testimony, Tarbell only states that the Mitchells suddenly turned back toward the herd without giving a reason. The specificity of Ray Mitchell's testimony on this aspect is much more compelling and is somewhat supported by the testimony of others who heard Tarbell call to Mitchell before he turned around (although only Jackson would confirm the quote).

As they faced each other for this final confrontation, an important question must be answered. Did Tarbell have a reasonable belief that Mitchell's fire was imminent and required his own action? Only one of these men had experience killing a man in self-defense at a shootout. In 1903, Ray Tarbell had killed a man in Bridgeport, Nebraska, during an argument and was cleared by the coroner's jury. Even if this Nebraska incident was a legitimate case of self-defense, it also demonstrates Tarbell's quick reflexes and coolness under fire.

It seems to be reasonable for Tarbell to have believed, perhaps only at that very moment, that George Mitchell posed a deadly threat. The fact that Tarbell himself had likely provoked Mitchell to such a state may be despicable, but it nonetheless was reasonable for him to defend himself. Considering the social cost of being considered a coward in the American West at the time, it seems likely to me that both men fired at the same time.

The days following the killing would prove vital to Ray Tarbell's future. He surrendered himself to the sheriff and was bailed out by Link Wilson. Tarbell obtained the services of the best lawyer in eastern Montana, former judge Charles H. Loud. The defense team clearly knew their client was going to trial and therefore were not aggressive at the preliminary hearing. At that hearing, they gained the advantage of getting the state's witnesses on the record while ever-so-gently laying the groundwork for self-defense. In doing so, however, they allowed the state's narrative to be repeated throughout Powder River country with little contradiction.

With much of the state's case now on the record, the defense then transformed George Mitchell's aggressive verbosity into the rabid threats of a dangerous man. Suddenly, almost a dozen eyewitnesses not used by the state in the preliminary hearing became available to testify for Ray Tarbell's claim of self-defense. Putting the victim on trial, Loud and his partner, Campbell, lined up a dozen men (some prominent cattlemen) to say Mitchell was belligerent and quarrelsome. Tarbell's own cattleman *bone fides* were used to quell anti-sheep sentiment and make Mitchell's ire seem unhinged. Until the trial transcript is found, we can never know how (or if) the state considered whether Mitchell's threats (if they even happened) may have had the effect of angering Tarbell and Woodley, rather than scaring them. The newspaper accounts give no reason to think the prosecution did so.

Indeed, there is some testimony that Tarbell and Woodley anticipated tragedy would occur that day. A.F. Kelly testified that Tarbell had told him days before the shooting that he (Tarbell) would shoot Mitchell if he "showed his head up over the hill," meaning if he came near the roundup. This testimony was severely

The George Mitchell ranch, purportedly by L.A. Huffman. The back of the photograph reads: "Broadus, Mont., 1893. George L. Mitchell, Maude Mitchell O'Keef—Joplin, Missouri, J. R. Mitchell, Ray Mitchell, Mrs. George L. Mitchell. Present Alan Steadman ranch, Sonnette." PHOTOGRAPH COURTESY OF THE RANGE RIDERS MUSEUM.

colored by Kelly's admission (under cross-examination) that he had consumed "half a skin full" before taking the stand. This clashes with the near unanimous testimony that Tarbell and Woodley were unarmed throughout the roundup until the day after Ray Mitchell and Jackson came to the roundup with their pistols. In a sense, the armed presence of Mitchell and Jackson the day before can also be considered a somewhat provocative act. It apparently caused Tarbell and his associates to arm themselves for a fight they showed virtually no interest in avoiding.

Hindsight being 20/20, it is clear that every party to this tragic affair had multiple opportunities to avoid the tragedy that ensued and that almost none did. The remarks of the trial judge, Sidney Sanner, seem to come to a similar conclusion when he pinned the tragedy on the common practice of carrying guns. Perhaps what would be most unfair would be to judge all the participants in this incident with the values of our present day.

From today's perspective, we can too easily blame the common practice of carrying guns and the social norms of not backing down from a fight. While that may be true, we have had the advantage of over one hundred years learning from all-too numerous tragedies such as this. Sheep spoiling a water hole for cattle today would not deprive ten children of a father and a wife of her husband, and for that we can perhaps be thankful.

NOTES ON CHAPTER 10:

- This article was first published in the *Powder River Examiner* on July 23, 2020.
- This is the fourth article in a series of four on the George Mitchell-Ray Tarbell incident.
- Trial Judge Sidney Sanner eventually became a justice of the Montana Supreme Court.
- Ray Tarbell was interviewed by Sheridan historian Charles Helvey. He does not discuss the Mitchell killing and only makes tangential mentions of key figures such as Woodley. The transcript of Ray Tarbell's interview with Charles Helvey is available from the Charles Helvey Papers at the American Heritage Center in Laramie.

Charley Flory, the wolfer. PHOTOGRAPH COURTESY OF THE TRAIL END STATE HISTORIC SITE, WYOMING DEPARTMENT OF STATE PARKS AND CULTURAL RESOURCES. MANVILLE KENDRICK COLLECTION.

11

The Fateful Ride of Charley Flory

On the early winter morning of January 16, 1927, Charley Flory got on his horse and left his homestead on Anderson Creek near Decker in southeastern Big Horn County, Montana. He was headed to the house of his father-in-law, E.T. Ostrum, who coincidently also went by the name "Charley." The sixty-five-year-old Ostrum worked as a ditch digger and was an immigrant from Sweden. The 35-mile trip at a horse-friendly pace would take two days during cold winter weather with at least one river crossing.

Flory was by trade a "wolfer" during the winter months, a man who specialized in trapping the predators that killed area cattle in large numbers. He was a particularly effective wolfer, and by 1903 he gained the patronage of the wealthy owner of the nearby OW Ranch, John B. Kendrick (as well as other cattlemen). By 1926, Kendrick was one of the most powerful men in Wyoming, then well into his second term (of three) in the U.S. Senate. Flory himself was a well-liked man and a respected trapper. In 1910, he had a serious bout with ptomaine poisoning, which substantially weakened him for the rest of his life.

Ostrum's rented cabin was across the border in Wyoming, near the Powder River and Kendrick's LX Bar Ranch. Flory's trapping range extended well into Wyoming, and he was especially familiar with the country around Kendrick's ranches.

Charley Flory had been a confirmed bachelor until he suddenly married Daisy Carola Ostrum in 1923. The social upheaval his marriage caused around Birney was a humorous anecdote told in the book *Hell Among the Yearlings*, by Ned Randolph. According to the marriage certificate, Flory was thirty-six years old when they married, while Daisy's age was listed as seventeen. In 1927, they had been married four years and had two children, a daughter (aged three) and an infant son (thirteen months). Daisy's parents had divorced only a few years after her birth, and the future Mrs. Flory had almost no contact with her father until the time of her own marriage. Charley Flory, on the other hand, had known Charley Ostrum for more than twenty years.

Ostrum had briefly re-acquainted with his daughter after she married, and in the summer of 1926, the Florys invited Ostrum for an extended visit at their homestead on Anderson Creek. He arrived the day after Thanksgiving and left the day after Christmas.

When Charley Flory went trapping, he would usually be gone for days at a time, leaving Daisy and the children in the company of his brother, Arthur, who lived in another cabin near the homestead. Daisy's mother, Etta, lived five miles away. Flory made several trapping rounds while Ostrum stayed at the house.

During his father-in-law's visit and at his prompting, Flory agreed to allow Ostrum to move in with them, as the ditch digger wanted to take advantage of employment opportunities with some nearby railroad construction. Daisy was supportive of the idea.

When Flory returned from a trapping trip on December 23rd, Daisy told him she didn't want her father to stay for Christmas. During his visit, the wolfer had begun making arrangements for Ostrum's new residence, only now Daisy did not support the move. Her father, she said, had been rude in his absence and "had acted like an animal." They agreed to not have the father-in-law live with them, and Charley invented a story to explain the change of plans. A few weeks later (around January 12th), while working on another trapping line in Wyoming, he ran into Ostrum and gave him the bad news. Ostrum seemed to accept the story and gave Flory a small package to deliver to Daisy, saying: "I asked Daisy how many more children she was figuring on having, and she told me none, so I told her when I was in town I would buy her something to prevent her having children. . . ."

Relieved that Ostrum had taken the news well, Flory returned to his homestead. When he did so, he gave Daisy the package from her father. Her face dropped as she looked at the package and blurted, "Oh God!" The box contained birth control devices for both of them. Daisy broke down and finally told Charley why she had changed her mind about her father moving in.

Flory approached his father-in-law's cabin around eleven o'clock that Tuesday morning, looking through the window of the front door to see if the old man was there. Not seeing him, he got off his horse and dropped the reins. He carried his hunting rifle, a Mannlicher Carbine with a double trigger system, when he entered the front door which gave way to the living room. Ostrum was in the kitchen adjoining the living room, apparently beginning to start a fire in the kitchen stove.

"Hello, Charley," Ostrum said, acknowledging his son-in-law.

Flory kept the cocked rifle in his right hand and walked toward Ostrum. "What made you rape Daisy, Charley?"

Ostrum, unarmed, came towards Flory with a "kind of grin," as the thin, sickly wolfer backed away from the larger man into the living room.

"Let's talk it over."

"Don't come any closer," replied Flory. Ostrum then turned back into the kitchen. Flory followed him, stopping at the kitchen door holding his rifle in both hands. As he got to the stove, Ostrum turned to Flory:

"Let's talk it over."

"Charley, do you know you just about ruined my family?"

Ostrum said, "I will keep the girl."

Flory responded, "you are a pretty son-of-a-bitch to keep your daughter."

At that moment, Ostrum sprang for the gun. As Flory backed away, the rifle was jerked back and fired off a shot. The big ditch-digger fell immediately, not making a sound as he hit the ground. Intuitively knowing that his father-in-law was dead, Flory immediately left the house and rode straight to his homestead, arriving late that night. He didn't stop to examine the body, nor did he inform any of Ostrum's neighbors (who lived less a mile away) of the incident.

Charley didn't tell Daisy what had happened until the next afternoon. She assured Charley she would testify to her father's assault, and he had resolved to turn himself in. His friend George Holmes had a truck and drove Flory to Sheridan that evening. The sheriff's office was closed for the night, and so he rented a room at the Rex Hotel.

The next morning, he turned himself into the Sheridan Police Department, who promptly turned him over to the Sheridan County Sheriff. It turned out that Ostrum's cabin was actually in Campbell County, and so arrangements were made to transfer him to the Campbell County authorities in Gillette.

The trial was a sensation all through Wyoming and Montana in 1928. The Campbell County D.A. charged Charles Flory with first-degree murder. Judge Harry Ilsley severely limited testimony on the sexual assault allegation because it did not justify homicide but was somewhat relevant to demonstrating Charley Flory's state of mind. Throughout the trial, the wolfer maintained that

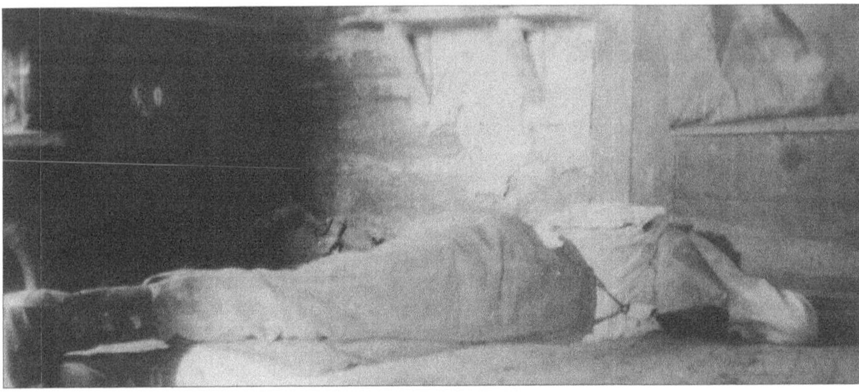

Photograph of the crime scene taken by Mary Kendrick. This image was not printed in the original *PRE* article. PHOTOGRAPH COURTESY OF THE TRAIL END STATE HISTORIC SITE, WYOMING DEPARTMENT OF STATE PARKS AND CULTURAL RESOURCES.

the shooting had been an accident and that he had only intended to make a citizen's arrest of his father-in-law after first obtaining a confession. He had brought the rifle, he said, because he feared the much larger and physical Ostrum would attack him if he were unarmed. The prosecution repeatedly railed against Flory's inconsistent testimony, as the wolfer's memory seemed to have some very convenient lapses. The defense tried to emphasize the rape allegation with only limited success. They also provided testimony about the hair-trigger nature of Flory's rifle and Ostrum's poor reputation. Daisy and the children were present during every day of the trial. Several members of the press were also among the spectators, as the story was front-page news throughout the area. The jury found Flory guilty of second-degree murder, and the judge sentenced him to twenty years in prison:

> *During the sentencing Flory came into the court room with his three-year old daughter in his arms. When asked if he had anything to say, he answered: "I have not." Flory's wife who appeared at his side, apparently was unaffected by the sentence.*

An appeal to the Wyoming Supreme Court reduced the charge to manslaughter, which at the time carried a sentence of between one and twenty years. The high court remanded the case back to Judge Ilsley for re-sentencing, and Ilsley promptly sentenced Charley Flory to eighteen years.

The supporters of Charley Flory, particularly around Sheridan and Birney, actively supported his parole by writing letters and signing petitions. Finally, in 1931, Flory received parole after acting Wyoming Governor A.M. Clark commuted much of his sentence. Many believed that the support of Senator Kendrick heavily influenced these decisions.

After his release, Charley and Daisy divorced. Both subsequently remarried. Flory continued to live in the Sheridan area until his death in 1973.

The description of the confrontation between Flory and Ostrum relayed in this column was drawn almost exclusively from the trial testimony of Charley Flory. Flory's testimony has considerable flaws and should be judged accordingly.

Charley Florey, several years before his fateful ride. PHOTOGRAPH COURTESY OF THE ARTHUR HAYES FAMILY.

NOTES ON CHAPTER 11:

- This article was originally published in the *Powder River Examiner* on August 27, 2020.
- The photograph of the crime scene was not included in the *PRE* article due to its subject matter, a decision that I fully agreed with.
- Charley Flory was interviewed by local historian Charles Helvey, but the subject of the trial was never touched upon. Flory makes some remarks about people he met in prison, but that is the extent of the interview. Based on this, it is clear that Helvey agreed to not ask Flory about this most important event in his life, a practice that repeated itself with many of Helvey's interviews. A transcript of Charley Flory's interview with Charles Helvey can be found in Helvey's Oral Histories housed at the American Heritage Center in Laramie.

Robert Guy, Rosebud County Sheriff from 1902 to 1908. PHOTOGRAPH COURTESY OF ROSEBUD COUNTY, MONTANA.

12

Sheriff Robert Guy's Deadly Chase

On Sunday, June 2, 1907, Rosebud County Sheriff Robert J. Guy was alerted by Forsyth resident James Anderson that three horses had been stolen from his pasture. Anderson discovered the trail of his stolen horses three days later, six miles southwest of Forsyth. That next morning, Sheriff Guy deputized Anderson and the two began a chase that ended with the formation of a posse, one man's death and inglorious burial, and another's daring escape and later arrest.

The two lawmen left Forsyth the morning of June 5th. There had been significant rain the night of the theft, and Anderson had picked up the trail of his horses heading south. That night they stayed at Charles Davis' camp on the head of Sheep Creek, where they learned the men they were pursuing had also stayed overnight. On Thursday, they traveled down Cottonwood, up Eagle Creek and over the divide to the head of Graveyard Creek. They crossed the Tongue River and found an unattended hot stove at Little Ed McGehee's place on Lee Creek, an indication that they were catching up to their quarry.

On June 9, when Guy and Anderson caught sight of the two thieves leisurely riding their stolen horses and using the third as a pack horse, their own horses were exhausted. Luckily, they were near John B. Kendrick's OW Ranch on Hanging Woman Creek in the southernmost point of the county. They quietly proceeded to the ranch house to procure assistance, which they received. Along with two fresh horses for themselves, Sheriff Guy formed a posse of himself, Anderson, and OW hands Joe Hertzler, James Burdick, Marian Fisher, and John H. Reavis. They caught up with the thieves as they maneuvered through a coulee, with Sheriff Guy and Anderson approaching them from the south while the remaining members of the posse rode up the north side to cut off their escape.

Guy and Anderson dismounted as they approached the two men, who were unaware they were being followed. Proceeding on foot, they identified themselves as lawmen and demanded at least three times for the suspects to throw their hands up and stop. The two men immediately spurred their horses into a run, with the trailing outlaw firing two shots from a pistol. One of these bullets came within inches of the sheriff's head. Guy fired his gun once above their heads as a warning, which was not heeded. Both Guy and Anderson then opened fire with deadly purpose, dropping the trailing outlaw from his horse. Sheriff Guy soon gained this position, found his victim dead, and continued the pursuit. The dead man's partner dismounted and ran some fifty yards to refuge in the coulee behind some rocks. The other members of the posse recovered the stolen horses along with the outlaws' pack.

The remaining horse thief was not in any mood to be captured and had armed himself with a 30-40 Winchester rifle. He took at least two shots from behind the rocks at Guy and Anderson. Sheriff Guy recalled to the coroner's jury that "one of the bullets from the Winchester 30-40 was so close I could feel the effects of it near all the afternoon." The surviving horse thief held them off until nightfall. Sometime during the night, he removed his spurs, allowing him to quietly slip away under cover of darkness by crawling out on his hands and knees.

At daylight the next morning, Sheriff Guy deputized Joe Hertzler, John Reavis, and Otter Creek legend Charlie Thex to assist him in bringing in the second outlaw. They soon discovered their target's escape (including the discarded spurs) and examined the body of the fallen outlaw. He appeared to be a young man, around twenty years old. Among the supplies recovered were approximately 250 rounds of ammunition for a 30-40 Winchester, a majority of which were poisoned lead cartridges. In addition, they found around 30 rounds of pistol cartridges and a pocketbook containing a small number of mail items from various parts of the country. Two spent 30-40 cartridges along with the spurs were found in the rocks were the remaining outlaw had sheltered.

Mary Kendrick took a photograph of the corpse before it was placed in a coffin of planks that had been hastily constructed at the ranch. The casket was buried where its occupant met his end. Sheriff Guy stated that the coffin should not be buried too deeply, as the coroner would soon come to collect the body. For unknown reasons, this did not occur, and the body was soon dug up by coyotes, and the remains scattered. Some years later, the remains were collected and again buried in the same place, only deeper.

The escaped outlaw was eventually captured in northern Wyoming on Dutch Creek. Because of the contents of the pocketbook, Sheriff Guy suspected

This image of Floyd Smith was taken by Mary Kendrick. PHOTOGRAPH COURTESY OF THE WYOMING STATE ARCHIVES. IMAGE IDENTIFIER SUB NEG 22226.

that the horse thieves had been involved in a heavily publicized train robbery of the Northern Pacific at Welch's Spur near Butte, which had resulted in the murder of the engineer. Newspapers throughout the eastern part of Montana repeated Guy's supposition until it was eventually debunked by the authorities investigating the robbery. The NP robbers had not accessed the mailroom, and the recovered mail was the primary reason for Guy's initial suspicion.

The man who escaped was named Robert Phillips, and he was convicted of stealing the horses and sentenced to two years in prison. The dead outlaw's name was Floyd Smith, from Arizona. In 1901, thirteen-year-old Floyd Smith was captured by a posse as part of a horse-thieving gang that had killed at least one man and seriously wounded an Arizona Ranger. The *Graham Guardian* of Safford, Arizona, also reported that "one of the boys had since escaped." When Phillips was captured, he was reported to have said, "it's a good thing that you killed him. If you'd have killed me instead of him, he'd have got some of you."

NOTES ON CHAPTER 12:

- This article first appeared in the *Powder River Examiner* on October 8, 2020.
- This article includes a photo that was not included in the original *PRE* article due to its content.
- Judy Musgrave gave me a copy of a letter Manville Kendrick sent to the Rosebud County Court several years after the capture of Phillips. Attached to this letter were written statements from some of the posse members. I am grateful for Judy's generosity and support.

A circa 1884 picture of T.B. Glover. PHOTOGRAPH COURTESY OF THE CONGRESSIONAL MEDAL OF HONOR SOCIETY, MOUNT PLEASANT, S.C.

13

The Medal of Honor Earned on the Mizpah and Pumpkin Creek

The citation reads:

> *The President of the United States of America, in the name of Congress, takes pleasure in presenting the Medal of Honor to Sergeant Thaddeus Brown Glover, United States Army, for extraordinary heroism on 10 April 1879 and 10 February 1880, while serving with Troop B, 2nd U.S. Cavalry, in action at Mitzpah [*sic*] and Pumpkin Creek, Montana. While in charge of small scouting parties, Sergeant Glover fought, charged, surrounded, and captured war parties of Sioux Indians.*

The Medal of Honor was presented to T.B. Glover over seventeen years after the most recent of the incidents cited. He entered the service in March 1876, and between 1877 and 1881 served under Colonel Nelson Miles in Montana. An ambitious man, he quickly rose to the rank of sergeant, stationed at Fort Keogh. As indicated by the citation, Glover was involved in two separate incidents, although only one involved the Sioux.

Capturing Black Coyote on the Mizpah in 1879

During the exodus of the Northern Cheyenne from Indian Territory (now Oklahoma) in 1878, Little Wolf's band split from Dull Knife's Band. Dull Knife went on to surrender to Lt. W.B. Clark at Fort Robinson. Little Wolf, however, had successfully brought around 150 of his people to the Powder River area. Among the band was an aggressive man named Black Coyote who was married to Buffalo Calf Road Woman, the "girl who saved her brother" at the Battle of the Rosebud.

Black Coyote often clashed with Little Wolf and advocated more violence toward whites. During an argument in a council meeting, he shot and killed

Black Crane. For this crime, Little Wolf banished him. His wife, two children, and several others (totaling eight in all) left the Powder River camp with him.

In early April of 1879, a sergeant and a private were repairing the Keogh-Deadwood telegraph line where it crossed Mizpah Creek. While they were having lunch, Black Coyote and others attacked the soldiers. The private was killed and scalped, while the sergeant was grievously wounded in the hip but managed to fight off the Cheyennes. He was discovered alive by three civilians who took him to Ft. Keogh. Colonel Miles dispatched Sergeant Glover along with ten men to arrest the perpetrators. After three days, Glover caught up with them and deployed his men:

> *Two Indians were standing on a rock, waving a white flag. Much to my regret they signified their intention of surrendering. I accepted the surrender and turned to my command, when suddenly, I heard firing behind me. The two Indians had been joined by others and they had treacherously begun an attack. Then we started in and captured the entire band.*

Black Coyote and two others were brought to Milestown for trial, but all three hanged themselves in the jail. While they were committing their crimes on the Mizpah, Little Wolf's band surrendered and joined Two Moons' band at Fort Keogh.

The Battle of Pumpkin Creek in 1880

Sitting Bull had taken his people to Canada in 1877, but small hunting and raiding parties continued to venture into Montana. On the third of February 1880, Fort Keogh learned of a local skirmish between some Gros Ventres and Hunkpapa Sioux, killing ten and wounding twelve. Two days later, "Catfish" Sandy Morris, a trapper and friend of eastern Montana adventurer Yellowstone Kelly, came to the fort detailing how he and his trapping partner had been attacked in a hay corral along Pumpkin Creek. Remembering his success ten months earlier, Colonel Miles again dispatched Sergeant Thaddeus Glover "to look them up." Miles was reported to have told the sergeant, "Glover, make a success of this trip and I will make a success of you."

When Glover, six enlisted men, eight Indian scouts, and Morris left Fort Keogh, the temperature was recorded at 32 degrees below zero. Also accompanying the party was Yellowstone Kelly, who was at the fort when his friend

Yellowstone Kelly, shown here in 1878, accompanied Sgt. Glover's party at the 1880 Battle of Pumpkin Creek. PHOTOGRAPH BY L.A. HUFFMAN, COURTESY OF THE BILLINGS PUBLIC LIBRARY, BILLINGS, MT.

brought news of the attack. Driving through deep snow, they reached the sight of the depredations, somewhere near thc head uf Pumpkin Creek. 'Ihey soon found the dead body of an Indian covered with leaves at the base of a large tree, along with "a very perceptible trail." Glover recalled later that:

At 11 o'clock that morning, while we were floundering through the snow-drifts girth deep, both men and animals suffering from the extreme cold, my scouts returned to the rear and refused further to lead the party. Their ponies, they said, were played out from breaking through the snow. Unwilling to abandon the trip, I took a corporal with me and, going to the front, assumed the lead, sending the scouts to the rear under arrest.

I immediately corralled my packs. Then I dismounted my men and sent half of them to the left of the ravine under charge of the corporal, taking the other half myself and going to the right. Each party was directed to advance, and, at a preconcerted signal, to open fire on the hostiles. Before the signal could be given, however, a shot was fired and the men were at once ordered to attack, although the most satisfactory position had not yet been reached.

The Indians withdrew in such a manner as to cover all assailable points and I at once ordered all the men to get out of range. Upon inquiry, I learned that the first shot had come from the Indians; that a private named Douglass, who had advanced too far along the ledge in an effort to get a shot at the Indians before the time agreed upon, had been shot and killed.

Not knowing at the time whether Douglass was killed or wounded, Glover called for volunteers to get the man. None did so. Glover then crawled out under heavy fire, tied a noose to Douglass' foot and pulled the body back to a place of safety. Satisfied that the hostiles could not be extracted with his resources, Glover sent one of the Indian scouts to Fort Keogh for reinforcements. He made a chain guard around the Sioux to prevent their escape, a tactic that required every man in his command to stay awake and alert until reinforced.

The next morning, I withdrew a part of my force and directed the balance to keep up the fire. After undergoing this for about two hours I was informed by one of the scouts that the hostiles desired to surrender. But having seen a body of men approaching from the post, I concluded to hold the Indians under fire until the relief arrived. Upon the arrival of Captain Snyder, I reported the state of affairs to him and was directed to accept the surrender.

Accompanying Captain Snyder's reinforcements was the Cheyenne Chief White Bull. White Bull finalized the surrender of the remaining Sioux. According to Kelly's memoirs, they had come from Sitting Bull's camp and were on a

Right: An undated photo of Major T.B. Glover with his Medal of Honor, presented for extraordinary heroism shown by then Sergeant Glover at Mizpah and Pumpkin Creek in 1879 and 1880. PHOTOGRAPH COURTESY OF THE CONGRESSIONAL MEDAL OF HONOR SOCIETY.

horse-stealing raid into Crow country when they encountered the white men in the corral.

Glover left the Army in 1881 but returned to serve as a Major in the Quartermaster Corps during World War One (1917–1919). He died in 1932 and is buried in Suffolk County, New York.

The precise location of the conflict between the Sioux and Sergeant Glover is not known to historians. If there are any readers with more information regarding the location of this incident, please contact me.

NOTES ON CHAPTER 13:

- This article first appeared in the November 5, 2020, edition of the *Powder River Examiner.*
- While I am still researching this subject, I have not been able to learn the precise location of these incidents.

Lakota leader Sitting Bull, 1885. PHOTOGRAPH COURTESY OF THE LIBRARY OF CONGRESS. LC-USZ62-112177.

14

When Sitting Bull Kicks Your Butt and the Perils of Oral History

Sometimes a story seems too good to be true, and history is often an inexact science. Because of this, using oral history is often like handling a lit firecracker. You trust it will operate as intended and hope it does not blow up in your face.

Recently, I attended the memorial service of two well-regarded family members. While there, a cousin of my father's told a family story that fascinated me, partly because I didn't believe a word of it. I have read and analyzed hundreds of pages of oral histories and knew many contained serious historical errors. Often these errors are the result of honest confusion and misremembered events. In rarer cases, these blunders are outright lies used to inflate egos or obfuscate sensitive subjects. As I listened at that moment, however, I recalled the many people I interviewed who were reluctant to tell their family histories, partly out of the suspicion that they might prove unreliable. I always asked them to describe what they knew, but I could relate to these generous storytellers upon hearing this story. A bad story is usually quickly forgotten. A good one, true or less so, can have a life of its own.

My great-great uncle was W.C. "Bill" Dunning. He was the elder brother of Grant and Luther Dunning, who settled on Otter Creek near the turn of the previous century. Bill Dunning eventually settled in Sheridan, Wyoming, and was that town's chief of police for several years in the 1920s. Other than knowing he also had a turn as a livestock inspector, he was a mystery to me. He was a name on a genealogical tree. That changed when my father's cousin told me a story about how Bill Dunning literally had his behind kicked by the famous Hunkpapa Lakota Chief Sitting Bull. Even more unbelievably, my relative was able to return the favor to the fabled medicine man a few months later.

I had a real sense of "George Washington slept here," but my father's cousin insisted that there was a newspaper article regarding the incident. When I returned home, I was able to access some of the online archives I have available to me. After a brief search, I found the *Billings Gazette* of June 27, 1926, and an article entitled "Sitting Bull Kicked Chief: Sheridan Officer was Victim of Indian Joke Long Ago."

> *Sheridan, Wyo. June 26—Sitting Bull has never been a romantic figure to Bill Dunning, chief of police here, for Dunning still remembers a kick which he received from the moccasined foot of the chief 39 years ago. Sitting Bull was then on the reservation at Standing Rock. Dunning, then 22 years old, and Johnnie Kelly, a youth of his own age, were riding range on the Grand River when nine Indians overtook the two boys.*
>
> *The Indians had an unpleasant habit of rounding up white men who came on the reservation and shooting at them if they showed fear or tried to run away. The Indians on this occasion held a parley and then ordered the two boys to go. Just as he started to get in the saddle, Sitting Bull gave Dunning boost with his toe which nearly sent him over his horse. . . . Later in that same year, Sitting Bull came to the ranch where the two youths were working to beg something to eat.*
>
> *The Indian chief recognized "Bill" Dunning because he extended his hand and uttered a guttural but evidently pleasant, "How."*
>
> *The young cow puncher ignored the proffered hand and gave Sitting Bull the Yankee version of "Go to the Devil." What else transpired has never been known. The chief left immediately.*

Upon reading this article, I silently gave my father's cousin the credit he richly deserved. He had considerably more backing for his story than many of even the most well-meaning storytellers I have interviewed. My attention, however, was now turned to the details of the story, of which I remained skeptical.

The main issue with the story is, of course, how braggadocious it is. It is almost too poetic in how it elevates Bill to the exclusion of nearly everyone else, including its infinitely more famous subject. Its obvious negative bias (reflective of the time) toward Native Americans very near the 50th anniversary of the Battle of the Little Bighorn also seemed highly suggestive. Still, nothing about the story was demonstrably false. Also, while this story was almost forty years old at the time, there were a great many people alive at the time to counter it if it was false, potentially to the great embarrassment of Bill Dunning. There was certainly enough to warrant more research.

Bill Dunning passed away in March 1942. Local obituaries repeated the generalities of the Sitting Bull story along with other considerable personal accomplishments, but obituaries are usually written by family and are hardly the place for historical nit-picking.

Last month, however, I found a document courtesy of the Wyoming WPA (Writers Project of America) from before World War Two. Dated October 1941, it is a piece on Bill Dunning written by Sheridan amatuer historian Ida McPherran. Significantly, it is dated before Dunning's death and describes details in what seems to be direct quotes from the posteriorly afflicted cowpuncher.

The piece reasonably answered at least one question I had, namely, how sure was Dunning that the man who kicked him was the famous Sitting Bull? Apparently, the young rancher had seen the great chief previously:

> *Young Bill listened to all the stories he heard about the recent battle between the whites and the Indians and he used to like to get a glimpse of Sitting Bull who had just surrendered to Major Brotherton and returned to the Sioux reservation.*

Sitting Bull did indeed surrender to Major John H. Brotherton in July 1881. In 1885, he was allowed to leave the reservation to perform in Buffalo Bill's Wild West Show for a period of four months before returning to Standing Rock.

McPherran continued:

> *In 1885 Dunning went to work for the Anglo-American or E6 outfit. It was while he was working for this company that he again met Sitting Bull. By that time young Dunning had lost his admiration for Indians and Sitting Bull, in particular. Perhaps that is why he never forgot his meeting, face-to-face, with the Indian he once so greatly admired.*
>
> *Some horses had strayed from the E6 and young Dunning and another cowhand had been sent to look for them. Sitting Bull had been known as a horse thief but young Bill and his companion didn't know that and neither were they looking for Sitting Bull or any other Indian-but they found them just the same.*

Here is where McPherran's document appears to quote Bill Dunning extensively and directly:

Johnny Kelleher and I had followed the horses' tracks to the fringe of the Sioux reservation on Grand River. It was late in the afternoon and we were hungry so we decided to make camp for the night and continue our search for the horses the next morning, but we soon changed our minds or, rather, had them changed for us, for no sooner had we dismounted than we saw a bunch of Indians ride into sight and come our way.

I had learned enough about Indian to know that they were quick to shoot at a man who acted frightened. It was the law of the under-dog, I guess, without their realizing it. They figured if a man or a couple of men acted nervous and started to get away that they were out alone, scouting around for horses or cattle, but if a man or a couple of men, suddenly surprised by Indians, acted unconcerned and indifferent, the Indians figured that there were other white men in close proximity or soldiers from one of the neighboring forts were around nearby. Many a man's bones have been left to bleach on the prairie because he did not understand the ways of the Indian.

I guess Johnny and I would have been among them if I hadn't known so much about the ways of the Sioux because, as soon as we saw the Indians coming, Johnny gasped, "Come on, Bill, lets vamoose."

"Ah, don't be a-scared," I told him, "just pretend you're not anyway."

On came the Indians and we stood, leaning against our horses, waiting for them. When they got near us I recognized Sitting Bull but I did not tell Johnny so. I didn't want him to scare me into running.

When they joined us Sitting Bull jumped off his horse and grunted. Johnny nor I knew anything about the Sioux language but I knew a lot of the signs that the Indians around there used to make themselves understood by the whites so I managed to make Sitting Bull understand that we were out looking for some cow ponies.

Well, Sitting Bull couldn't talk but a few words of English but he made us understand that we were to move on. We didn't need any coaxing but we didn't want him to know it and we started to mount our horses as if we had all the time in the world. I guess we weren't hurrying fast enough to suit Sitting Bull and when I put my foot in the stirrup of my saddle and had just thrown my other leg up to mount, Sitting Bull kicked me right in the seat of my pants.

Johnny didn't need the extra impetus and he was several yards gone when I sat my saddle. Then I joined him but we did not run until we were out of sight of Sitting Bull and his handful of warriors and then did we race.

The timing of this incident would be 1886. While there are still a great many questions regarding this story, only a few details are contrary to known evidence. Sitting Bull did indeed have a limited knowledge of English and was known to be wary of white men encroaching on Indian land (he famously opposed the sale of Indian land then part of the Great Sioux Reservation to whites).

With regard to Sitting Bull's later comeuppance, Bill recalled:

> *That fall Sitting Bull and half a dozen other Indians came to the E6 asking for something to eat and the cowboys beat up on them for scaring the life out of a couple of kids. Of course, Johnny and I helped with the beating.*

It was not unusual, particularly given the scarcity of rations at this time, for a group of traveling Indians to seek food from homesteaders and ranchers. Still, while I cannot find any contradictory evidence, I consider this last part of the story unlikely at best. I can find no corroboration from any other source, and the notion that a bunch of cowboys beat up the famous Sitting Bull with only one willing to tell the tale is a stretch too long for my tastes. For all I know, there could be several families in the region with a similar account. However, it is simply too entertaining a story not to be passed along. That is perhaps the best quality of oral history, its ability to entertain us and give historical context.

NOTES ON CHAPTER 14:

- This article was first published in the January 28, 2021, edition of the *Powder River Examiner.*
- For clarification, the location of this (alleged) incident was in Dakota Territory (1885 or 1886).

Arthur Ross Brown (left) in the custody of Deputy U.S. Marshall James Comerford (right). PHOTOGRAPH COURTESY OF BETTMANN/GETTY IMAGES.

15

THE MANHUNT FOR ARTHUR ROSS BROWN

Sheridan County (WY) sheriff Willard Marshall entered the Rex Hotel in Sheridan on September 1, 1955, to question a transient ex-convict regarding a recent house burglary. As he went to the front desk, he inquired if an Art Brown was staying there. The proprietor said no one with that name was registered there. Marshall gave the man's description and confirmed that his suspect had been registered under the name "Bob King" at the hotel for three nights. The sheriff sat a few minutes in the waiting room, and when his subject arrived at the hotel from the back stairs, Marshall followed.

Several shots rang out, and the proprietor heard the sheriff yell, "call an ambulance and a doctor at once. I've been shot!" At the bottom of the stairway, Marshall was found with two .38 caliber bullet wounds, one through the abdomen and one in the leg. He underwent four hours of surgery at Sheridan Memorial Hospital. Attendants reported that Marshalls' first words when he regained consciousness were, "Did I get him?" The sheriff had got at least one shot off at his assailant.

Unfortunately, he did not "get him." Witnesses reported hearing three shots and seeing a man leave the hotel with a gun and briefcase in his hand. Another witness said the fleeing man brandished his gun at him as he fled down the alley.

Thus began one of the biggest manhunts the area has ever seen. The *Billings Gazette* reported that:

> *Police Chief Ray Dow said three highway patrolmen from Billings and Hardin, Mont. and Gillette, Wyo., had been sent to Sheridan to assist local officers in the manhunt, which is being concentrated in downtown Sheridan, a community of 11,500 persons.*
>
> *A score of National Guard radio-equipped Jeeps patrolled the foothills of the Big Horn Mountains west of here in the event the suspect might have fled on foot.*

Dow said the suspect is believed to be Art Brown, a 29-year-old ex-convict recently released from a California penitentiary.

As the suspect eluded capture, the net was widened throughout the area. The Interstate Highway System would not be constructed through the area for several more years. Throughout a matrix of state roads and U.S. highways, they looked for a 1950 two-door green Ford reported stolen at Sheridan:

The Yellowstone sheriff's office reported a roadblock had been established in the Hardin area and local deputies have been put on the alert.

At 10 p.m. Wednesday, pursuers believed the gunman was traveling on a dirt road north of Decker, which is a short distance north of the Montana-Wyoming border in Big Horn County.

Billings police received reports that a stranger had inquired for directions to Decker. Roadblocks were promptly set up near Broadus and in the Miles City area.

As a young man, former Otter resident Neil Thex recalled game wardens staffing a roadblock on the Otter Creek road. There were many tips, most of which proved to be untrue. Local officers were sent to Birney, where a hitchhiker resembling Brown was sighted and where he had some distant relatives. The officers returned with no results.

On October 15, over a month later, the green ford was found abandoned on Ellsworth Air Force Base near Rapid City, South Dakota. A liquor store in Rapid City was robbed, and the victim identified Brown as the perpetrator. In November, Brown's estranged wife Jean was forced into a car at gunpoint by her husband near her home in Kansas City.

By late October, Sheridan Memorial Hospital released Sheriff Willard Marshall after seven weeks of recovery. Contacted during the manhunt, Brown's mother said that her son suffered from mental problems. "If only people understood," she was reported to have said.

Finally, on November 14, the manhunt ended in San Francisco. Brown's aunt reported a prowler in her home that was possibly her nephew. The FBI and the San Francisco Police found their subject asleep in a car near the aunt's house. Brown was apprehended 75 days after he shot Willard Marshall. Only when the FBI interviewed him did the full horror of Arthur Ross Brown become apparent.

Sheriff Willard Marshall. PHOTOGRAPH COURTESY OF SHERIDAN COUNTY, WYOMING.

FBI agents questioned Brown about the Willard Marshall shooting when he blurted out, with no prompting: "I'm really wanted in Kansas City." Beginning with that declaration, Brown confessed to a notorious unsolved crime: the murder of Wilma Allen, the 34-year-old wife of a wealthy Kansas City auto dealer and mother of two young children. Ross gave three separate confessions to the FBI, and only on the third did he admit everything, including the fact that he had raped his victim before shooting her twice in the back of the head.

After an extensive missing person search, police had discovered Wilma Allen's body on August 7, 1955. But, because Allen had no known association with Brown, he was not on anyone's list of suspects for the crime. Brown's confession to the FBI was the first indication he was involved. He erroneously believed the Kansas City authorities had his picture and were looking for him.

He confessed to the FBI that he had made a decision that fateful morning to rob someone and was walking in a parking lot "looking for a good prospect that looked wealthy." He eventually spotted "an expensive-looking woman," and when she got in her car, Brown opened the passenger door, displayed his weapon, and ordered her to "start driving and behave." They eventually drove to a remote field where Brown committed his gruesome crime.

Brown was taken back to Kansas City, where he led authorities to the places he hid several of Wilma Allen's personal effects. Despite a long history of psychological problems, a three-person expert panel declared the accused mentally competent and fit for trial. During that trial, Brown offered no defense. In fact, when the prosecution was through with its case, his court-appointed attorney simply stated, "the defendant offers no evidence and rests his case." He wanted no mercy and received none. In less than six months, Arthur Ross Brown was executed in Missouri's gas chamber on February 24, 1956. Willard Marshall continued serving as Sheridan County Sheriff until 1962. He passed away in 1983.

NOTES ON CHAPTER 15:

- This article article first appeared in the February 25, 2021, edition of the *Powder River Examiner.*
- Art Brown's reported relatives in Birney were not in any way associated with the Brown Cattle Company.

Federal hunter H.P. Williams and rancher R.R. Richardson stand in a corral over the carcass of the Custer Wolf, supported by a metal frame. PHOTOGRAPH COURTESY OF THE DENVER PUBLIC LIBRARY. STANLEY PAUL YOUNG PAPERS, CALL NUMBER Z-15553.

16

"HIGH POWERED" WILLIAMS AND THE CUSTER WOLF

"The Custer Wolf is Dead."

So began a remarkable press release dated January 17, 1921, by the U.S. Department of Agriculture Press Service. This incredible story was picked up by hundreds of newspapers throughout the country, describing the nearly six-month effort of Harry P. Williams to eliminate perhaps one of the most calculating and vicious livestock killers nature had ever produced.

The USDA's press release, entitled "World's Greatest Animal Criminal Dead" did not mince words:

> *He was the master criminal of the animal world.*
>
> *Throughout the region around Custer, SD, that day, the telephone lines were busier than they were on the day the Armistice was signed.*
>
> *For 9 years this wolf had lived as an outlaw-the cruelest, the most sagacious, the most successful animal outlaw that the range country had ever known. His cruelty was surpassed only by his cunning. He killed with the refinement of animal ferocity.*

While this press release may seem overly dramatic, it was less so than those of us in more modern times might think. By the time of his death, the Custer Wolf had killed over $25,000 worth of livestock (an astounding amount of money in the 1920s). The massive $500 reward and the efforts of several talented government hunters, along with hundreds of amateurs, failed to bring him down.

Finally, in March 1920, the USDA Biological Survey (forerunner of today's Fish & Wildlife Service) ordered its best hunter, 44-year-old H.P. Williams, to the Black Hills with orders to "stay after the wolf until he was taken, no matter how much time was required." It took Williams more than six months.

Harry Percival Williams was born in Elbert County, Colorado. Already an excellent horseman in his early twenties, he came to Buffalo, Wyoming, around 1900. Williams worked for several area ranches and even had a run-in with Arapahoe Brown, the man who led the attack against the Invaders in the Johnson County War. Another time, while at the Sheridan Inn, he hung a new hat on the rack before entering the dining room. When he exited, he found his hat was gone. The proprietor of the inn told him, "Tom O'Day has your hat, he's drinking and mean. Don't bother about it, I'll get you another hat."

Williams' reply was "you won't get me another hat." After a brief discussion, the horseman punched O'Day "right from my knees up under the jaw and he went down and out and I picked up my hat, took the gun off him and handed it over to the bar keeper." Williams had no idea Tom O'Day was a notorious member of the Hole-in-the-Wall gang. The two would meet later in a saloon, where the outlaw acknowledged being in the wrong and apologized.

The outlaw Tom O'Day, pictured here without his mustache. This is O'Day's mugshot from the Wyoming State Penitentiary #460-2192. PHOTOGRAPH COURTESY OF THE WYOMING STATE ARCHIVES, 13761.

"He was a pretty good guy", Williams recalled.

Like many cowboys, Williams spent his winters trapping predators for bounties, and he quickly developed a reputation for being an effective wolfer. By 1920, he was employed by the USDA Biological Survey's Predator Control program. While adept at using traps, his preferred method of killing wolves was shooting them with his Springfield rifle. Indeed, he became so successful at shooting wolves that people started calling him "High Power" Williams, a play on the "H.P." initials he often used instead of "Harry Percival."

The Custer Wolf had already successfully evaded some of the area's most respected hunters. One of them had killed the Custer Wolf's mate and cubs four years before. This act, Williams said, disordered the Custer Wolf's life, making him a loner and extremely unpredictable (thus the term "lone wolf"). He never took another mate, and as his legend grew, people attributed the wolf's seeming cruelty to a depraved need for revenge.

The Custer Wolf was known to be "trap-wise," eluding tracker's attempts and even springing them purposely, as if in contempt. Actions like this furthered his growing reputation. However, his behavior in his later years drove the public's imagination to extremes. During this time, the Custer Wolf killed far more than what he needed to live. The $25,000 figure mentioned earlier included over 500 domestic animals, and there were reports of him killing several dozen in a single night. Many ranchers gave up trying to kill him and resolved to wait until he died a natural death.

Now, he seemingly enjoyed mutilating animals (including bob-tailing cattle) and directly attacking the sex organs of livestock. Many were left alive only to be put down when their owners found them. The practice that got the populace's imaginations burning was his habit of killing pregnant cows and eating only the unborn calf. The Custer Wolf was now more than an intelligent nuisance; he was a demon with four legs.

It was March of 1920 when H.P. Williams received the telegram from Washington to track this maniac down. The two adversaries jousted with each other for six months. Viewing the wolf with binoculars, Williams saw him "come upon a horse herd. Of course, they spooked all over the area. That wolf rounded them up like a sheep dog would and then had them all bunched up. He sat there and watched them for a minute, then trotted off."

Williams also discovered that his shrewd opponent could evade tracking by climbing a nearby mountain mesa topped with rock. From this vantage, he could then change direction without detection.

By October, Williams discovered that the Custer Wolf had help in the form of two coyotes who followed him everywhere and scavenged on his kills. Traveling 100 to 200 yards on the wolf's flanks, when danger approached, they would run away, and in this manner, warn him. This was unusual behavior for a wolf, who typically kill coyotes when they can. Williams was initially reluctant to shoot the pair for fear of spooking his primary target, the wolf.

I kept trying and one day saw him with an old carcass, probably an old kill. I eased up on him and was just about in position when those blasted coyotes

> *jumped up again. The wolf took off and this time, though I hated to make the noise, I shot the coyotes.*
>
> *Because I didn't want him to know what happened, I dumped their bodies in a deep wash and then set some traps around the old carcass. It didn't do any good. He returned the next day, dragged the coyotes up on the rim of the wash, then took the carcass and dragged it over every trap, springing them.*

The Custer Wolf was playing with him, and Williams knew it. The wily hunter then used the wolf's curiosity against him:

> *I took that same old carcass, moved it up the hill a ways and set traps. Sure enough, he moved it back to the original spot and never touched a trap.*
>
> *Then I scooped up a big pile of dirt beside the carcass, as if another animal was fooling with it. I set a circle of traps out from the carcass—the path I figured he'd follow while looking the situation over.*
>
> *He put his right forefoot smack in the middle of one. About 150 yards away he jerked the trap against a tree with such force the drag hook snapped loose.*

Although his target was free of the trap, he was also now leaving tracks on the top of the rocked mesa. After tracking him for three miles, Williams found and shot him.

> *He has been so lucky that I expected the gun would fail to shoot, but it worked OK. He is smaller than the average male wolf, weighed about 98 pounds and measured just six feet from tip to tip . . . He is an old wolf with a fur that is almost white.*

The "vicious" and "excessive" habits of the Custer Wolf that terrified the local populace are now understood to be the result of sudden (from an ecological perspective) disruption of the wolf's natural predatory habits. Wolves are highly intelligent, social animals and therefore highly adaptable. The practice of focusing on fresh kills and not returning day upon day to a kill prevented them from falling victim to traps and poison by humans. The practice of "surplus killing" has also been firmly established as a rare but normal behavior in many mammalian predators.

NOTES ON CHAPTER 16:

- This article first appeared in the *Powder River Examiner's* March 25, 2021, edition.
- While the story of the Custer Wolf's demise has been pretty well documented, H.P. Williams' story was lesser known, and substantially so. One author even claimed that H.P. Williams' real name was unknown. Williams eventually settled in Casper, Wyoming, and died there in 1970.
- The story of Williams' life in Wyoming was related by the man himself in an interview with Charles Helvey in the 1960s. A transcript of that history is available amoing Helvey's papers housed at the American Heritage Center in Laramie.

Portrait of Levi Howes as a younger man.
PHOTOGRAPH COURTESY OF THE AMERICAN HERITAGE CENTER, PAPERS OF LEVI S. HOWES, LARAMIE, WY.

17

When Levi Took Command

In late May of 1897, John Hoover was found dead. The young sheepherder, employed on Fred Barringer's ranch north of Ashland, had been missing for several weeks. One of several search parties eventually found Hoover's body near his sheep camp, situated very close to the boundary of the Northern Cheyenne Reservation. Hoover had been shot to death. "Three empty cartridges, horse hoofprints, and a beef carcass nearby persuaded Barringer and others that Hoover had fallen victim to Cheyennes caught in the act of slaughtering white-owned stock."

Throughout the early years of its establishment, the Northern Cheyenne Reservation (along with many other plains reservations) suffered from severe food shortages primarily caused by federal government mismanagement. For the previous ten years, ranches on the reservation border repeatedly found their stock slaughtered by Cheyenne seeking to feed themselves and their families. As these white settlers' appeal to the reservation and federal authorities proved ineffective, tensions grew. When some Cheyenne started killing whites who witnessed their crimes, the escalation was viewed extremely seriously outside the reservation borders. While these murders were rare (less than ten confirmed between 1890 and 1898), they further enflamed the local white population.

Hoover's body was taken to a nearby ranch for a coroner's inquest. Custer County Sheriff John Gibb and Coroner Bateman established that a group of unknown Cheyenne Indians had committed the crime. This conclusion was instantly spread to the sixty people waiting outside the building, and they demanded justice. Armed with general warrants for the arrest of anybody involved and demand for the Northern Cheyenne to give them up, Sheriff Gibb deputized a group of approximately twelve people and headed for the reservation.

A few miles to the south, another group of white ranchers also gathered with earnest intention. One hundred to two hundred men from ranches neighboring the southern edge of the reservation had tired of nearly ten years

Joseph T. Brown, in his U.S. Volunteer Cavalry uniform. When the Spanish American War began in 1898, Brown commanded a group of Montana Volunteer troops, which is why he is known around the area as "Captain Brown." PHOTOGRAPH COURTESY OF THE HAYES (BROWN) FAMILY.

of Cheyenne troubles and were determined to do something about it. They disagreed, however, on exactly what strategy to pursue. Those strategies were personified by two men: Joseph T. Brown of Birney and Levi S. Howes of Otter.

At this time, Joe T. Brown was representing the area in the Montana Legislature. Originally from Mississippi, Brown had run away from home at the age of fourteen to serve in the Confederate Army in the Civil War. Superficially wounded, he was returned home with a letter to his parents:

July 5, 1864

Dear Pete and Sister Mary
This will be handed to you by the Young Hero, Joseph T. Brown. You must not scold him, as he has more than acted well his part. Joe borrowed a gun—went into the fight—fought like a tiger. Got a bullet through his pants! He is the admiration of all. God bless and preserve him.

Yours truly and affectionately,
Colonel Roberts.

After the war, Brown attended the Virginia Military Institute, graduating in 1879. In 1886, he drove the first of several herds of cattle from Indian Territory (now Oklahoma) to the Tongue River Valley, where he established the Three Circle Ranch. Becoming a successful pioneer stockman and being active in politics, Brown was soon one of the most highly respected men in the state. He had closely followed the deteriorating situation with the Cheyenne for years, and his military background made him believe that decisive action was needed. According to Levi Howes, Brown wanted the party assembled at the reservation border to take on White Bull's band of Cheyenne (the one thought to harbor the killers of John Hoover) all at once and "eat them up" to teach them a last lesson.

Levi Howes preferred a different course.

Levi was the second son of Captain Calvin Howes, a successful former sea captain from Massachusetts. Captain Howes "left the sea" and traveled west to start a cattle ranch in Montana. In 1882, he partnered with Judge J.W. Strevell to form the Circle Bar Ranch on Otter Creek. By 1883, the Circle Bar had brought several thousand head of cattle up from Texas under the direction of Ed McGehee. A young Levi Howes was part of these drives. By the middle of the 1890s, Howes claimed the Circle Bar had between 8,000 and 10,000 head of cattle and horses, making it one of the most significant outfits in the area. Levi Howes almost single-handedly got a post office established at Otter by getting petitions signed and personally meeting with postal officials in Washington D.C. He, too, had been closely following the situation with the Cheyenne. A practical man, he was not convinced a glorious charge into the heart of the reservation would bring any success, much less justice.

Howes counseled against Brown's vigilante-like course, preferring instead to have the law on his side. Howes recalled in 1956:

> *It's a question of lives and things, but if you want to go over there, you haven't got men enough. You'll just get a bunch of somebody killed. If you're going, we ain't even going to the reservation. We're going back and prepare for war. And when I got up and made the talk to him. First one, and then another said to him (Brown) "you ain't goin' alone we're goin' with you!" And when Captain Brown started off, he only had a few men, the whole crowd was with me. And then they told me: we'll do as you say, you go ahead. So right then, I was foremen for Circle Bar, and I took charge. And I was one of the youngest men there. But I had to take charge.*

Howes and this group met up with Sheriff Gibb. Agreeing with Howes about the need to operate within the law, Gibb deputized twelve of the new group members, including Howes. The sheriff's band now included around twenty-five men. The rest returned to their homes to await instructions.

The basis of all this mobilization was a generalized certainty among the white settlers that the Cheyennes were about to violently "break out" of the reservation. This certainty, however, had very little basis in fact. Immediately upon hearing of the discovery of Hoover's body and that the Cheyenne were suspected, the Indian agent, George W.H. Stouch, requested two troops of cavalry from Fort Custer. He also ordered White Bull and his entire band to Lame Deer.

On May 26, 1897, White Bull arrived at Lame Deer, where Stouch informed him of the situation and the need to assist the agent in finding the killers. They agreed to meet again that evening. Later that day, Sheriff Gibb and his twenty-five men arrived at Lame Deer.

The presence of the ranchers greatly disturbed the Cheyennes, and Stouch proceeded to parley with the sheriff. The agent refused to cooperate with the sheriff and explained he was in the process of investigating the murder. He told Gibb that the sheriff's men were a dangerous complication he did not need and would thwart his investigation. Gibb and Houch negotiated a compromise, wherein four deputies would remain on the reservation to assure the white settlers that Houch's investigation would proceed. Howes stated that they would be back in two weeks, and if the killers were not turned over, there would be war between the Cheyenne and the settlers.

That afternoon, Captain Robert D. Read of the Tenth Cavalry arrived with his troops. The presence of the cavalry significantly lowered the tensions among the Cheyenne, who now felt some measure of protection from the ranchers. After a few days, White Bull told Stouch that a brave named David Stanley had confessed to the murders, but there was conflicting evidence that more Cheyenne were involved. Stanley was eventually released to Sheriff Gibb, but the controversy regarding the other suspects did not quell the simmering anger in the white community.

After he left the reservation, Howes and the settlers did as they said: they prepared for war. White women and children surrounding the reservation were loaded on wagons and sent to the nearest city (Rosebud, Miles City, or Sheridan). At the Circle Bar Ranch, Captain Howes and his son Levi built a stone fort on the top of an isolated hill near their ranch. They supplied it with food, guns, and ammunition. A small fighting force of local men was recruited to man the fort. The fort was named "Fort Howes," and the men who occupied it were the Fort Howes Defenders. The fort exists to this day on the property of the Circle Bar Ranch.

In hindsight, the effort to determine who would lead the white settlers becomes incredibly significant. The Cheyenne were not in an "outbreak" of any kind. Racism and justified dissatisfaction with the situation inflamed the local settlers into a mob mentality that required skillful leadership to manage. Had Joseph Brown emerged the leader of white ranchers, it seems likely that his bold military-style campaign would have become a self-fulfilling prophecy. The Cheyenne may very well have resorted to violence to defend themselves against a group, ironically attacking them in the name of restoring order. Young Levi Howes kept a cool head and charted a compromise path that eventually resulted in "the Cheyenne Outbreak of 1897" being no outbreak at all.

NOTES ON CHAPTER 16:

- This column first appeared in the *Powder River Examiner's* June 24, 2021, edition.
- Levi Howes recollections were recorded by Charles Helvey in 1956. Both the transcript and the audio are available from the American Heritage Center in Laramie.
- My great-grandmother, Beatrice Tucker Dunning, was among those evacuated to the fort. In *Echoing Footsteps,* she recalled spending the night in Fort Howes as a young girl.
- White Bull and Levi Howes have an even more personal conflict described in my article "He Wanted to Eat a White Man's Heart," included later in this collection.

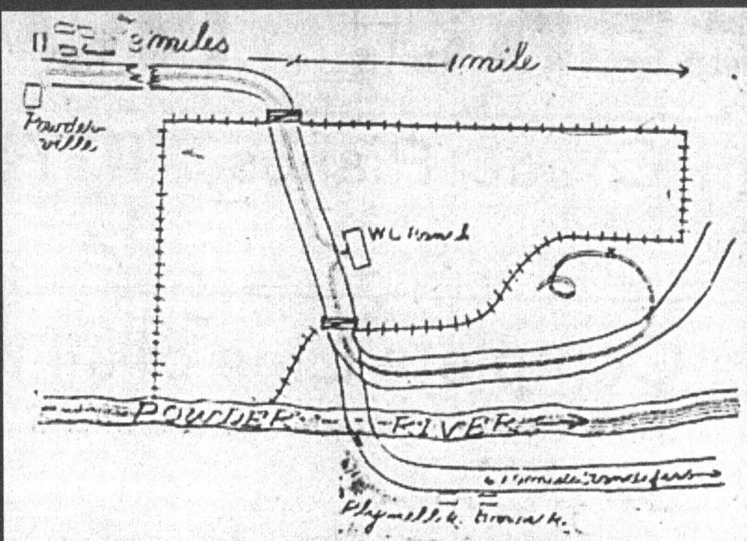

The hand drawn map published in the *Yellowstone Journal* on June 13, 1903. The original caption read: "The cut was prepared by the *Journal* to give readers a general idea of the ground where the Standifer tragedy occurred. Some positions are exaggerated and others diminished for purposes of illustration, but the relative position of the important points can be gathered to a certain extent. The parallel lines running from Powderville is the road and the center line shows the course of the buggy in which Standifer and wife were riding. Where the buggy leaves the road is the spot where the fatal shot was fired, about a mile below the WL and 100 feet from the point marked X, near the fence, which is where Standifer fell from the buggy. The body fell 25 feet from the fence. The buggy tracks showed the short turn drawn, which was only nine feet across. Standifer's ranch from where he and his wife drove to Brown's in the morning, was on the same side of the river as Brown's, 10 miles below." Author note: The term " below" meant downstream, to the right of the picture, or generally in a northerly direction.

18

THE CURIOUS END OF POWDERVILLE'S DEADWOOD DICK

The term "Boot Hill" was commonly used for the cemeteries utilized when the deceased were violent criminals who "died with their boots on." The most commonly known Boot Hill is located at Tombstone, Arizona, where Billy Clanton and the McClaury's were buried after the gunfight at the OK Corral. Another Boot Hill Cemetery is located at Powderville. Among those reputed to have been buried there is a man named "Deadwood Dick.".

This particular nickname has been used by several people over the years, perhaps most notably by actor Richard Clarke in the late 1920s. The name was made famous as the fictional protagonist of a series of dime novels written by Edward Wheeler, published between 1877 and 1897. The identity of the man buried in Powderville's Boot Hill is a matter of some conjecture since only one grave has a marker (that marker is for John Church). The Powder River County Genealogy book *Echoing Footsteps* identifies the "Deadwood Dick" buried in Powderville as Dick Stannifer, killed by his ex-wife, Leo Brown.

His real name was Eldridge M. Standifer, but he was also called Richard and, most often, "Dick." Harry McKenzie, in the book *Powderville: A Personal History* (by Mary Jensen Hill), described Standifer like so:

> *I'll admit one thing, that he was crazy, he was unbalanced, not insane, just crazy. He would do the darndest things. He was one of the best riders that ever lived, but m'gosh he'd get throwed every day by some fool antic he would pull off.*

On June 8, 1903, Leo Brown shot and killed Standifer near the old WL Ranch outside Powderville. The circumstances of that death created a sensation, not the least because of the salacious family dynamics that further colored the story. Leo Brown was not only Dick Standifer's ex-wife. His grieving widow, Carol Standifer, was the killer Leo Brown's own sister.

Powderville in 1886, the main crossing of the Powder River between Miles City and Deadwood. PHOTOGRAPH BY L.A. HUFFMAN, COURTESY OF THE MONTANA HISTORICAL SOCIETY, 981-397.

After shooting her ex-husband in the back as he drove a horse-drawn buggy, Leo Brown then rode to Miles City with her then-current husband (Joe H. Brown) and turned herself in to Custer County Sheriff William Savage. She claimed self-defense, an assertion later disputed in some detail by her sister.

According to the accused, the incident started when her sister Carol and Dick were over at Leo's ranch. While in the barn, Standifer asked Leo why she never came over and visited them. When Leo told him she didn't want to, he hit her in the face and hit her again when she got up. She escaped and started towards her house to get her gun but was blocked by Standifer. Leo then got on a horse and left. Later that day, Standifer and Carol met Leo on the road. Dick asked Leo where she was going.

She said: "To town to have you arrested."

According to Leo, Dick reportedly said: "If you do, I'll kill you. I guess I'd better kill you right now."

Standifer reached towards his bootleg, where Leo knew he usually kept a gun. Taking no chances, she admitted to shooting him in the back as he stooped over. Dick fell out of the buggy and died of his wound very quickly. The horses took off at the shot and were stopped minutes later by some hands from the nearby WL Ranch.

As stated before, the grieving widow painted a much more deliberate tale to the coroner's jury. According to Carol, an argument in the barn began with negotiating a horse deal between the two. The discussion escalated when Standifer complained about Leo's past remarks concerning his marriage to Carol. Specifically, he alleged Leo had written his mother:

> *Dick said he thought this was the dirtiest thing that was ever done, to write to his poor old mother this way. Dick told Leo she had written to his mother that himself and her sister (the present Mrs. Standifer) had slept together time and again before they were married in her house that's why she left him.*

Again, according to Carol's statement, Leo did not respond well to Dick's accusation.

"I won't take nothing off of you nor any other son of a b____, if you want to fight, I'll fight this out right now." The two exchanged blows until Carol intervened and stopped the fight. Leo then got on a horse and went to her mother's house.

Later that day, Leo met Dick and Carol on the road, and they again discussed a proposed livestock trade. Leo stated she wanted to see some cattle further down the road and followed the Standifer's buggy as they rode along. "We were riding that way, and she shot. I heard the shot. Standifer was driving with the lines in his right hand, I believe, leaning forward slightly. When the shot was fired, I noticed the blood on Dick's back and saw Leo behind with a weapon of some kind." Significantly, Carol also claimed that after Dick fell from the moving buggy, Leo fired a second shot at Dick while he was on the ground.

The coroner's jury discovered later that Standifer did not have a gun on his person and was not wearing boots at the time of his death (he was wearing shoes). He had been shot only once. They also discovered marks around Leo's neck consistent with her story about the assault in the barn.

Dick Standifer had a bad reputation, and the matter was quickly resolved in Leo's favor. Richard Standifer was buried on Powderville's Boot Hill, even though he didn't precisely die "with his boots on." I could find no contemporary account of Standifer's life, or death that includes any reference to the moniker "Deadwood Dick." Also lacking is any known connection between Standifer and Deadwood (other than Powderville's location along the trail between Fort Keogh and the Dakota gold town).

Both Leo and Carol married again before passing away. Leo Rodman, (as she was then known) passed away in 1952.

NOTES ON CHAPTER 18:

- This article first appeared in the August 5, 2021, edition of the *Powder River Examiner.*
- Most of the information for this article was obtained from Standifer's coroner's report obtained at the Custer County Courthouse in Miles City.

John Kendrick's massive OW Ranch was situated on Hanging Woman Creek, southwest of the raid site. Kendrick organized and carried out the attack to keep Robert Selway's sheep from overtaking the cattle country of the Tongue River basin. PHOTOGRAPH COURTESY OF TRAIL END STATE HISTORIC SITE, PHOTO HOFPX182, HOFF COLLECTION.

19

The Right Man to Do a Wrong Thing: Charlie Thex, the Bear Creek Sheep Raid, and the Primacy of Fear

On December 28, 1900, eleven masked men surrounded a lone sheepherder near the confluence of Otter, Tooley, and Bear Creeks in southeastern Montana, then in Custer County. A gunman pointed a Colt revolver at the herder while his co-conspirators clubbed to death 2,200 head of prize ewe lambs. The *Yellowstone Journal* published a worrying lament under the headline "Another Range War" as fears of further violence spread throughout the Powder River country. "For the first time in its history Custer County since it became identified with the range stock interests, there comes this morning the news of a clash between opposing or antagonistic range interests," the *Journal* reported, "the first blow struck—if reports be true—a stagger. From the best information gathered within a few miles of the scene of operations, a band of 2,000 sheep have been killed by masked marauders."[1]

Despite a sizable reward of $2,000, none of the participants ever faced justice, although locals speculated on the identity of the perpetrators. Perhaps because the sheepherder was not physically harmed, or perhaps out of fear, what community outrage existed quickly dampened, especially in the isolated areas of Custer County. The matter settled into hushed rumor, curious speculation, and veiled threats. Sheep never returned in large numbers to the Otter Creek valley. Not one participant was conclusively identified during his lifetime. In fact, those rumored to have been involved seemingly reveled in their success and justified any alleged actions as the reasonable response of upright citizens who were simply beating back an unsavory threat to everyone's livelihood. One of the alleged raiders, Frank "Booker" Lacy, rationalized the raid nearly six decades later:

[1] "Another Range War," (Miles City) *Yellowstone Journal*, Jan.3, 1901.

This photograph of the Kendrick's Dutch Creek (Wyoming) cavy in 1897 include at least three known raiders. Walt Snyder is the third horse backed cowboy from the left. Bill Munson is the cowboy in the back center. Charlie Thex is the man posing beside his horse on the bottom right. PHOTOGRAPH COURTESY OF THE TRAIL END STATE HISTORIC SITE IN SHERIDAN, WY, MANVILLE KENDRICK COLLECTION, H9517425. THIS IMAGE AND CAPTION WAS NOT INCLUDED IN THE ORIGINAL *MMWH* ARTICLE.

> *You couldn't blame them fellows because that was just like anything else, an army or anything coming into your country and they [sheep] was going to overrun it. . . . Well, it was just one of those things that was done . . . nobody hurt, and why if somebody had been killed they would have whipped on that until they would have known, but nobody was killed, nobody hurt and it was just a matter of let it die.*[2]

The Bear Creek sheep killing was conducted with impunity because of careful planning and the calculated use of terror. This deliberate fear was instrumental in maintaining a decades-long regional silence about the perpetrators of the attack and in keeping large numbers of sheep out of the Otter Creek valley.

[2] Frank "Booker" Lacy, interview by Robert Helvey, Jul. 23, 1957, Collection 1465, box 18, Robert T. Helvey Collection, American Heritage Center, Laramie, WY (hereafter AHC).

This triumph of the cattlemen emboldened others in eastern Montana and Wyoming to do similar things, leading to a wave of violence against sheep and the people who owned and handled them over the next decade. As a result, the open range's precious water holes and grasses remained the domain of local cattlemen.

The victims fumed for years to no avail, but they never received justice for the slaughtered sheep. When they eventually passed on, any incentive for pursuing justice died with them. The perpetrators were either forgotten entirely or, worse, admired for their craftiness and daring. As decades passed, the entire incident became legend, chock full of exaggerations, confusion, and outright lies.

In 1974, an article in *Montana, The Magazine of Western History* brought some clarity on the Bear Creek sheep raid. Lyman Brewster named the eleven men who participated and made public previously unknown details about the incident. Most importantly, Brewster's article confirmed what had been rumored for years: the raid was largely the work of John B. Kendrick and George W. Brewster, Lyman's deceased father. Owners of the large OW and Quarter Circle U cattle ranches, respectively, Kendrick and Brewster became

John B. Kendrick, horseback, at the OW Ranch in 1895. PHOTOGRAPH COURTESY OF THE TRAIL END STATE HISTORIC SITE, WYOMING DEPARTMENT OF STATE PARKS AND CULTURAL RESOURCES, H9517015.

successful politicians in the years following the raid. Kendrick became governor of Wyoming in 1915 and then served three terms as Wyoming's U.S. Senator from 1917 until his death in 1933. Brewster served three terms as a state representative for Montana, winning election in 1904, 1906, and 1908. Lyman Brewster also identified Horton Boal (Buffalo Bill Cody's son-in-law), Frank "Booker" Lacy, William Munson, Mahlon "Tug" Wilson, Frank McKinney, Barney Hall, Walt Snider, John "Shorty" Caddell, and Charlie Thex as the remaining members of the eleven.[3]

One hundred and eighteen years after the raid, an old Colt Single Action Army pistol, a leather holster, and a few hand-loaded shells were found in the closet of a Rosebud County residence.[4] Uncovering the story of this revolver puts an ominous and revealing new perspective on perhaps the most devastating sheep raid in Montana history. The gun's owner was Otter Creek cattleman Charlie Thex, a complex, brutal man. His proclivity for violence was instrumental in the raid's success. Although Charlie's name is only mentioned once in Brewster's article, new sources have revealed Thex as the triggerman in the Bear Creek sheep raid. These sources challenged the sanitized, even entertaining accounts of this incident, replacing them with the details of a deadly serious operation, well-planned and implemented, in which violence engendered silence and allowed cattlemen to profit on terror. The raid's success had lasting historical implications, as it freed Kendrick to expand his OW operation into an enormous cattle empire with multiple ranches in Montana and Wyoming and to enter the political arena. By building on the fear of violence, Kendrick and Brewster's raid put an end to large-scale sheep ranching in the Otter Creek valley and ensured, instead, their own prosperity and that of their fellow cattlemen.[5]

---

[3] Lyman Brewster, "December 1900: The Quiet Slaughter," *Montana* 24:1 (Winter 1974): 82-85. This short piece was not a scholarly analysis of the raid; rather, it was a collection of personal insights based on family history and a confession by the last living raider, Shorty Caddell. Given the significance of Brewster's revelations, he probably assumed that more professional historical analysis would follow. Unfortunately, it did not, and the article became just another citation on the long list of cattleman-sheepman conflicts without much comment. See Bill O'Neal, *Cattlemen vs Sheepherders: Five Decades of Violence in the West, 1880–1920* (Burnet, TX: Eakin Press, 1989), 70-72. Wayne Gard, "Range Wars," in *The Book of the American West,* ed. Jay Monaghan (New York: Bonanza Books, 1963), 291. Cynde Goergen, *One Cowboy's Dream: John B. Kendrick* (Virginia Beach, VA: Donning Company Publishers, 1995, rev.2003), 33; Maude Beach, "John Daut History," in *Faded Hoofprints—Bygone Dreams,* ed. Robert Thaden Jr. (Broadus, MT: Powder River Historical Society, 1989), 1–2.

[4] A search of the serial number indicates the pistol was originally sold in 1893, https://colt.com/serial-lookup, serial number 153590.

[5] Brewster, "December 1900," 82-85. See O'Neal, *Cattlemen vs Sheepherders,* 70-72; Gard, "Range Wars," 291; Goergen, *One Cowboy's Dream,* 33; Beach, "John Daut History," 1–2.

Standing left to right, Luther Dunning, unknown cowboy. Seated on the bottom row: Grant Dunning, alleged Bear Creek raider Frank McKinney. THE PHOTOGRAPH IS CIRCA 1900, COURTESY OF THE CHARLIE DUNNING FAMILY. THIS IMAGE AND CAPTION WAS NOT INCLUDED IN THE ORIGINAL *MMWH* ARTICLE.

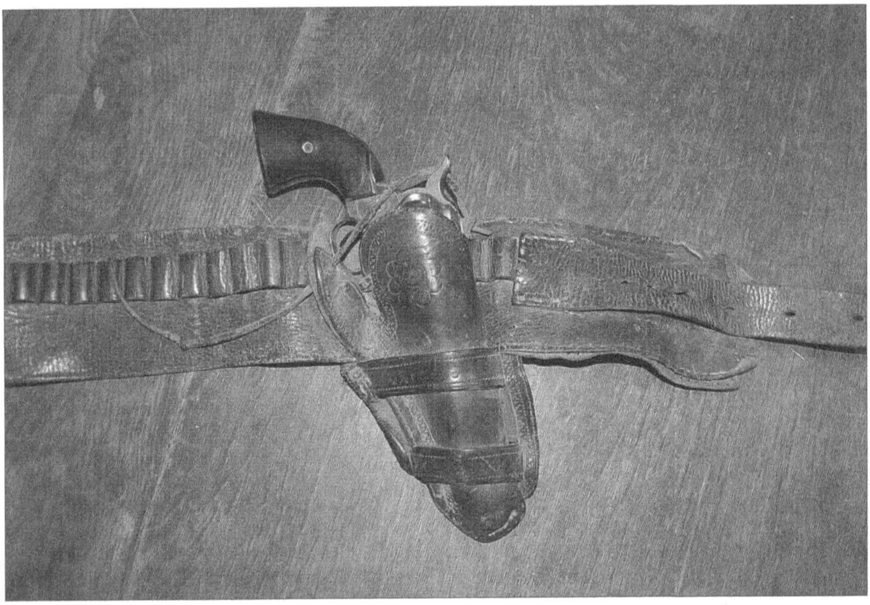

A descendant of Charlie Thex discovered his Colt Single Action Army revolver, used to intimidate the sheepherder in the Bear Creek raid, in a closet in 2018. The raid's organizers counted on Thex's reputation for violence to prevent anyone from speaking openly about the Bear Creek sheep slaughter. PHOTOGRAPH BY SHANE DUNNING.

An enlarged portion of the "Fort Howes Defenders" photograph focusing on Charlie Thex. THE ORIGINAL PHOTOGRAPH IS COURTESY OF THE AMERICAN HERITAGE CENTER, PAPERS OF LEVI S. HOWES.

The history of the raid begins with federal land and homesteading policies. Under the 1862 Homestead Act and the subsequent Desert Land Act of 1877, a single homesteader could claim up to 640 acres in arid regions, with their spouse claiming another 640 acres. As the act initially allowed claiming small, narrow tracks of land, homesteaders chose land along the few precious waterways. The homesteader could then restrict water access to other livestock that grazed on the neighboring unclaimed and unfenced "open range" federal land. Large livestock operations often had their employees file on the water holes in their range and would buy them out once the claim was "proven" and had title. These land-grabbing actions were well-known and well-established manipulations of federal land policy, and in the late 1880s, an enterprising sheep rancher named Robert R. Selway took advantage of this practice when he expanded his sheep operation on Pumpkin Creek in southeastern Montana. In 1900, he started bringing sheep into the firmly established cattle country around Otter Creek.

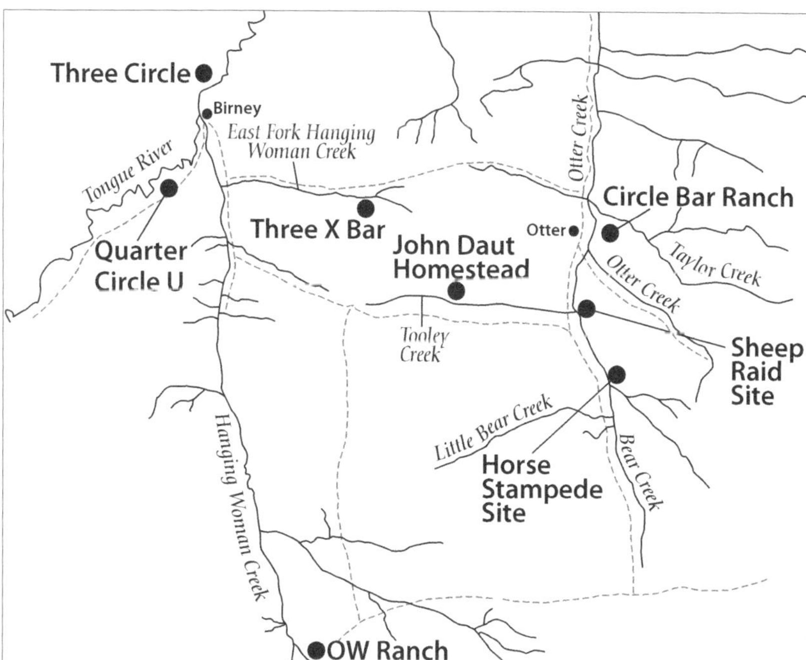

The Otter Creek valley in 1900. When John Daut, partnering with "Sheep King" Robert R. Selway, brought his sheep deep into the cattle country of the valley, local cattlemen considered it an invasion. The massacre of Daut's sheep occurred near the junction of Bear and Otter Creeks. MAP BY SHANE DUNNING, USED WITH PERMISSION FROM *SLAUGHTER ON THE OTTER*, BY FOREST DUNNING.

Selway became known as the "Sheep King" of eastern Montana. He built an impressive empire by partnering with enterprising sheepherders and homesteaders on a shares system. Taking on some of Selway's financial burdens and risks, the settlers filed homestead claims and raised their sheep on the few water holes in the arid breaks of southeastern Montana. Controlling the water monopolized the surrounding open-range pasture. Using these tactics, Selway and his partners had previously taken control of the land surrounding their headquarters on Pumpkin Creek, roughly twenty-five miles northeast of Bear and Otter Creeks.[6]

When he began expanding his ovine empire toward his new hometown of Sheridan, Wyoming, Selway alarmed the cattlemen in his path. In the late fall of 1900, John Daut, Selway's foreman, established a homestead on Tooley Creek and brought 8,000 head of sheep in two bands. The presence of surveyors hired by Selway at several scattered water holes in the Otter Creek area alerted local ranchers to the Sheep King's intended "invasion," and set Kendrick and Brewster scheming about putting an end to his competition.[7]

Conflict over sheep and grazing was nothing new in the American West in 1900. First introduced to the Americas by the Spanish in the 1500s, domestic sheep formed a sizable industry in New Mexico by the end of the Mexican-American War in 1848. As ovine production expanded into neighboring Arizona and Texas, conflict with existing cattle interests arose over control of range territory. Texas lost an estimated $30 million in tax valuation because of the Fence-Cutting Wars of 1883, where conflict between homesteaders —including several sheepmen—caused miles of barbed wire fencing to be regularly destroyed and just as regularly rebuilt. In Arizona, in 1887, the introduction of sheep accelerated the already violent Pleasant Valley War, leaving fifteen dead, both sheepmen and cowboys.[8]

More than just an economic enterprise, cattle ranching created a cultural persona that emerged in this period: the cowboy. An important aspect of the cowboy persona was a hostile aversion toward sheep and the men who worked them. Mutual antipathy between cattlemen and sheepmen was rooted in the

---

6 John T. Ganie, "The Desert Land Act in Operation, 1877-1891," *Agricultural History* 11:2 (Apr. 1937): 142–57; Maude Beach, "Historical Outline of Powder River Country," in *Faded Hoofprints*, 19.

7 Beach, "Historical Outline of Powder River Country," 19; Brewster, "December 1900," 82–85.

8 Edward Norton Wentworth, *America's Sheep Trails* (Ames: Iowa State College Press, 1948), 21-27: O'Neal, *Cattlemen vs Sheepherders*, 24–26, 43–65. A list of Pleasant Valley War casualties appears on page 57.

different management techniques of the animals and the social norms that sprang from them. Cattlemen believed that sheep ruined pasture. Sheep, they claimed, bit grass closer to the ground using their upper and lower jaws, depleting the pasture more thoroughly than cattle, which only use one set of teeth to pull grass. Cattlemen also believed that a sheep's hooves excreted a smelly oil that cattle avoided, which became more important as herds of sheep gathered around water holes. Sheepmen, particularly herders, were often older men who worked alone with their timid, vulnerable flocks, usually on foot. In the southwestern United States, sheepmen were often of Mexican or Basque origin. In contrast, many cattlemen were of northern European descent. The cowboys hired by the cattlemen were often young men. Driving, herding, and branding cattle was dangerous and required cowboys working together on horseback to control their livestock. As early as the 1860s, range-depleted Lone Star cattlemen began moving large herds of cattle to the plains of Montana and Wyoming Territories. Along with his cattle, the Texas cowboy brought with him all the bravado and baggage of his profession and a distinct enmity for sheep. It is no coincidence that of the eleven Bear Creek raiders, at least six had come up the trail from Texas. [9]

The West's cattle-sheep conflict was one of several aspects in a violent era known as the Range Wars. Historian Richard Brown termed the overall violence that occurred in the American West between 1850 and 1920 as "the Western Civil War of Incorporation," giving the victory to the "wealthy and powerful individuals, companies, and corporations [that] sought either to force settlers off the land or overcharge them for their occupancy. In effect, this was a land-enclosing movement, which in the West engendered instability and discontent." Economically motivated violence and vigilantism characterized these western land-use conflicts, which arose between white settlers and Native Americans, corporations and labor, and cattle barons and homesteaders, among others.[10]

[9] Beach, "John Daut History," 5; O'Neal, *Cattlemen vs Sheepherders*, 2-5. Many working cowboys were Black, Native American, or Hispanic, but non-white cowboys were often regulated to subordinate roles in ranching operations or otherwise marginalized. See Bruce Glasrud and Michael Searles, eds., *Black Cowboys in the American West: In the Range, on the Stage, Behind the Badge* (Norman: Univ. of Oklahoma Press, 2016); Michael K. Johnson, *Hoo-Doo Cowboys and Bronze Buckaroos* (Jackson: Univ. Press of Mississippi, 2014); Peter Iverson, *When Indians Became Cowboys: Native Peoples and Cattle Ranching in the American West* (Norman: Univ. of Oklahoma Press, 1997); Allison Fuss Mellis, *Riding Buffaloes and Broncos: Rodeo and Native Traditions in the Northern Great Plains* (Norman: Univ. of Oklahoma Press, 2003).

[10] Richard M. Brown, "Violence," in *Oxford History of the American West*, eds. Clyde Milner, Carol O'Connor, and Martha Sandweiss (New York: Oxford Univ. Press, 1994), 393–425

The 1892 Johnson County War in Wyoming has gained the most attention of the Range Wars. During its climax, key members of the Wyoming Stock Growers Association (WSGA) and corrupt state officials brought a group of armed men—mostly Texans—to Johnson County for the purpose of killing local ranchers and homesteaders who refused to bend to the WSGA's political and judicial will. The established cattlemen claimed the county's new settlers and smaller ranchers were "rustlers" who stole cattle from WSGA members without legal consequence. The WSGA's targets—local homesteaders—asserted that the open range was available to all and that the association had manipulated state law to the severe detriment of homesteaders.[11]

John B. Kendrick was a member of the WSGA from the 1880s through the Johnson County War and was its president from 1912 to 1913. In April 1892, when Kendrick learned that the WSGA's hired militia were surrounded at the TA Ranch south of Buffalo by an armed group of local ranchers, he took steps to come to the aid of the invaders. In her diary, Kendrick's daughter Rosa-Maye recalled that "Father organized a band of men to rescue the bedraggled cattlemen…but before they assembled to go to the rescue, he sent Arthur Christian to find out the conditions and to report back to him." Kendrick called off the rescue when he learned that the U.S. Cavalry had resolved the standoff by taking the militia into custody. This incident demonstrated the power of an organized local community to overcome a well-financed threat from outside interests, a key element of the Bear Creek sheep raid. In this case, Selway was the well-financed outsider.[12]

---

[11] Tom W. Davis, *Wyoming Range War: The Infamous Invasion of Johnson County* (Norman: Univ. of Oklahoma Press, 2008), 140-145. Early histories concentrated on establishing the facts and declaring one side or the other morally justified; see A.S. Mercer, *Banditti of the Plains, or The Cattlemen's Invasion of Wyoming in 1892* (Norman: Univ. of Oklahoma Press, 1894, rep. 1954.) Modern examinations focus on the complex motivations and realities facing the WSGA and the homesteaders. Daniel Belgrad described in the Johnson County War in an environmental context, noting that conflict often occurred in winter, when most cowboys were unemployed and under the most financial stress. Daniel Belgrad, "'Power's Larger Meaning': The Johnson County War as Political Violence in an Environmental Context," *Western Historical Quarterly* 33:2 (2002): 159–77. Marilynn Johnson also compares the political violence of the Johnson County War with that of Colorado's Ludlow Massacre and discusses how the Johnson County War had a far greater influence on popular culture. Marilynn S. Johnson, *Violence in the West: The Johnson County War and the Ludlow Massacre* (Long Grove, IL: Waveland Press, Inc., 2009), 145–55.

[12] Goergen, *One Cowboy's Dream,* 33; Rosa-Maye Kendrick, "The Diary of Rosa-Maye Kendrick," 16–17. Wyoming Room, Sheridan County Fulmer Public Library, Sheridan, WY. A portion of Rosa Kendrick's diary was discovered in 2011 in a drawer holding the files of Sheridan historian Elsa Spear Byron. Bucky King, *The Empire Builders: The Development of the Kendrick Cattle Company* (Sheridan, WY: Self-published, 1992), 15.

A longtime cattleman in Wyoming and Montana, John B. Kendrick (here, ca. 1900) was one of the key leaders of the sheep raid. Kendrick later entered politics, serving as Wyoming's governor and U.S. Senator in spite of rumors of his involvement with the sheep killing. PHOTOGRAPH COURTESY OF THE TRAIL END STATE HISTORIC SITE, SHERIDAN, WY. PHOTOGRAPH HOFPX025, HOFF COLLECTION.

In Montana, the formation of vigilance militias to defend cattle interests dates to 1884, when Granville Stuart led a vigilance committee, aptly known as Stuart's Stranglers, throughout central and eastern Montana and hanged several dozen alleged horse thieves and cattle rustlers. Controversy existed at the time whether all the men executed were guilty of their supposed crimes. Authors Mark Brown and W.R. Felton describe how the Stranglers attacked the Stringer Jack Gang with "a cloak of secrecy [that] still covers for the most part . . . the events that followed. Aided by a few well-placed observers, the Stranglers struck ruthlessly and without warning. Stuart personally led the raid on Stringer's gang." George W. Brewster's family history reveals that he acted as a dispatch rider for the group. It is plausible that the planners of the 1900 Bear Creek raid deliberately used the same tactics of stealth, quick action, and discipline used by Stuart's Stranglers.[13]

[13] T.A. Clay, "A Call to Order: Law, Violence, and the Development of Montana's Early Stockmen's Organizations," *Montana* 58:3 (Autumn 2008): 48-63, 95-96. "'Mr. Montana' Revised: Another Look at Granville Stuart," *Montana* 36:4 (Autumn 1986): 14-23; Mark Brown and W.R. Felton, *Before Barbed Wire: L.A. Huffman, Photographer on Horseback* (New York: Henry Holt and Company, 1956), 114-15; Warren Brewster and Eula Ebeling, interview by Margot Liberty, Aug. 27, 1977, Wyoming Room Oral Histories, Sheridan County Fulmer Public Library, Sheridan, WY.

In 1900, the Bear Creek raid's organizers knew they would have to rely on more than honor among thieves to keep their men silent. Any hint of cooperation with legal authorities would require immediate suppression, and homesteaders inclined to partner with Selway needed to be convinced that the Otter Creek valley was cattle country. Even years after the raid, when the perpetrators' fear of legal and financial sanction faded, public exposure could still threaten the prospects of its leaders. In short, they needed a violent man who could put the credible fear of death into a man instantly to keep the herder peaceful and to prevent all participants from confessing. Of the eleven named raiders, only Charlie Thex even remotely meets that description.

Charles Houston Thex was born Sheely Scott in about 1860. In 1877, he came up to the short grass country of Montana Territory from Marion County, Texas. After trailing a herd of cattle from Texas to Dakota Territory, he and a much older friend were exploring the country and stopped at the Stoneville (now Alzada) saloon. During a dispute over a card game, the teen's friend was shot and killed.[14] He retold the story in 1941 to local historian Maude Beach:

> *There was a free-for-all, and my pal was killed before my eyes. I was a kid spectator and had no hand in the game, but I saw red, and when I got outside with my gun in my hand, I had shot the man that killed my pal. I made for my horse and in twenty minutes I was out of there and riding towards the Black Hills.*[15]

After a short, unsuccessful attempt panning for placer gold near Deadwood, Scott returned to the Texas panhandle and to life as a cowpuncher for the Matador and Bridle Bit Ranches. He enlisted for three months in the Texas Rangers around 1879, during which he claimed to have killed three Native Americans during a furious fight as part of a scouting party. Another bloody bar fight solidified his reputation as a singularly dangerous man when provoked. At some point during this period, Scott changed his name to Charlie Thex. Recovery from a serious case of malaria convinced him to return to Montana Territory.[16]

---

[14] Neil Thex, interview by author, Oct. 26, 2020; Maude Beach, "Charles Thex, Old Cattleman," in *Faded Hoofprints*, 269.

[15] Beach, "Charles Thex, Old Cattlemen," 269.

[16] Family history includes an unconfirmed account of a bar fight in Texas with several African American men in the 1880s. After the fight, Thex allegedly returned to the bar with a gun and killed several people. Neil Thex, interview by author, Oct. 2020; "Chas. H. Thex saw Otter Creek in 1877," (Broadus) *Powder River Examiner*, Apr. 2, 1954.

Charlie Thex (back row, far right), Barney Hall (back row, second from left), and Levi Howes (third row, third from right) pose with their guns for this group portrait of the "Fort Howes Defenders." Thex was the gunman for the Bear Creek raid, but Howes denied knowledge or involvement despite the proximity of his Circle Bar Ranch to the raid site. PHOTOGRAPH COURTESY OF THE AMERICAN HERITAGE CENTER, LEVI S. HOWES PAPERS, COLLECTION 4430, BOX 1.

He returned to the Powder River country in 1882, established a homestead neighboring the Circle Bar Ranch on Otter Creek, and associated with Levi Howes' Circle Bar Ranch. In 1897, he married Bertha Hagen and started his own successful cattle operation. Also in 1897, Levi Howes formed a small fighting force in reaction to the killing of a sheep rancher by Northern Cheyenne earlier that year and rumors of an Indian "outbreak." Nicknamed the "Fort Howes Defenders," they built a small fort on the Circle Bar ranch. A heavily armed Thex was part of this group.[17]

While planning for the raid, Kendrick and Brewster had to account for the possibility that it could turn deadly, and fast. Charlie Thex later told historian Beach that "the herder was scaring the cattle out of the country with guns,

[17] "Chas. H. Thex saw Otter Creek in 1877." The threat posed by the Cheyenne was greatly exaggerated by area ranchers, as there was not actual "outbreak," and the only casualty was the sheepherder. See Lonnie E. Underhill, Daniel F. Littlefield Jr., and Hamlin Garland, "The Cheyenne 'Outbreak' of 1897 as Reported by Hamlin Garland," *Arizona and the West* 15:3 (Autumn 1973): 257-74; photographer unknown, Fort Howes Defenders, 1897, Collection #4430, bx1, The Papers of Levi S. Howes (1897-1967), AHC; Maude Beach, "Captain Howes and his Sons and Stone Fort," in *Faded Hoofprints*, 149.

shooting to scare off coyotes," he said. "What the stink of sheep didn't the guns did." In his memoirs, Levi Howes called Daut's herders "a strong crew of armed men of doubtful reputation." Kendrick and Brewster believed Daut's herders were armed, but chose to risk this danger to send a distinct message to Selway and Daut. To do so, the raiders needed a threatening gunman. None of the other Bear Creek raiders had any documented history of deliberate violence against people. George Brewster's family history claimed he was involved with Stuart's Stranglers, but only as a dispatch rider. Horton Boal, the son-in-law of Buffalo Bill Cody, served in the Illinois National Guard and earned some distinction quelling the Haymarket Riot in 1886. Other than this, none of the identified raiders had anything close to the violent reputation, much less the violent past, of Charlie Thex.[18]

Earlier that fall, Daut had been warned about the consequences of bringing Selway's sheep into the Otter Creek valley. Levi Howes of the Circle Bar Cattle Ranch had confronted Daut as he moved his sheep down Taylor Creek:

> *Howes told him that if he wanted to make a home there, no one would disturb him, but that Bob Selway could not overrun that country with his sheep.*
>
> *Daut said, "Do you mean to say I can't run sheep on my own land if I wish?"*
>
> *Howes said, "There are seventeen of us that say you can't run Selway sheep in country; you can run what you like on your own land, but you can't run Selway sheep on this range, and Daut, you had better keep out of it.*[19]

John Daut did not heed this warning, and soon several of Levi Howes' Circle Bar horses stampeded through his sheep, killing several dozen. Even this provocation did not cause the sheepman to alter his course.[20]

---

[18] Brewster, "December 1900," 82-85; Beach, "Charles Thex, Old Cattleman," 272; Levi Howes, "Montana Territory" (unpublished manuscript, n.d.), Collection #4430, bx 1, The Papers of Levi Howes (1897–1967), AHC; Warren Brewster and Eula Ebeling, interview by Margot Liberty, Aug. 27, 1977, Wyoming Room Oral Histories, Sheridan County Fulmer Public Library, Sheridan, WY; Richard Tuthill, George Shattuck, and John Stockton, "Horton St. Clair Boal," in *Memorials of Deceased Companions of the Commandery of the State of Illinois, Military Order of the Loyal Legion of the United States* (Chicago: The Commandery, 1912), 88-90.

[19] Beach, "John Daut History," 1.

[20] Levi Howes denied involvement in the planning or execution of the raid, but, given the involvement of Charlie Thex and Howes' cousin Barney Hall in the raid itself and the proximity of Howes' Circle Bar Ranch to the site of the slaughter, it is possible he may have deliberately avoided being in the raid so as to keep some deniability. After the raid, Howes provided half of the $4,000 paid by Kendrick to John Daut to buy him out. Lucille White, "Sheep Killing on Bear Creek as told by Levi Howes," Jul.8.1966, interview notes courtesy of Sandy and Paddy Bard.

To the cattlemen, Daut's recalcitrance demonstrated a need for more extreme measures to get him to take his sheep and leave. By December, the nascent threats had Daut's wife, Lillian, almost paralyzed with fear. Life for a woman on the open range "was lonely, miles from any settlement or womankind; winter in a small cabin, in an unfriendly and isolated community would have been bad enough, but her fear and apprehension at what might happen at the camps or otherwheres was unsettling her reason." John would find Lillian "clasping a kitchen knife, and wildly declaring she would kill anyone that disturbed her household." Given the tension, the raiders had to assume that an armed herder, alert for mischief, awaited them.[21]

In the dark winter morning of December 28, two raiders, Charlie Thex and Shorty Caddell, quietly moved to just outside the herder's wagon. The herder needed to be surprised and threatened in so complete a fashion that his compliance was assured, and this required a gunman who knew how to make an instantly credible threat. If they could not obtain the herder's compliance, then they had two alternatives: abandon the raid before any serious criminal acts or shoot the herder. Charlie Thex could be relied on to instill significant fear in the herder to ensure his compliance, or, if that failed, to take his life. With this plan in mind, the raiders sprang the trap on the lone herder, Dan Squires:

> *The herder of these sheep was petitioned by a stranger (said to be a man from Wyoming, where the Johnson-countyites grow thickest) asking for something to eat. The herder accommodated, but as he had his back to the stranger, when he went to throw out the dishwater, he was mightily surprised to find himself peeking into the barrel of a six shooter when he reversed. It needed little persuasion to win his consent to being tied to a tree, and when that formality had been gone through . . . a mob of about a dozen husky men turned loose on the sheep and the cudgels removed the menace of the inoffensive baa-baa's.*[22]

The hungry stranger was Caddell, who had lived in Sheridan before beginning work for Boal's 3X Bar ranch less than six months prior. Caddell confirmed his presence with Thex at the drop, recounting how Thex not only threatened Squires with his Colt Single Action Army revolver, but also demanded

[21] Beach, "John Daut History," 3.

[22] Nomination of John Daut to the Range Riders Hall of Fame (biographical sketch), Miles City, MT, Dola Wilson & Charles M. Boucher Papers, 1939-1954, MHS.

his captive make him coffee, adding a psychological menace to his physical threat. "Charlie was there, though, he was there with a big gun," Caddell later described the moment. "He put a six shooter up to this old fella's face and he said, 'Put a little sugar in that coffee, please. Put a little more, a little sweeter.' That old six shooter was right up in this fella's face, you know."[23]

Dan Squires was no coward. He had a shotgun in the wagon and was a recent veteran of Montana's Troop I, Third Volunteer U.S. Cavalry that mobilized for the Spanish-American War. He had no wife or children, so family obligations were not a factor, yet he acquiesced, as Kendrick and Brewster hoped he would. His compliant behavior during and after the raid can only be fully explained as an act of self-preservation when faced with a loaded revolver held by a killer.[24]

With Thex holding Squires at gunpoint, the rest of the hooded raiders drove the herd into a nearby roundup corral and began clubbing the sheep. The herd consisted of 2,200 ewe lambs separated several days earlier from the larger herd of adult sheep. With softer skulls than mature sheep, these lambs were more susceptible to clubbing, a relatively quiet killing method. Using ash wood clubs weighed down on the end with ball bearings, space in the corral quickly became unworkable as the piles of carcasses grew and as the frozen ground became slick with blood. The raiders herded the remaining lambs to a large cut bank nearby, where the majority of the sheep met their end. Shorty Caddell said the culling took all the daylight hours, and recalled that the thing he most remembered about that day was being "terribly tired."[25]

After killing all the lambs, one of the hooded men told Squires, "It is a vote from the crowd that you go to the wagon and stay there one hour, and you had better do it." The herder wisely complied. After the requisite sixty minutes,

---

[23] 1900 Federal Census of the United States, Sheridan, Sheridan County, WY, entry dated Jun. 9, 1900; John H. "Shorty" Caddell, interview by Robert Helvey, Mar. 21, 1960, The Paper of Robert T. Helvey, AHC. Caddell also related this story in a conversation witnessed by this author's nine-year-old father in 1958. See Forest B. Dunning, *Slaughter on the Otter: The Kendrick Sheep Raid* (Helena: Sweetgrass Books, 2018), vii-viii.

[24] Beach, "John Daut History," 3; *Butte Miner*, Oct. 24, 1899, 14. Squires served as a private in Troop I, which mobilized for the Spanish-American War. The Third Volunteer Cavalry did not see service overseas but deployed for training at Camp Thomas in Georgia. Squires died in 1914 and was buried in Miles City with a veteran's headstone. Applications for Headstones for U.S. Military Veterans, 1925–1941, NAID: A1, 2110-C, Record Group Number 92, Record Group Title: Records of the Office of the Quartermaster General, National Archives at Washington, DC.

[25] Frank "Booker" Lacy, interview transcript, Jul. 23, 1957, Collection 1465, bx 18, Robert T. Helvery Collection, AHC. Elmer "Deke" Reisch, interview by Margot Liberty for the Montanans at Work Project, OH 510. Reisch was a former employee and friend of Frank Lacy. Beach, "John Daut History," 3; Brewster, "December 1900," 82–85.

he left the site of the slaughter and headed to John Daut's homestead, staying only long enough to tell Daut what happened. Despite the gunnysack masks, Squires recognized some of the raiders, particularly Thex, whose homestead was less than ten miles from the raid site. After a quick stop at the Three Circle Ranch near Birney—home of his former cavalry commander, Joseph T. Brown—Squires left the area and did not return for several years. He did not even stay to cooperate with the sheriff's investigation. When Squires returned to southeastern Montana in 1909, to work for the LO Ranch near Powderville, he refused to discuss the raid.[26]

After reviewing the scene of the slaughter, Daut telegraphed Selway and the Custer County sheriff. Once the sheriff completed his investigation, the sheepman contacted the nearby Northern Cheyenne Reservation with a message to bring wagons. When the Cheyennes arrived, Daut kept the hides but let the Indians butcher the dead lambs. They hauled the carcasses back to the reservation where "there was a big feasting and celebrating and dances, according to their tribal customs, in gratitude for this great amount of meat." Daut had another, larger band of mature sheep some miles away under the management of another herder. Near this band, a handwritten note turned up: "Move these sheep as far east as pens on Bradshaw creek or every damned one of them will be killed."[27]

Intimidated by the raid, Daut and his wife decided they would be willing to leave if their personal losses could be ameliorated, and made that known to a nearby fence-post crew. Within days, Daut was visited by Kendrick.[28] The cattleman claimed he represented a group of ranchers who thought Daut had been used by Selway and offered him $4,000 if he would leave the area and agree not to bring sheep into the country for fifty years. Daut maintained he needed a year to make arrangements, to which Kendrick agreed. The Dauts eventually resettled at the mouth of the Little Powder River, where they established another sheep operation and endured several financial ups and downs. John Daut died in an asylum in 1947.[29]

---

[26] Beach, "John Daut History," 1–4; Brown and Felton, *Before Barbed Wire*, 93.

[27] Beach, "John Daut History," 4; "The Sheep Killing," in *Sheridan (WY) Enterprise*, Jan.5, 1901.

[28] Beach, "John Daut History,' 4

[29] Sheridan (WY) Post, Jul. 6, 1901; Beach, "John Daut History," 4. The original title document where Lillian Daut relinquished her homestead claim back to the federal government can still be found today in the files of the Kendrick Cattle Company, who were not a party to the abandonment. Desert Claim Title for Lillian Daut (1900), Collection H94-29, "Legal Records, Miscellaneous Real Estate Documents 1899, 1902-1970," Kendrick Cattle Company Papers, Wyoming State Archives, Cheyenne, WY. Beach, "John Daut History," 84-84; Nomination of John Daut to the Range Riders Hall of Fame, Dola Wilson & Charles M. Boucher Papers, 1939-1954, MHS.

With the dirty work done, it was time for the raiders to make their exit. According to Shorty Caddell's confession to Lyman Brewster, they rode during the night, following the tracks of wild horses to obfuscate their tracks. Their destinations were at least one, possibly two "alibi dances" that had been arranged at nearby ranches to account for the raider's whereabouts, indicating a level of community complicity. Community-wide dances were held throughout the year (such as for New Year's Eve, in this case), and the men involved could be witnessed by multiple people in the hours after the raid. Before they split up and went their separate ways, "the men who had killed the sheep were all sworn to secrecy and had taken an oath if any one of them ever talked the others would kill him."[30]

This open-range omertà is key. Kendrick and Brewster knew they could not rely on mere loyalty to ensure silence. For this threat to be taken seriously, the raiders had to believe the oath would be enforced by at least one among them who had both the means to administer the penalty and the fortitude not to talk. Again, the key man is Charlie Thex, who was not a person to squeal when the heat was applied. Thex himself told the story of a visit from Selway, who offered Thex $50,000 to turn "state's evidence." Denying any involvement in the raid, Thex refused Selway's money, saying:

> *I am in no immediate need of any money at all, but if I were, I couldn't take up your proposition, as I've never handled any sheep, I am not familiar with their diseases, and wouldn't know anything regarding the cause of their death; but if I did know anything about it, you nor your whole sheep association couldn't dig up enough money to hire me to tell it.*[31]

The absurd notion that all the sheep may have died in a single night from some sort of disease became a standard canard of the men involved.

On January 15, 1901, the *Yellowstone Journal* of Miles City received an ominous advertisement from Hanging Woman Creek, the location of Kendrick's OW Ranch.

Is This a Warning?

It is not the habit of the Journal to print anonymous communications or nonsensical stuff contributed in a spirit of spite towards any particular person or

[30] Brewster, "December 1900," 82-85; Brown and Felton, *Before Barbed Wire*, 93.
[31] Beach, "Charles Thex, Old Cattleman," 272.

> *persons. A communication has been received from Hanging Woman creek, however, that is both anonymous and nonsensical but the* Journal *gives it space for the reason that there may be a deeper meaning to it than is apparent at first glance. Whether this voices the feeling of the people of Hanging Woman or is a veiled threat to sheepmen to keep out of that section can best be judged by those familiar with that section. With this apology we present the communication verbatim:*
>
> *Hanging Woman Creek,*
> *Jan. 1, 1901*
> *The Pneumatic Sheep Killer, Patent applied for. When completed will be Second to none on the Market; it is light durable easy running having Ball Bearings easy to carryon horse back.*
>
> *Works either in the corrall or on the Prairie having a killing capacity of 1,000 head per hour.*
>
> *All you have to do is wind it up and the machine will do the rest; it also works well on sheep men. This machine will be thoroughly tested in the Near future in the vicinity of Bear Creek. When all interested will be in attendance; this machine is fully protected by patents and will be used exclusively on hanging woman creek & tributary upper Tongue River and vicinity and Bear Creek and that locality. All Persons using this Machine else where will be Prosecuted to the full extent of the Law. Yours Very Respectfully,*
>
> *Knock 'Em Stiff & Bust 'Em*
> *Propr—.*[32]

County sheriff Osceola C. Cato came down from Miles City to investigate. Selway immediately offered a reward of $2,000 to persons with information that would lead to a conviction. Cato was a lame-duck sheriff, having narrowly lost reelection that November, and would leave office in less than thirty-five days. The county sheriff was also a longtime cattleman and the former manager of the well-known XIT ranch. Selway did not have faith in Cato's investigation and told him so. Cato replied, "I have a scheme that will catch all of them. I went out to the corral, looked the situation over thoroughly, found all the clubs, and now have them in the office at the jail. And the first man that comes

[32] "Is This a Warning?" *Yellowstone Journal*, Jan. 17, 1901.

Before winning election as Custer County sheriff, Osceola C. Cato, pictured here, was the manager of the sprawling XIT Ranch's Montana operations. Cato's shoddy investigation into the sheep raid relied on the participants to admit their guilt. PHOTOGRAPH COURTESY OF THE RANGE RIDERS MUSEUM.

in and claims one of those clubs I intend to arrest them." This absurd plan confirmed Selway's lack of confidence in Cato. Indeed, identifying the clubs became a source of local amusement. Several people stopped by the sheriff's office to examine the clubs and joshingly remark, "Well, you can't do anything to me. My club isn't there. Whose club is that? Must belong to [so-and-so]. He's the only one big enough to handle a club like that." The notion that the sheep had suddenly fallen victim to some sort of illness became such a popular joke among the cattlemen of the area that it was given the name "the club disease." Cato's tenure as sheriff ended on February 1, 1901, and the investigation faded away.[33]

[33] "The Sheep Killing," *Sheridan (WY) Enterprise*, Jan. 5, 1901; "Custer County Election Returns," *Yellowstone Journal*, Nov. 15, 1900; Michael M. Miller, "Cowboys and Capitalists: The XIT Ranch in Texas and Montana, 1885-1912," *Montana* 65:4 (Winter 2015): 4, 11-28; J. Evetts Haley, *The XIT Ranch of Texas* (Norman: Univ. of Oklahoma Press, 1929, rep. 1953), 128; Brown and Felton, *Before Barbed Wire*, 93; Charles Flory, interview by Robert Helvey, Jan. 11, 1961, Collection 1465, bx 17, Robert T. Helvey Collection, AHC.

Having established mechanisms for keeping their own participants silent, the organizers had to appeal to the pro-cattleman sentiments of the community or ensure the area's silence through fear. Their neighbors' silence effectively hampered the sheriff's investigation and set up important barriers to further encroachment by any sheep-friendly parties. The economic domination of the cattle industry was incentive for the people of close-knit communities like Otter and Birney to keep their mouths shut, and loyalty to their friends would ensure it. Antipathy for the sheep industry further encouraged silence. Wyoming pioneer Count Frederick Thorne-Rider recalled that when he first arrived in Sheridan around 1899, "Sheep men, why, were not in particular favor and sometimes to avoid open, little arguments on the street, why one had to step across the street if you saw your brother sheepman in the vicinity so as not to run, encounter him."[34]

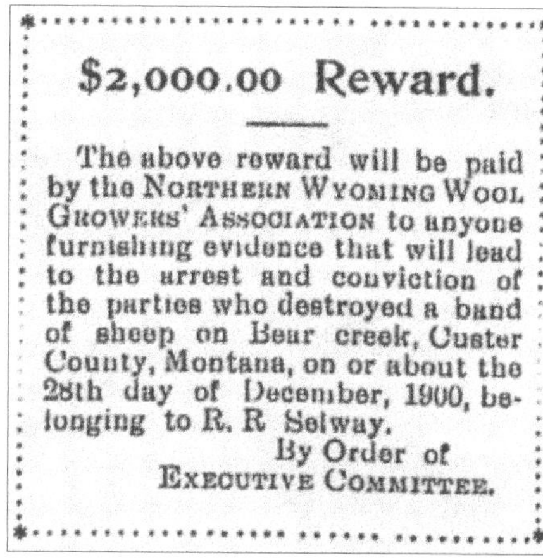

$2,000.00 Reward.

The above reward will be paid by the NORTHERN WYOMING WOOL GROWERS' ASSOCIATION to anyone furnishing evidence that will lead to the arrest and conviction of the parties who destroyed a band of sheep on Bear creek, Custer County, Montana, on or about the 28th day of December, 1900, belonging to R. R Selway.

By Order of
EXECUTIVE COMMITTEE.

This advertisement ran in several area newspapers over multiple weeks to get information on the Bear Creek Sheep Raid. This image and caption was not included in the original *MMWH* article.

The fact that the raiders directed their violence towards the lambs while sparing the sheepherder dampened community outrage. From the cattlemen's perspective, Selway had provoked the cattlemen and had received a measured, even welcome response. Nonetheless, steps taken, such as the "Pneumatic Sheep Killer" ad, warned any locals inclined to cooperate with the investigation of the consequences. The situation created a strange dissonance. The same community that took assurance from the fact that not one person was hurt in the raid became subject to indirect threats of violence. Their silence, coupled with Cato's bias toward cattlemen, ensured that the investigation went nowhere.

Unsurprisingly, Selway took personal affront to the raid, to the lack of justice, and to the men he identified as its leaders: Levi Howes, Charlie Thex, and John B. Kendrick. When $15,000 was anonymously deposited in a Miles City bank to the credit of the sheep's owner, Selway declined the money.

[34] Frederick Thorne-Rider, interview by Robert Helvey, date unknown but prior to May 5, 1963, Collection 1465, bx 19, Robert T. Helvey Collection, AHC.

Overseen by cowboys (ca. 1902), cattle graze near the corral where the Bear Creek raiders began killing John Daut's ewe lambs. As the corral filled with carcasses, the raiders herded the rest of the sheep to the nearby cut bank and dispatched the remaining animals. PHOTOGRAPH COURTESY OF THE ASHLAND RANGER STATION, U.S. FOREST SERVICE.

As it became clear that justice would not come easily to Otter Creek, the Sheep King made his own attempts to buttress his position. Levi Howes recalled in 1966: "Then Selway hired a crew of several men, supposed to be dangerous men with guns. They went to the camp on Tooley Creek and stayed there all winter.[35] According to Howes, Selway's men confronted Charlie Thex, but nothing came of it.

> *Some of them also came down to Thex's. They left notice there that if any one showed upon those hills on Tooley Creek they would probably be shot at. Charles Thex took down his Savage rifle, got on a horse and rode around sheep camps near by . . . Then one of the warriors came down to Thex's. "We are paid to shoot," he says, "but I'm not dangerous. I won't shoot." He drew the money but would not fight. After that everything went on as usual.*[36]

Soon after the raid, Kendrick moved his personal residence to Sheridan, Wyoming, where both he and Selway became active in the social scene. Suddenly, in June 1906—over five years after the raid—Custer County district attorney Thomas J. Porter charged Kendrick with grand larceny. The basis of the charge was a "confession" by one of the supposed participants, along with an affidavit from Selway. Daut later claimed that Selway personally delivered

[35] Brown and Felton, *Before Barbed Wire*, 93; White, "Sheep Killing on Bear Creek as told by Levi Howes."
[36] White, "Sheep Killing on Bear Creek as told by Levi Howes."

the indictment papers to Kendrick in his office at Sheridan's First National Bank. Kendrick responded by grabbing Selway by the collar and throwing the Sheep King unceremoniously into the street. The county attorney's reason for bringing the case may well have been politically motivated. Porter was, at that time, serving on the executive committee of the Eastern Montana Woolgrowers Association. Whereas the district attorney during the initial investigation had valued the sheep at misdemeanor levels, Porter's indictment valued Selway's sheep at $9,500, clearing the monetary hurdle for felony charges.[37]

The legal case imploded when the confession was revealed as the handiwork of Selway's agents, who forced the confession from the previously unknown—and whiskey-drunk—Jesse Bowe of Bell Fourche, South Dakota. He wrote a letter to Kendrick via the court in Miles City:

> *I was on a drunk there and the Selway Boys got holt of me and kept me drunk there two weeks, giving me money and trying all the time to get me to make some kind of a statement against you but I would not, but they kept me drunk til I was crazy from the whiskey and they say that I made a statement before a notary public. If I did the statement is a fraud because I don't know what is in the statement. The cliques is all in together and they have got it in for me.*[38]

The court quietly dismissed charges against Kendrick in October of that same year; news of their existence never appeared in any newspapers. Selway's attempt to bring down Kendrick had failed miserably.[39]

[37] *State of Montana vs John B. Kendrick,* Custer County Courthouse, Case #387 of the Seventh Judicial District, Custer County, 1906; Beach, "John Daut History," 4. Daut's source for this story was Selway's brother-in-law, Charles Lewis. "Sheep Growers in Miles City where Industry is Discussed," *Anaconda Standard,* Apr. 17, 1906; *State of Montana vs John B. Kendrick.* In the initial investigation, the DA declined to bring charges. According to reporting in the *Yellowstone Journal:* "Under the present law the offence was only a misdemeanor, and in the opinion of the county attorney that 60 days in jail was the most severe punishment they could be given and that if such liberal rewards were offered, he might be tempted to plead guilty and get the reward." "Wool Growers in Session," *Yellowstone Journal,* Apr. 17, 1901.

[38] The original letter reads: "I was on a drunk thar and the sellway Boys got holt of me and keep me drunk thar for too weak giving me money and trying all the time to get me to mak som kind of a thatment against you but I would not but they kep me drunk till I was crasey from whiskey and they say that I mad a statement before notra republic iff I did the statement is frud because I dont know what is in the statment the clike is all in together and they hav got it in for me . . ." Jesse Bowe to John B. Kendrick, R.R. Selway Suit, Collection 342, bx, 1-6 and bx 150, The Papers of John B. Kendrick (1873-1961), AHC.

[39] State of Montana vs John B. Kendrick.

As the years progressed and the statute of limitations passed, the specter of criminal consequences for the raiders faded. Motivation to keep the crime under wraps, however, persisted due to the fear of public exposure that could derail the fledgling political careers of Kendrick and Brewster. Brewster entered the political arena first, when Montanans elected the Republican to the state legislature in 1904, and reelected him in 1906 and 1908.[40] Even with the veil of secrecy, rumors of Brewster's involvement in the raid were prevalent enough during the 1906 election to prompt the staunchly Republican *Forsyth Times* to address the subject.

> *The Times can make right and deny, through the publicity of its columns, that George W. Brewster is not guilty of any connection whatsoever in the widely celebrated sheep killing case known as the Selway affair . . . The people of Rosebud County love justice. They will make the false reports concerning Mr. Brewster react upon his political opponent, and the "Selway affair" will prove a boomerang which will return the Hon. George W. Brewster to the state house as our next representative by an unprecedented majority.*[41]

The source of the allegations was "a confession [that] had been obtained by a man said to have been employed by the sheep killers." Most likely, the *Forsyth Times* was referring to the Bowe confession introduced in the Kendrick indictment weeks before their editorial. Brewster did not seek reelection after 1908. He became president of the Montana Livestock Association in 1911, serving until his death in 1912, at the age of fifty-five.[42]

After moving to Wyoming, Kendrick also became active in politics. Elected as a Democrat to the Wyoming State Senate in 1910, he quickly rose through the ranks of the state Democratic Party and gained the nomination for the U.S. Senate seat in 1912. He narrowly lost that election to Francis Warren but won election as governor of Wyoming in 1914. As Kendrick began his rise in political circles, Selway saw another opportunity to seek revenge.[43] A pair of

---

40 Ellis Waldron, *Montana Legislators, 1864-1979* (Missoula: Bureau of Government Research, Univ. of Montana, 1980, 44.

41 "How's This?" *Forsyth Times*, Oct. 16, 1906.

42 "How's This?" *Forsyth Times*; Burton Brewster, *They Came and They Stayed: Rosebud County History* (Billings: Western Printing), 1970, 36.

43 Goergen, One Cowboy's Dream, 33.

cattlemen related a second-hand story, describing a confrontation between the cattleman and the sheepman.

> *Kendrick met Selway here in the evening and he told them that they were going to come out in the Post about Kendrick being in on that sheep killing . . . Kendrick stopped Selway and he said now if that comes out in the Republican paper you'll be [the] one that will be dead when the sun comes up in the morning.*[44]

The source of this story was Sheridan sheepman Tom Stout, and the confrontation probably occurred during the 1912 election. The purported piece in the *Sheridan Post* did not appear.[45]

Throughout 1912, Kendrick began receiving personal correspondence from John Daut asking for money to "do right by me," suggesting Daut knew the cattleman was responsible for the raid but declining to challenge Kendrick beyond monetary compensation. Daut claimed, "The trouble between your people & Selway has nothing to do with them and I, and I never changed my mind just from what I said that time that two rongs [*sic*] would not make one right." Hard up for money, Daut continued, "I am sure I done all that I think is right . . . Three thousand dollars is nothing to such big ranchers like there is up in that country and now I have asked nothing but a friendly deal between all of us and leave Selway out." There is no evidence that Kendrick ever paid Daut anything after 1901.[46]

Selway left the area in 1921, moving to Iowa to live near the family of his second wife. There, he was indicted for fraud in 1922 while raising capital for his bankrupt steel fence-post company. During those proceedings, Selway died of pneumonia. Much of the energy and certainly all the money spent to obtain justice in the Bear Creek sheep raid faded with his death.[47]

Kendrick's skyrocketing political career meant that Selway's death did little to relax the wall of secrecy around the raid. Any real threat to his political career

---

[44] Hale Jeffers and Deyo Hasbrouck, interview by Robert Helvey, Jun. 24, 1958, Collection 1465, bx 17, Robert T. Helvey Collection, AHC. The transcript misspells "Hasbrouck" as "Hasbrook."

[45] Ibid.

[46] John Daut to John B. Kendrick, Aug. 13, 1912, Collection 341, bx 1-6, series 1, subseries 1 (early correspondence, 1912), The Papers of John B. Kendrick (1873-1961), AHC.

[47] Maude Beach, "Charles Daly and the Selway Ranch," in *Faded Hoofprints,* 80-81; Death Cheats Court in Trial of Selway Post Co. President," Waterloo (IA) Courier, May 23, 1922; "Bob" Selway Dies at Des Moines Home," *Powder River Examiner* and *Broadus Independent,* Jun. 2, 1922.

became less likely as the years passed. He was so popular with some of his constituents, particularly around Sheridan, that they chose not to believe rumors tying him to nefarious activity, or tacitly accepted his actions as a necessary part of range politics.[48]

Of the other members of the raid, Horton Boal committed suicide in 1902. George Brewster passed away in 1912. Dan Squires, the herder, died in 1914. Kendrick himself was dead by 1933. Yet intriguingly, the veil of secrecy surrounding the raid remained until the late 1950s. Given the lack of legal and political consequences, how was this possible? Daut still lived to tell the tale until 1947, but he had little standing to make anything happen without Selway's money. The Western mythos might explain the silence as loyalty to old friends who rode for the brand, However, a more direct explanation existed to reinforce the surviving raider's inclination toward silence: Charlie Thex was still alive.[49]

In the years after the raid, Thex became prosperous but kept some of his violent tendencies. In 1929, local homesteader Archie Carnes was arrested for stealing two milk cows. When local ranchers discovered four more head of cattle killed with their brands removed, they gathered around the grisly evidence.

> *It was thought the brands on these cattle had been tampered with and the parties responsible had become alarmed over Carnes' arrest. One old time cowboy who had come up the trail from Texas said "We know who the sons-of-bitches are. Let's go hang them." Some of the other men thought the country was a little too modern for that and that the law should deal with the guilty ones.*[50]

The "old time cowboy from Texas" was Charlie Thex, whose penchant for summary justice remained despite progress in community standards and legal accountability.[51]

Thex and Kendrick maintained their association after the raid. Correspondence between the two can be found among Kendrick's personal files, in which each man refers to the other repeatedly as "friend." Their friendship extended beyond letters. In 1907, two horse thieves were discovered on Kendrick's OW Ranch. One was killed in a shootout and the other escaped in the night. The next morning, Thex, who then lived over thirty miles

[48] John Ray Shreve, *Ride the Divide* (WY: self-published, 2002), 25.

[49] "Gone on his Last Roundup," *Semiweekly Billings Gazette,* Oct. 31, 1902; Montana Death Records, Custer County, May 1914; Goergen, *One Cowboy's Dream,* 43.

[50] J. Fred Toman, *Echoing Footsteps* (Butte: Ashton Print & Engraving, 1967), 43.

[51] Neil Thex, e-mail to Forest Dunning, Jun. 25, 2020.

away, joined the posse to pursue the surviving horse thief, who was eventually captured by law enforcement in Wyoming. Thex's loyalty to Kendrick, and Kendrick's dependence on Thex, may have been rooted in friendship, but it was cemented by their damning secret.[52]

Thex lived on Otter Creek until passing away in 1955, at the estimated age of ninety-four. Assumptions that the old man would have been too feeble in the final years of his life to be a threat are belied by this 1951 encounter, recorded in the *Billings Gazette* under the headline "Hardy Montana Farmer Speeds Haying Job at Ripe Age of 92." The newspaper reported that the *Gazette's* journalist, while "trying to interview 92-year-old Charlie Thex at work in a nearby field, was brushed off with: 'I'm to busy to talk, I have to get this haying done.' Thex has been in Montana since trailing a herd of cattle up from Texas in 1877." If Thex was hardy enough to gather hay in 1951, he could still handle a gun.[53]

The power of Thex's menacing presence is validated by the fact that within two years of his death, the first cracks appeared in the vows of secrecy surrounding the raid. First, George Brewster's son, Lyman Brewster, confronted his old friend, Shorty Caddell, in 1955 and obtained his confession. Cadell later talked to Robert Helvey in 1960. It was most likely Frank "Booker" Lacy who admitted his involvement to author Mark Brown but demanded anonymity, a request Brown honored. Whether or not Lacy was Brown's anonymous source, the fact remains that the raider finally felt free to discuss the matter with an outside author after Charlie Thex passed away. In 1956, only Lacy, Caddell, and McKinney, three of the eleven raiders identified by Lyman Brewster, were alive to confess to Brown and Felton.[54]

---

[52] Charles Thex to John B. Kendrick, Oct. 13, 1913; Kendrick to Thex, Nov. 30, 1912, Mar. 7, 1913, Nov. 30, 1913, Collection 341, bx 1-6, series 1, subseries 1, *Correspondence of John B. Kendrick* (1873–1961), AHC; "Sheriff Kills Horse Thief," *Billings Gazette,* Jun. 11, 1907; statement of John H. Reavis regarding criminal proceedings of Robert Phillips, Jul.27, 1971, included in correspondence between Manville Kendrick and the Clerk of District Court, Rosebud County.

[53] "Rites Accorded Pioneer Rancher," *Billings Gazette,* Aug.2, 1965; "Hardy Montana Farmer Speeds Haying Job at Ripe Age of 92," *Billings Gazette,* Aug. 25, 1951.

[54] Brewster, "December 1900," 82-85. John H. "Shorty" Caddell interview. Lacy's cooperation is revealed when comparing two separate comments about the raid. "The mystery was never solved but there used to be a lot of joshing done about it. One night at a dance, Mrs. [William Smith] said to me, 'You are a mighty little fellow to handle one of those big clubs killing those sheep.' I said, "Why Mrs. [Smith], I did not handle a club. It kept me busy carrying water to [William]." The bracketed name is fictitious. Brown and Felton, *Before Barbed Wire,* 231. A similar story is recorded in an interview with Birney matron Mary "Peachy" Cox by Floyd Alderson: "They tell me funny stories about that. Fay Humpries, you know. She used to kid Booker Lacey [*sic*] She said, Mr. Laccy (sp), how many sheep [they] did not kill? They weren't supposed to have been there, these fellows you know. And Lacey said, "Well, I tell you Mrs. Humphries I didn't get a chance to kill very many because I was too busy packing water for Matt.' He had a great sense of humor." Mary "Peachy" Cox, interview by Floyd Alderson, Jul. 10, 1969, SC 1338, MHS.

At its core, the Bear Creek sheep raid was a struggle between two well-financed, strong-willed men, Kendrick and Selway, each of whom dominated his industry. Issues that complicated other sheep raids—such as race, class, and religion—were not central factors in this incident. Both sides had plenty of money and influence. Kendrick was victorious because he and Brewster had planned carefully, chosen their raiders well, and taken steps to enforce a general silence, knowing, too, that public sympathy tended to lean in their favor. The raid's success at preventing the expansion of sheep into the Otter Creek valley demonstrated to all stockgrowers in northern Wyoming and southeastern Montana that violence, when applied with careful discipline and used to instill fear in the victims, perpetrators, and local population, could provide a leg up in the waning years of the open range.

In the decade after the 1900 slaughter at Bear Creek, sheep raids in southeastern Montana and northern Wyoming took on a more brutal character, escalating with the deaths of several men. In a shootout in 1907 near Selway's home ranch on Pumpkin Creek, Ray Tarbell killed cattleman George Mitchell. Two years later, a bungled raid ended with the murder of three sheepmen near Ten Sleep, Wyoming. The incident, called the Spring Creek raid, was a sensation throughout the West and finally outraged a community enough to act against the perpetrators. Seven men were arrested, with two turning state's evidence. The five raiders who did not testify for the state eventually pleaded guilty during a dramatic trial. Raider Herb Brink received a life sentence, while Milton Alexander and George Saban pled guilty to second degree murder and were sentenced to at least twenty years in prison. Even then, significant numbers of the local populace supported clemency. In 1915, Spring Creek raider Milton Alexander received a pardon from Wyoming's governor, none other than John B. Kendrick.[55]

NOTES ON CHAPTER 19:

- This article was published in the Summer 2021 edition of *Montana, the Magazine of Western History. MMWH* is the official journal of the Montana Historical Society, headquartered in Helena.

[55] "Tragedy at Selway in Which Geo. L. Mitchell Looses [*sic*] Life," *Miles City Independent*, Sep. 11, 1909; John W. Davis, A Vast Amount of Trouble: A History of the Spring Creek Raid (Norman: Univ. of Oklahoma Press, 19930, 232-33); Report of Convicts Discharged, #1442: Milton Alexander, State Penitentiary, Wyoming State Archives, Cheyenne, WY.

"The Right Man to Do a Wrong Thing" won the 2022 Spur Award from the Western Writers of America for Outstanding Non-Fiction Journal Article in 2021. This photograph shows author Shane Dunning, left, accepting the award from WWA President Phil Mills. The image and caption were not included in the original *MMWH* article. PHOTOGRAPH BY JOHNNY D. BOGGS.

- This article won the 2022 Spur Award for Best Short Non-fiction of the year from the Western Writers of America.
- My father, Forest B. Dunning, authored a short book on the raid, *Slaughter on the Otter*. Researching that book for my father jump-started my own writing.

A younger White Bull, also known as Ice. PHOTOGRAPH BY L.A. HUFFMAN, COURTESY OF THE MONTANA HISTORICAL SOCIETY, 981-083.

20

He Wanted to Eat a Piece of a White Man's Heart

During the summer of 1897, talk of war between the Northern Cheyenne and local settlers was seemingly on every tongue. John Hoover, a white sheepherder working for Fred Bollinger just north of Ashland, had been shot and killed, presumably by Indians. In a previous article, I described how a group of 200 armed white men led by Levi Howes gathered outside the reservation and were persuaded by Custer County Sheriff Gibbs to seek justice through the law instead of vigilante action. The killers were believed to be part of a band of Cheyennes led by White Bull. These Cheyennes were given an ultimatum to turn over the persons responsible for Hoover's death. Disregarding the demand, Levi Howes stated, would mean war.

White Bull, also known as Ice, was a well-known chief and medicine man among the Northern Cheyenne. He was best known for a miracle he performed near Busby, purportedly around 1884. According to John Stands-in-Timber, White Bull had a hole deep enough for a man to sit in produced at a site near Busby. A few large rocks that took several men to move were placed near the hole, which was covered by a tipi. After performing several ceremonies, White Bull sat in the cavity, with the rocks used to cover him completely. "Go outside now," he ordered them, "and I will sing, and then give the signal for you to come back and lift the rocks off." When this was done, White Bull was gone. They searched for him to see if he was hiding, to no avail. Putting the rocks back over the hole as instructed, they soon heard the signal. Ice was back, sitting in the hole. Eventually, White Bull became the recognized leader of the Cheyennes near the Lame Deer agency.

White Bull was also known for claiming he had a bad heart, and said he needed to eat a piece of a white man's heart to cure this condition. This was well-known to the white settlers. Whether this claim was a boast, a threat, or straight-forward medical advice is not clear.

The St. Labre Chapel, circa 1963. PHOTOGRAPH TAKEN BY NED RANDOLPH, COURTESY OF THE AMERICAN HERITAGE CENTER, THE PAPERS OF EDMUND RANDOLPH.

The Cheyennes did turn over the suspected killer (David Stanley) and some witnesses to the crime, but tensions remained high. Levi Howes built a stone fort on a hill overlooking his Circle Bar Ranch and supplied it with guns, ammunition, and provisions. The Cheyennes witnessed these preparations with increasing concern. While not implicated in the murder, White Bull feared for his own life at the hands of the ranchers and fled to the Catholic mission at Ashland. Two Dutch priests, Father Vandervelder and Father Vandepaugh placed him under their protection and sent for Levi Howes. White Bull believed Howes was pursuing him personally.

Levi told the rest of this remarkable story on a least two occasions. One was in November 1962 to author Edmund (Ned) Randolph. He also gave an interview to Bob Helvey in December 1956:

The old priests down there sent for me, and I went there. He told me, there were two of them there at the mission. They said, "we're white men, but we're here for doing, working with the Indians, but we're white men. If there is anything, warning we can give you, we will do it." "But," he says, "we have got to, not lose our influence with the Indians." So, they sent for me to come down and talk things over.

According to Howes, the priests contributed to White Bull's paranoia.

And there was one old Indian down there, kind of a chief, a medicine man, old White Bull. And he'd been, they said, telling everybody all around his heart was bad, he wanted to eat a piece of a white man's heart. . . . his old father Vandervelder, he talked to him, what was his trouble?

There were 200 men, white cowboys gathered on the other side of the river. "Yes," he [Father Vandervelder] said, "they mean to fight." "If this thing ever starts," he told this old White Bull, "the first man they are going to get is the man that wants to eat a piece of a white man's heart." And old White Bull was so scared he asked them to hide him. They took him and hid him under the chapel on a floor.

This was the situation when Levi Howes arrived at the mission. They provided the young manager of the Circle Bar Ranch with a nice clean bed in the chapel. The priests supposedly informed Howes, "the man who wants to eat a piece of a white man's heart is laying on the dirt underneath." The two antagonists spent that night, one sleeping in comfort directly over the other.

According to Randolph's notes:

The priests wrangled a peace. Levi and White Bull departed without incident. The next time Levi saw White Bull, the two were crossing Tongue River at flood time, Levi in a buggy, White Bull on horseback. Levi made light of the incident and paid White Bull a dollar to test the depth of the water by riding into it and across.

The veracity of this fascinating story is deserving of some scrutiny. Although he did tell it multiple times in formal interviews, this tale comes from a single source: Levi Howes in his advanced years. Their lack of corroboration characterizes the

A portrait of Levi Howes as an older man. PHOTOGRAPH COURTESY OF THE AMERICAN HERITAGE CENTER, THE PAPERS OF LEVI S. HOWES.

apocryphal nature of stories such as this. What corroboration exists is often contradictory, and such is the case here.

Randolph's notes claim that White Bull helped Levi navigate a flooded river in a buggy. In Howes' unpublished memoirs, he identifies the man who helped him as Badger (the father of David Stanley, Hoover's killer). Also, Howes' memoirs do not mention the chapel incident but do reference White Bull's heart trouble and his plan to relieve them. Still, an article in the *New York Times* (June 1, 1897) about the Hoover incident does state: "The Sheriff learned that the crime was committed by three of the bands led by White Bull, who said a day or two previous that his heart was bad—that he wanted to eat a white man's heart." Unfortunately, it seems, most of the best stories seemingly can't be proven either way.

Notes on Chapter 20:

- This column first appeared in the *Powder River Examiner's* September 10, 2021, edition.
- Edmund (Ned) Randolph was the author of *Hell Among the Yearlings,* among others. His papers include his interactions with Levi Howes and are available from the American Heritage Center in Laramie.
- As mentioned before, Levi Howes also gave an interview to Charles Helvey in 1956. The transcript and audio recording are available among Helvey's papers, which also are stored at the American Heritage Center in Laramie.

John L. Tucker (right) is pictured alongside Jess Barclay, date unknown. PHOTOGRAPH COURTESY OF THE CHARLIE DUNNING FAMILY.

21

The Unsolved Murder of John L. Tucker

My great-great-uncle John L. Tucker was murdered on Otter Creek in 1911. His murder was, and remains, officially unsolved. Florence Shy, in *Echoing Footsteps,* wrote that "People were terribly upset over this but were too divided in their opinion, so no arrests were made."

He was discovered shot in the back of his neck at his residence during the evening hours of March 28th. The body was found initially by Tucker's friend James Maxwell, who immediately notified Rosebud County Sheriff N.G. McMullin (who also resided in Ashland).

Tucker's residence was a mile and half east of Ashland, officially in (at that time) Custer County by a matter of only twenty feet. The Rosebud County Sheriff set guards on the scene and traveled to Miles City to inform Custer County Sheriff Lavalley of the crime.

McMullin, who had formerly operated a store in Ashland, was a friend of Tucker's. McMullin being among the very first to the crime scene was memorialized in the initial newspaper accounts of the tragedy. "Sheriff Finds Body of Friend" was blazoned across newspapers across Montana.

Tucker was killed when he was only 33 years old. He was unmarried, a moderately successful stockman, and the brother of Robert Lee Tucker (my great-great-grandfather), a prominent homesteader on Otter Creek. Stock rustling proliferated in the area at this time, and initial newspaper speculation on the murder pointed to this as the motive: "There has been considerable feeling over stock rustling in that territory, and Tucker had been assisting the authorities in ferreting out the criminals," according to the *Forsyth Times.*

When Sheriff Levalley arrived with the coroner, they found Tucker dead with a single bullet wound that entered the back of his neck and exited his forehead. Tucker had entered his cabin in the early evening hours and attempted to light his stove. When he was shot, he fell forward, struck his face on the stove, and then fell backward. They found Tucker's own six-shooter undisturbed in his trousers. Another pistol was discovered lying on the dead man's chest, and "it looked as if an attempt had been made to close his fingers around the butt." This pistol belonged to Tucker's good friend, Ves Hall, who declared to the inquest that the gun had been stolen sometime before. The inquest concluded that death had been instantaneous and that the crime had been committed between seven and ten o'clock the evening of the 28th.

Any initial thoughts that Tucker may have committed suicide, as indicated by the hand closed on the gun, were dismissed almost immediately. Not only were there no indications of depression in Tucker's demeanor that day, the location of the entry and exit wounds with no powder burns squarely pointed to another person.

The most immediate suspicion fell upon local stockman J.W. "Billy" Coleman. Ves Hall testified to a conversation he and Tucker had the day before the killing:

> *The other day as we were going to Ashland, inside of the last three weeks, and we were talking about Mrs. Coleman, Mrs. Bill Coleman, he says she is coming back. I got a letter from her and he says she wrote and told me to be on the lookout, that Bill was going to kill him and when we got off at the gate he took the letter out of the vest pocket and handed it to me, but I handed it back and said I don't want to read your letter. And he insisted my reading it, but I didn't even look at it.*

Several people testified to seeing Bill Coleman on a black horse around the area in the late afternoon. Coleman was also seen near Ves Hall's residence earlier in the day. Seventeen-year-old Ora Ferris testified that she was with Tucker most of the afternoon and witnessed Tucker get his pistol. When she asked why he was getting his gun, he reportedly replied that he "wanted to play cowboy."

Billy Coleman briefly testified to arriving at Elmer Landers' place (about two miles from the killing) at seven o'clock and staying the night. Frank Jordan also stayed there that night and testified to Coleman's presence until morning, although he placed the suspect's arrival at half-past seven. Dusk had arrived around seven o'clock that night. Coleman made no statement to the inquest about threatening Tucker, only a description of his activities that day.

Suspicion of Coleman had been communicated to Sheriff McMullin by Hall, because one of Sheriff McMullin's first acts on discovering the body was to send his deputy, J.C. "Kid" Anderson, to arrest Coleman and notify the Custer County authorities of his actions. Anderson found Coleman in time to give minimal testimony before the inquest.

The final witness before the inquest was thirty-year-old Mrs. J.W. Coleman. She testified that she and her husband had returned to Otter Creek from Siloam Springs, Arkansas, the previous Saturday. Her testimony to the coroner confirmed several elements of the letter described by Ves Hall, but she obfuscated on some key points.

> ***Coroner:*** *Did you hear Mr. Coleman, while you were down there, before coming back here, make any threats against John Tucker?*
>
> ***Mrs. Coleman:*** *Well, I don't know. I don't remember.*
>
> ***Coroner:*** *Did you, before starting home from down there, write a letter to John Tucker, deceased, stating in that letter that Mr. Coleman had threatened his life and to look out for him?*
>
> ***Mrs. Coleman:*** *I wrote and told him that he had better be on the lookout, and I was afraid. That he would deal me lots of misery. And that the best thing I could do was to stay there.*

In the written record of her testimony, Mrs. Coleman, as other witnesses, had been allowed to review and correct her statement. In that document, a phrase has been scratched out by the witness where the stenographer had recorded the above testimony. The sentence was originally recorded as "better be on the lookout, and I was afraid *he would take my life.*"

In the final questioning, the coroner followed up on the letter:

> ***Coroner:*** *Did you ever write to Mr. Tucker more than this one letter while you were down there?*
>
> ***Mrs. Coleman:*** *I wrote him one or two or three letters while there.*
>
> ***Coroner:*** *Did you know of your husband having any ill-feeling towards Mr. Tucker?*
>
> ***Mrs. Coleman:*** *Not that I know towards him, but he did towards me.*
>
> ***Coroner:*** *Did your husband know you were writing these letters to Mr. Tucker?*
>
> ***Mrs. Coleman:*** *No, he did not.*

The inquest concluded that an "automatic pistol had killed John Tucker, Savage make, 32 caliber, then and there in the hands of persons unknown to this jury." A grand jury in Miles City was also allowed to indict any suspects but did not. To this day, the crime remains unsolved.

As mentioned before, this lack of action caused considerable tension along Otter Creek. Coleman's "alibi" did not seemingly cover the period immediately around seven o'clock. Witnesses did not definitively see Coleman until approximately seven-thirty, two miles from the crime scene. Coleman's wife seemingly corroborated Hall's testimony regarding the letter, including that she had warned Tucker and she considered her husband a violent man. Many years later, Otter Creek resident Ernest Coon stated that "Lav Jordan and Bill Coleman were two of the Ashland toughs.... He said he was sure Billy Coleman killed John Tucker." Lavie Jordan was also questioned briefly by the inquest and was the brother of Frank Jordan, who provided part of Billy Coleman's alibi. Within three months, Lavie Jordan eloped with Ora Ferris (the girl who testified to Tucker's actions the day of his death), against her parent's wishes.

Ves Hall, whose stolen pistol was found on Tucker's body, was a known friend of Tucker's and was apparently not suspected as having a role in his death. In later years, Ves Hall became infamous as the first man arrested for loudly criticizing President Woodrow Wilson's pro-British policies in the frenzied run-up to World War One. I wrote a column about that incident several months ago (see Chapter 5).

It seems likely that Billy Coleman did, indeed, kill John Tucker. The evidence, however, is circumstantial at best. Coleman appears to have had several possible motivations for the deed. Coleman's wife was admitted to communicating privately with the unmarried stockman. It is possible those letters indicated a romantic relationship, although Tucker's willingness to show Ves Hall the last letter casts some doubt. Mrs. Coleman's testimony indicates tensions between herself, her husband, and John Tucker. Perhaps Billy Coleman knew Tucker was cooperating with law enforcement, which threatened his (and others') criminal interests. Mrs. Coleman may have also known this and, having some affection (romantic or otherwise), chose to warn Tucker via her letters.

Even so, the performance of Custer County officials also seems strange and no doubt contributed to the community's hard feelings. The coroner, O.M. Lanphear, resigned from his post within weeks of this case. He objected that the county was not paying his expenses, including his travel costs from Miles

City to Ashland. Perhaps his unhappiness contributed to a less-than-vigorous investigation. As mentioned before, the grand jury convened that month also refused to indict Coleman or anyone else.

John L. Tucker was among the first buried in Willow Creek Cemetery, the land for which was donated by Robert Lee Tucker, the deceased's brother. The tragedy clearly had a significant impact on the family. If you go down to the cemetery along Otter Creek, you will find, near the graveyard's center, an obelisk headstone nearly three feet high that dwarfs every stone near it. It marks the final resting place of John L. Tucker. This obviously expensive and ornate headstone reflects the Tucker family's considerable grief.

John L. Tucker's gravestone is one of the more prominent monuments at the Willow Creek Cemetery, on Otter Creek. PHOTOGRAPH BY SHANE DUNNING.

NOTES ON CHAPTER 21:

- This column first appeared in the October 15, 2021, edition of the *Powder River Examiner.*
- After publication, I heard from another family member who relayed another story about John L. Tucker's funeral. The source of this story is Bryan Tucker (John's nephew), who stated that Lav Jordan attended the funeral and said something along the lines of "good riddance." One of the Dunnings (Grant or Luther, mentioned in Chapter 14 and detailed in Chapter 30) pointed a pistol at Lav's head. Others at the funeral told the pistol-pointing cowboy, "Don't do it; it's not worth it."
- John L. Tucker's coroner's report was used in this article. It is available from the Custer County Courthouse in Miles City. ⇠

HAUNTED BY DEAD COWBOY

STRANGE STORY ROSEBUD COUNTY MAN TELLS.

INDIANS WERE HIS SLAYERS

Ghost of Bob Ferguson Nightly Visits Ranch Where He Lived Years Ago.

The headline referencing the ghost of Bob Ferguson, from the January 13, 1903, edition of the *Billings Gazette*.

22

THE GHOST OF BOB FERGUSON

In January 1903, "a gentleman who has long resided in Rosebud County and spoke in all seriousness" gave a curious interview to the *Billings Gazette*:

> *No, I'm not joking; neither have I become locoed by the many ghost stories of a political nature that have been sent out from our country. Thirteen years have passed since it first became noised about that the house of which I am speaking was disturbed by visits from an inhabitant of shade land.*

The speaker identified the ghost as the spirit of Bob Ferguson, a stockman murdered in 1890 by Cheyenne Indians. Ever since the murder, the source claimed, Ferguson's former residence on Little Rosebud Creek near Kirby had been reported by several parties as haunted.

On May 6, 1890, Bob Ferguson rode out into the Upper Rosebud Creek area to search for stray horses. He was twenty-seven years old, unmarried, and a moderately successful stockman. He was last seen alive borrowing a horse and field glasses from the Thompson ranch. His disappearance was not discovered until a week later when Ferguson's brother started a systematic search. Even then, it was not until May 24th that evidence of a terrible crime was discovered.

Ferguson's dead horse was discovered first, shot through the shoulder and removed of all its trappings. "A few days later," a body was found:

> *buried in a sand draw, loosely covered in earth and about 600 yards from where the dead horse lay. The body was wrapped up in the saddle blanket and a rope tied about it and the coat was wrapped about the head. His saddle, bridle, slicker and field glasses were also found buried. There were two bullet wounds in the body, and one through the left wrist and the face of the corpse was bruised showing it had been dragged some distance to the place*

> *of burial. Moccasin tracks in the sand clearly demonstrate that Cheyenne Indians did the bloody deed.*

Footprint evidence indicated that Ferguson had come upon a group of Cheyennes butchering a couple of beef carcasses. At the time, conditions on the reservation were dire. Federal government food rations had been grossly inadequate to feed tribal members, with the result that young men often went off the reservation seeking food for their families. Frequently, the result was the clandestine slaughter of cattle belonging to white settlers who bordered the reservation. This practice had been going on for years and, by 1890, had caused a considerable amount of racial tension.

A group of Cheyennes was immediately identified as the killers. However, investigators soon demonstrated that the suspects were observed at Fort Keogh near Miles City at the time of the murder. With these alibis firmly established, they were released. No other suspects were arrested.

Ferguson's sister disposed of her brother's property to a married couple, and that is when (according to the *Gazette's* informant) strange things began happening:

> *It was not long after the new owner had taken possession when nightly the house's occupants were awakened by someone rapping on the door. Beattie, the man who bought the ranch, was away from home considerably, leaving his wife at home alone. She was anything but a timid woman, and whenever she heard the rapping she would go to the door and open it, always with the same result—nobody was to be seen. Determined not to be driven away by a ghost or a trick he believed somebody might be playing on him to frighten him and cause him to sell out, Beattie hung onto the ranch, his wife bravely standing by him.*

In 1900, the Northern Cheyenne Reservation was expanded, and the government included the old Ferguson property. Beattie sold his ranch to the federal government. Before the transfer took effect, Beattie's wife died. He remarried, but his new bride soon realized all was not well with the property. "The second Mrs. Beattie heard the rapping, making it tolerably clear that it had not been a trick of the imagination that had caused the first Mrs. Beattie that something was wrong with the place."

The property had many desirable features, and when the federal government took possession, there were several applicants among the tribal members to live there.

> *One of the many applicants for the place secured it and moved onto the land, using the house and stables built by Ferguson. They did not remain long, though. The rappings that had annoyed and mystified the white occupants continued and the Indian moved. Another moved in and then out. Several others tried it, but none would remain. All declared that a "bad spirit" was there and would permit nobody to live on the place.*
>
> *Several years have passed since the last occupant left and the buildings have begun to go into decay and are tumbling down, and unless the ghost of Bob Ferguson gets tired and goes elsewhere the ranch will probably be never occupied again, at least by any of the Cheyennes.*

While Bob Ferguson's murder is officially unsolved, it is believed that Head Chief, the Cheyenne who killed Hugh Boyle under very similar circumstances a few months after the Ferguson affair, was the guilty party. Before his dramatic

Bob Ferguson's lonely grave, located along Highway 314, south of Kirby. The marker reads: "Robert Ferguson at 27 years of age killed by Cheyenne Indians at the head of a fork of Tulluch Creek north of here. May 6, 1890." PHOTOGRAPH BY SHANE DUNNING.

"suicide-by-soldier" near Lame Deer in September 1890 (see Chapter 3), Head Chief admitted to killing three white men, including Hugh Boyle. Speculation is that Bob Ferguson was one of these others.

The identity of the *Gazette's* only source for the ghost tale was not provided with any specificity, so it is impossible to evaluate the credibility of this story. Nothing about the behavior of this supposed specter can be identified with Bob Ferguson. The ranch was not the location where Ferguson was killed, nor is any reason given why the ghost would haunt white occupants as well as Cheyenne. A considerable amount of time between the murder and the body's discovery caused significant decomposition. The inquest caused even further delay. Because of this, Bob Ferguson's body was finally laid to rest near his family's land just south of Kirby the Saturday following the inquest.

To this day, Bob Ferguson lies by himself, with no other graves in the vicinity. A lonely headstone marking the final resting place of Bob Ferguson can still be seen a few yards east of Highway 314, about two miles south of the Kirby Saloon. Perhaps he still ventures out at night. Who can say for sure?

NOTES ON CHAPTER 22:

- This column first appeared on October 28, 2021, in the Halloween edition of the *Powder River Examiner.*
- Head Chief's suicide-by-soldier was discussed previously in this collection in Chapter 3, "An Artist's Firsthand View of History."
- *Death at Lame Deer,* a historical novel by my father, Forest B. Dunning, accurately describes many of the issues surrounding Ferguson's and Boyle's deaths.
- Robert Ferguson's coroner's inquest was used for this article and can be obtained at the Custer County Courthouse in Miles City.

Frank Lavigne (left), Montana's Chief Stock Inspector, with Billy Richardson, in 1916.
PHOTOGRAPH COURTESY OF THE FRANK LAVIGNE PAPERS, MONTANA HISTORICAL SOCIETY.

23

Billy Richardson vs Poker Jim Roberts

Last month the good people at the *Powder River Examiner* asked me to follow up on an item they discovered in their regular review of past issues. The *Examiner* issue in question was dated November 4, 1921, and headlined "Protection for Stockmen."

> *The legitimate stockmen of southeastern Montana are being reassured of protection in the event they attend the big meeting called for November 19 at Piniele. At that time, an organization will be perfected to assist in ending the unlawless traffic in horses and cattle and to drive the alleged gang of thieves from the country.*

The article was an oblique reminder that news, as it is happening, often occurs in bursts followed by lulls. Based on a tidbit of an article from 100 years ago, present-day readers could be forgiven for thinking the former residents of this area seemed a bit reactionary. Such a notion would be wrong. This meeting was, in fact, a minor point in a serious range crisis that occurred throughout southeastern Montana and eventually forced state officials in Helena to action. This column will focus on the prelude to this meeting, namely, the conflict between "Poker" Jim Roberts and Stock Inspector Billy Richardson.

By 1921, Powder River County and Carter County had recently been established as separate authorities distinct from Custer County. Fifty-two-year-old James Roberts came to Montana from Beeville, Texas, in 1895. After 1920, he resided near Ridge, Montana, in the tri-state border country where Wyoming and South Dakota meet the Treasure State. By early 1921, Roberts and his associates had established a history of playing loose with other people's livestock. The *Ekalaka Eagle* reported in February of that year:

A broadside view of Piniele, Montana in 1917. In late 1921, a stockman's meeting was held here to assuage the local populace that alleged rustling activity would be dealt with. PHOTOGRAPH COURTESY OF THE POWDER RIVER HISTORICAL MUSEUM IN BROADUS, MT.

> *County Attorney Nelstead was in the south of the county last week looking after some criminal cases. Jim Roberts, known as "Poker Jim," was accused of selling beef without having the hide inspected. The case will be heard before a jury in Justice S.B. Martin's court in Alzada on the 11th. Jim lives in the Ridge country. He gave bonds for his appearance in the sum of $200. Andy Anderson and Babe Ellis were also held on a charge of larceny, and their hearing set for the 11th also. Harry Atwater of Sturgis will appear for all defendants in these cases.*

Roberts eventually pled guilty and received a $150 fine. Anderson and Ellis were released due to "lack of sufficient evidence." It appeared that Roberts was running a significant operation in the southeastern part of the state that involved multiple men and took advantage of the difficulties enforcing livestock laws across three states, with capitals in far-off Helena, Cheyenne, and Pierre.

Things started to become much more serious that summer. In June, Stock Inspector Billy Richardson arrested Poker Jim for rustling livestock at his headquarters on Willow Creek. Roberts was released on $2,000 bail, and, according to the *Ekalaka Eagle* in early July:

When he reached his habitat, he found that during his enforced absence somebody had burned his "layout," his house and buildings. It is said that he accused one Whitehurst of having had a hand in the burning and proceeded to work him over in the old fashioned way with his fists.

Stock Inspector Richardson is said to have made a move toward arresting "Poker Jim" on the charge of assault in a high degree. Some gun play is said to have taken place between Richardson and Jim and that immediately each side secured reinforcements. The battle raged on and off for some time between the Richardson posse and "Poker Jim's" adherents, about a dozen men participating. It appears that most of the shooting was done at long range, and nobody was wounded except a pet saddle horse belonging to Bill McCracken. The story goes that Jim and his followers headed for the McCracken ranch, being followed by the Richardson crowd and that at this place some long range shooting took place also.

It is said that the war has quieted down for the time being and that some arrests are likely to follow. The general belief is that things will "pop" loose again and that more serious results will no doubt follow. Just who is at fault and the cause of the trouble has not been definitely established, and it appears to many that all sides are on the "outs" down in that section, a section of the country that has furnished its share of the excitement in time gone past.

The *Eagle's* rather anodyne version of events suffered compared to Richardson's, which was related in a letter to State Livestock Inspector Frank Lavigne and published throughout Montana under the headline "Reads Like Yarn of Old Montana."

*One night recently Richardson attended a dance at Ridge and, according to a letter received by Stock Inspector Levigne [*sic*], a fellow by the name of McCracken, whom Richardson is gathering evidence against on a horse stealing case, tried to pick a quarrel with him at the dance and told him he would get him.*

The next day Richardson went to the home of rancher MacMains, from whom a black horse was stolen, and with MacMains started on a trip to look for evidence against McCracken. Richardson went ahead

> *early in the morning and MacMains was to meet him at a neighbor's, a rancher named Martin. Richardson had his breakfast at Martin's and while waiting for MacMains, laid down in the shed to take a nap. While asleep, Mrs. Martin saw two men, who were on horseback, going after a man on foot some distance from the Martin house. She awakened Richardson, who discovered that the riders were "Poker" Jim Roberts and Mack Whitehurst. They "beat up" William Heron, the man on foot, because he wouldn't tell where the black horse alleged to have been stolen was hidden by the officers. Their object, according to the letter from Richardson, was to do away with the evidence against McCracken. Following the beating given Heron, the two men told him to go and tell Richardson to come out of the Martin place because they would get him (Richardson) anyway.*

It was around this time that MacMains arrived on the scene, and, after exchanging some ineffectual gunfire, Poker Jim and Whitehurst fled the scene. Richardson sent to Ridge for assistance. "I sent for four men and ten came." The stock detective's posse located their quarry at sundown near McCracken's place, but the fading sunlight prevented Roberts' capture. "About fifty shots" were fired at this location:

> *We went on into McCracken's and got close enough to see them corral four horses. Three of us went to the east of the house, and three went to the west and left four of the boys to watch the north.*
>
> *Then four men came towards us from the McCracken place, mounted and armed. I told our men to hold their fire and let them come. Just then, their rifles cracked and a shot just missed Ormesher, who was on my right, and one bullet hit on my left. We opened up on the four men, Jensen shooting also. They then turned back and went northwest past the house and Jensen opened up on them again. It was so dark by this time that we could not see at all and about 11 pm we went home.*

Richardson was able to get a bench warrant against Roberts for assaulting Bill Heron but could not get the warrant served, as the *Ekalaka Eagle* quoted the *Broadus Examiner.* The Carter County paper then chose to add its ending when it reprinted the *Examiner's* story:

> *Richardson failed to get "Poker Jim." Sheriff Boggs does not employ any press agent or stage any big battles, but he went quietly down to the south end last Friday and returned with the redoubtable "Poker Jim." Boggs didn't get up any posse nor use any handcuffs, but his man is now in custody and will be arraigned on Saturday before Judge Felt who will hold a short term of court here.*

Poker Jim was arraigned by Judge Felt and released on bail, with trial to begin that October. Once released, Roberts hauled lumber to his place and quickly built a new cabin, which did not last long. Stock inspector Billy Richardson was himself arrested by Carter County Sheriff Boggs for "tearing down the new cabin recently erected on Poker Jim Roberts' place on Willow Creek." Richardson was released on $1,000 bond.

These episodes exhibited the decidedly odd environment that existed in southeastern Montana at that time. It appeared that Roberts and his friends had some sympathetic ears in Ekalaka proper, the Carter County legal system, and out-of-state livestock interests. Bill Richardson was branded an aggressive show-off with a personal antagonism towards Roberts. Whether most of the local populace felt this way or was scared into acquiescence is impossible to know.

What is clear is that livestock interests further removed from the tri-state border (such as Broadus) were more than concerned about this chain of events and demanded action from Helena. To them, horse and cattle rustling had become such an "industry" in Carter County that it controlled the local levers of power. To respond to this challenge, the attorney general of Montana, Wellington Rankin (a scion of the famous Rankin family), traveled to Broadus with a slew of local dignitaries to deliver an address. This remarkable speech sparked the Pienele meeting referenced at the beginning of this column and nearly started another vigilante wave in Montana. That story, however, is a story for a future column.

NOTES ON CHAPTER 23:

→ This article first appeared in the *Powder River Examiner's* December 2, 2021, edition. ←

Wellington Rankin, Montana Attorney General in 1921. Rankin gave a fiery speech in Broadus on the subject of cattle rustling. PUBLIC DOMAIN PHOTOGRAPH OBTAINED FROM *A HISTORY OF MONTANA* (1913), BY HELEN FITZGERALD SANDERS.

24

Rankin's Barn Burner in Broadus

My previous column described the violent back-and-forth between stock inspectors and a gang of livestock rustlers in southeast Montana. Much of the excitement was instigated by stock detective Billy Richardson or "Poker" Jim Roberts, suspected ringleader of the rustlers in the summer of 1921. Richardson sent a report to his boss, Montana's Chief Livestock Inspector Frank Lavigne, describing a day-long shootout with Roberts in southern Carter County.

The situation came to the attention of the newly elected attorney general for the State of Montana, Wellington Rankin. Rankin, a Republican, had been elected in 1920 and was the brother of Jeannette Rankin, the first woman elected to Congress and a noted pacifist. Wellington Rankin took office in early 1921.

Rankin came out of the gate swinging. By September 1921, newspaper reports out of Helena described the AG's impending "war on rustlers." The scale of cattle and horse rustling in southeast Montana was so widespread that it was being described as an "industry." In a statement before leaving Helena for a stockmen's meeting in Broadus, Rankin said:

> *In cooperation with the state livestock commission and the county attorneys, this office is making a special effort to stamp out cattle stealing. The cattle rustlers are going to receive considerable special attention throughout Montana in the matter of law enforcement.*

Perhaps the most disturbing aspect of the cattle rusting problem was the relative silence of the local community, particularly in Carter County. It was unclear if the populace in the border country were scared into cooperation or were actively encouraging it to their own economic benefit. Rankin believed that an aggressive publicity campaign would reinforce the area's legitimate law enforcement and encourage those officials who had been less cooperative to change. To that end, he and a procession of dignitaries arrived at livestock meeting in Broadus on September 30th.

Listeners were greeted to hearing the currently serving attorney general of the State of Montana come uncomfortably close to advocating vigilante action by evoking the spirit of Virginia City:

> *The time is going to come, and it is here now, when the man who would employ men of questionable reputation, the men who would render comfort and aid to these men, is going to be confronted with public sentiment, more deadly than bullets, more deadly than the hands of the law or officers and that public sentiment that you are going to develop and are ready to crystallize will clean up this county and the adjoining counties in the state. That is the spirit which cleaned up Virginia City. You can go into Virginia City now and they will show you where they hanged those men, because it was essential to the growth of the city. The thought crystallized that these men should have been hanged. The officers are not to blame for the rustling in this corner of Montana. You are to blame for not crystallizing this public sentiment sooner.*

As if invoking the spirit of Virginia City wasn't enough, the attorney general (and WWI veteran) publicly challenged the rustlers by name. The *Examiner* reported:

> *"Is Poker Jim Roberts greater than the law?" he asked, "I am not going to mince words in talking of these men and I hope some of their friends and associates are here and I wish this man and his bunch were here today. They are: Poker Jim Roberts, Bill McCracken, Babe Ellis, Andy Anderson, Jasper Brooks, Denver Woods, Oscar Woods, Gander Oliphant, Tom McCrorey, Mack Whitehurst.*
>
> *And there are also others to be listed with them. There is a time coming when they will stop defying the law, and the others associating with them, lending aid and comfort to them. I ask Powder River and Carter Counties, how long are you going to stand for men of this kind? They are saying to you: "What are you going to do about it?" That is their spoken word and*

> *their attitude. And why, and how long, I say, are you going to stand for it? You are not going to stand for it. You are going to clean them up and they can be cleaned up. The man who is robbing the homesteader is robbing the cattleman. The men who are preying on these homesteaders and cattlemen are cowards, and a strong organization, determined, can clean them up.*

Newspapers across the state reported on Rankin's speech. An article titled "War on Cattle Thieves to Be Started; When Cowboys Cleaned Up Rustlers," began with extensive quoting from the speech, then recounted its readers with details of Granville Stuart's vigilante campaign in the 1880s. This article itself was printed in almost every newspaper in the state.

The result of these actions was the calling of an organizational meeting in Piniele (in southern Carter County) on November 19th to form the "strong organization" Rankin advocated in his speech. The organizers of the meeting publicly reassured legitimate stockmen of protection. It was the description of this reassurance, which recently appeared in the "100 years ago" section of the *Powder River Examiner,* that spawned this article and its predecessor.

Another result of the speech was that Rankin's targets threatened to sue the attorney general and the *Powder River Examiner* for publishing the address. Interestingly, there appears to be no such threat made to the *Ekalaka Eagle,* which also extensively quoted the speech in its November 19 issue. Perhaps the *Eagle's* previously sterile coverage of the rustling crisis played a role in that decision. The *Helena Independent-Record* covered this legal maneuvering:

> *Ekalaka, Nov. 24. - There is much interest in the story about stock men of the south part of this county suing Attorney General Rankin for statements he made about men rustling cattle. It is believed that one or more of the men who have a better case than the others will carry the matter into court and make a fuss about it. Many of the local people who are in a position to judge look upon the matter as a joke or mistaken judgment. Reports here say that several attorneys have been consulted and would not take up the case.*

The Piniele organizational meeting occurred as scheduled with Sheriff Boggs of Carter County, Sheriff Sutter of Powder River County, Billy Richardson, and other law enforcement present. Also present were accused rustlers Bill McCracken and Tom McCrory:

The meeting resolved itself into a round table discussion of livestock conditions in southeastern Montana. It seemed the consensus of opinion that to stop the cattle thievery in southeastern Montana, the stockmen must perfect an organization.

It was decided that those attending meeting were not fully representative of the local livestock interests, and so another meeting was suggested.

One party recommended that the meeting be postponed until after the annual election of the Tri-state Stockmen's Association at Bell [sic] *Fourche coming the first of the year. "If you don't organize until then, it will give me a chance to get away with considerable beef," taunted one of the spectators.*

Roberts and McCracken's criminal enterprise dried up. By 1925, Roberts was serving three to six years in Deer Lodge for grand larceny as a result of stealing a horse from R.C. Price of Alzada. Grand larceny would return "Poker" Jim to the state prison again in 1935, this time sentenced to fourteen years, for the theft of a stallion belonging to Oscar Williams of Ekalaka. The threatened lawsuit against Rankin and the *Examiner* fizzled away. Rankin's efforts had engaged public sentiment in such a successful fashion that law enforcement could be reliably instituted in southeast Montana. In an editorial, the *Examiner* concluded:

In a campaign of publicity in which the Examiner *has occupied the lead among the newspapers, public sentiment has crystallized against the unlawful traffic in horses and cattle in southeastern Montana, for there are fewer animals being stolen now than ever before known. And the amazement is heightened by the knowledge that his result has been achieved without resort to process of law, unless we concede that law really is defined as public sentiment. There have been no arrests and no trouble in inducing the rustlers to "lay off." How long the present conditions will obtain, no one knows but to make it permanent means continued publicity and vigilance on the part of the newspapers, officials, stockmen and the public in general.*

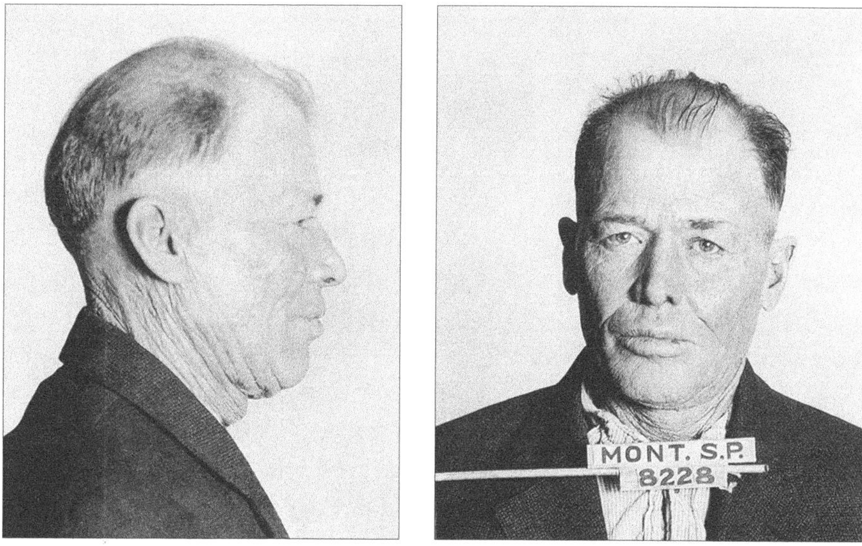

Poker Jim Roberts, circa 1925. COURTESY OF HIS INMATE FILE AT THE MONTANA STATE PRISON AND THE MONTANA HISTORICAL SOCIETY. MSP 8228.

NOTES ON CHAPTER 24:

- This article first appeared in the December 19, 2021, edition of the *Powder River Examiner.*
- There is no known connection between Poker Jim Roberts and Poker Jim Butte/Lookout/Creek, located in the Otter (Custer) National Forest. The earliest reference to Poker Jim Creek I have found is from 1897, which predates Poker Jim Roberts' adulthood.

The original caption of this picture reads: "Start of the First Marathon race to be run in Montana Covered Distance of 153 miles from Billings to Miles City along US 10 and 12. Time: 19 hours, 13 min, 14 sec. Sponsored by Range Riders Reunion of Miles City." The winner (Merle Hillyer) is supposed to be the twenty-second rider from the left. The original caption's claim that the race was the first ever marathon race in Montana is questionable. PHOTOGRAPH COURTESY OF THE CHARLIE DUNNING FAMILY.

THE RACE WAS ON . . . 75 YEARS AGO

June of 2022 marked the 75th anniversary of a most extraordinary Montana horse race. In 1947, the Range Riders Rodeo Association sponsored a 153-mile horse race, starting in Billings and ending at Miles City, just in time for the 1947 Range Riders Reunion. At 4:00 P.M. on Sunday, June 23, 1947, fifty-one horses and their riders gathered at the fairgrounds on Alkali Creek and started east along old Highway 10 in a race:

> *Before that time they had weighed in, man and equipment could not weigh more than 175 pounds. Pictures were taken and the starting gun fired.*

"They left on a gallop, some on a high lope, and some at a high trot," John Williams said. This was not a casual-constructed event. The race would occur along the highway, with mandatory rest stops at Custer and Forsyth. The Montana Highway Patrol assigned fourteen patrolmen between Billings and Miles City, who were instructed to ensure that "no motorist can park along highway" and no motorist could follow the horses "too closely." The horses were shod with rubber shoes. To keep "amateur riders out of the race," organizers set a $100 entry fee:

> *Race officials ruled that riders should use the same mounts the entire distance theorizing that it would be "easier on the horses in that they would not be asked for exhausting bursts of speed, common to relay riding." Stamina—that will be the telling point.*

Race judges John Williams and Don Pyle of the Range Riders followed the lead horses in a car the entire race ensuring the competition's integrity. Highway 10 was selected as the road "best adapted to the race," because its grades were filled and the hills cut down. According to race organizers, visibility of the highway would also cut down on "fudging," such as sneaking in relief riders or hauling the horses in a trailer along sideroads.

Physicians were present at the checkpoints to care for riders. Veterinarians Dr. H.F. Wilkins (Helena), Dr. A.W. Elting (Miles City), and Dr. George W. Wright (Billings) also judged for the race, as did Kirby rancher Willis Spear, Jr. The purpose of these judges was to ensure the safety of both horse and rider:

> *The endurance race was carried out in spite of protests from the Humane Society and judges all agreed at its conclusion that only a suggestion to riders was necessary for them to drop out when judges told them the horses were tired. "True western sportsmanship showed up, for the riders without exception dropped out when we told them to and some of them dropped out of their own accord."*

Two entrants quit at Pompey's Pillar. Another two did not get further than Custer, where the first of two mandatory breaks occurred. There, the veterinarians checked the horses. First to arrive at the check station at Custer was Eugene Fuchs of Plevna, who came at 9:07 P.M. Fuchs and his horse exited the

An advertisement for the race that was printed in the *Miles City Star* in the weeks before the race.

race ten miles from Forsyth, however. "Both rider and horse were played out," Williams was quoted as saying. At Forsyth, the three leaders (Clifford Hunter, Merle Hillyer, and Bud Hunter) rode into town at the same time and split a $100 purse:

> *Miles City radio station KRJF broadcasted the start of the race on delay the next morning. They reported the results coming out of Custer and Forsyth live. The portion of the race from Forsyth to Miles City was tracked by an airplane, with observers using short-wave radio updates to the radio station and the assembled crowd at the Miles City rodeo grounds. The winning horse did not get to the lead until 20 miles west of Forsyth. Every hour and at the last part of the race, every mile, the horse was stopped, the saddle slid off. It was given a quick sponge, "braced" with liniment and witch hazel, given a sup [sp] of water, all within a minute's time by Larson and Harry Miller and Jack Wicker.*

Precisely 19 hours, 13 minutes, and 14 seconds after the starting gun fired, Merle Hillyer of Sand Springs and his horse, Bucky, crossed the finish line at the Eastern Montana Fairgrounds in front of thousands gathered. Hillyer had been a last-minute substitute rider for Clem Larson, Bucky's owner. Coming in second was Lester Stovall of Billings, finishing in 19 hours, 25 minutes, and 7 seconds. Also coming in the money was third place winner, T.J. Saye (Miles City), at 21:12:1, and fourth place Clifford Hunter (Butte) with 22:31:18.

The winning horse's owner, Clem Larson, was thrilled with the win. "Bucky is home on the range and will never have another saddle on him." Weighing in at 1,125 pounds, Bucky was an eight-year-old, barrel-chested buckskin. Larson bought him as a three-year-old for $125. Larson picked his 36-year-old neighbor Merle Hillyer to ride Bucky in the race because "he is a good hand with a horse." Hillyer "used neither spurs or quirt during the race." The victorious rider and his mount rode a truck in the rodeo parade the day after the race. Bucky wore his winning wreath. The winning team took home $2,080.

The picture taken at the start of the race is captioned "Start of First Marathon Race to Be Run in Montana. Covered Distance of 153 Miles from Billings to Miles City Along US 10 and 12. Time: 19 hours-13 min-14-sec. Sponsored by Range Rider's Reunion of Miles City." The claim to the first marathon race in Montana is debatable, but the 153-mile race was still quite an accomplishment.

The Range Riders sponsored another endurance race, the "Hell Creek Race" the next year.

Today, endurance horse racing is still an active sport held under the auspices of the American Endurance Racing Conference. The AERC provides professional management of the sport with rules designed to protect rider and horse. Locally, the Fort Howes Endurance Ride occurs at Otter's Circle Bar Ranch. In 2021, Fort Howes hosted the AERC's National Championship 100-mile ride.

A lot has changed in seventy-five years.

NOTES ON CHAPTER 25:

- This article first appeared in the *Powder River Examiner* on January 27, 2022.
- The web edition and this collection have corrected an author's error printed in the *PRE* physical edition. The error has been fixed on the *PRE* online edition and the website. The name of the second endurance race sponsored by the Range Riders was the Hell Creek Endurance Race. The printed version identified it as "XXXXXX."
- I could not find confirmation that my great-uncle Jimmy Dunning participated in this race until after its publication. Jimmy rode Standish Johnson's horse in the race (representing the Ranger Riders Bar) and may be seen in the picture.

The hilltop of the mysterious "Soaring Hawk" site. PHOTOGRAPH BY SHANE DUNNING.

26

THE MYSTERY OF SOARING HAWK

Deep into a dry creek valley in southern Rosebud County is a structure whose origins are mysterious. A small hill on the south side of the valley commands a broad view of the surrounding country. The top of the hill is flat, covering about 9,000 square feet. The dry creek runs into the Tongue River, and the entire structure is located on private land.

The summit of this hill contains three man-sized rings constructed of stacked rock. One is on the northeast corner of the hill, with an excellent view of the valley below. A second ring is located on the butte's southern point, where

One of several rock structures at the "Soaring Hawk" site is pictured. PHOTOGRAPH BY SHANE DUNNING.

A view from the inside one of the "rifle pits." PHOTOGRAPH BY SHANE DUNNING.

the slope is most gradual. The third ring occupies a central position between the other two, on the highest elevation point. In addition to the three dominant rings, at least four additional rock structures, irregular in shape, also exist along the outside rim of the crest.

The structure has been known since at least the 1930s. My great-uncle John Moreland worked that valley in his youth and had a homestead in the 1940s near this location. His daughter Sharon grew up with my father (Forest Dunning) and, during a recent visit, told us of these formations. Phil Wood also knew the structure's location and obtained the land owner's permission to travel up the dry creek valley to what we were initially calling "robber's roost." The trip took place in 2021 in the early fall.

The robber's roost moniker originated from the only story we heard regarding the origin of this place. According to this story, a group of outlaws fought off a posse from the top of the hill. To be clear, the existence of this structure was unknown to almost everyone, including the area's local history oracles. This outlaw story, such as it was, was not communicated with much confidence in its veracity.

We took the most direct and practical hike to the summit, up the west slope from the two-track road that eventually wound its way to our destination. This rock-strewn slope was very steep at 70 degrees and continued for a good two hundred yards of climbing. Once there, I took several pictures. The structures resembled breastworks created as a defensive position, but not obviously so.

As I mentioned before, the existence of this structure was unknown to almost everyone. After a few months of being unable to obtain any information, I queried the fine folks at the Montana State Historic Preservation Office (SHPO) in Helena. After showing them a few pictures, they told me they were familiar with similar structures and offered two other possibilities. One was hunting blinds along animal trails; the other was fasting beds for Native American vision quests. The fasting bed explanation was one I previously considered since I had seen pictures of these structures, which looked very similar to the formation on the top of this hill.

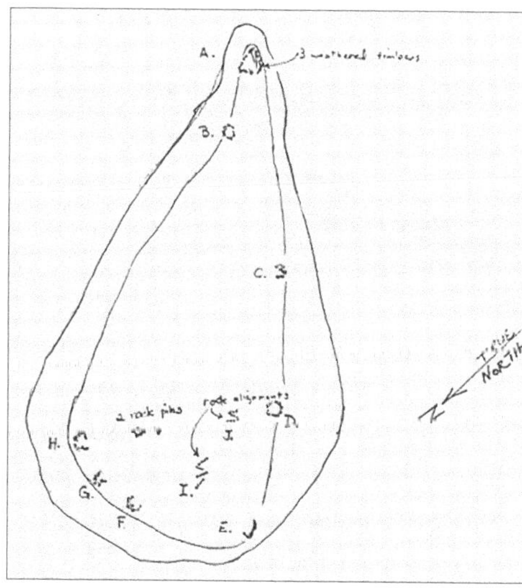

A hand drawn map of the "Soaring Hawk" site, by archeologist Tom Schley of the BLM. COURTESY OF THE MONTANA STATE HISTORIC PRESERVATION OFFICE.

The SPHO looked up the location in their database and found that the site had been previously recorded. In 1979, a BLM archeologist named Tom Schley visited the site as part of a larger area archeological survey to obtain information on cultural resources potentially impacted by mining. His one-page report identified the site as "Soaring Hawk" without explanation. Perhaps the archeologist saw a hawk in the sky and named the location on the spot. According to SPHO:

The form shows 10 rock features positioned at the edges of the hill. The recorder believes that this could either be a defensive formation or potentially fasting location. However, they were leaning towards defensive based on the fact that the features are located at the edge of the butte facing multiple directions. Typically fasting beds all face one location, usually the rising sun.

I sent the office a few more pictures to attach to their files (they didn't have any). I could not find the slightest evidence to corroborate the outlaw story. These structures were built deliberately, taking quite a bit of planning, energy, and time. It is inconceivable that this site was thrown together on the fly by a group of outlaws upon the arrival of a posse. It is possible that an outlaw gang made their home below the hill and constructed the breastworks in anticipation of a fight, but that explanation is still unsatisfying. Outlaws would have preferred escape to a last, desperate stand, and the natural cover surrounding the hill would have given them plenty of it.

My father, a retired Army Lt. Colonel of Artillery, is convinced the site shows clear indications of United States military doctrine:

> *There are at least nine rock structures which appear to be fighting positions on the top of the hill. Eight of the positions are on the extreme military crest of the hill with a ninth large position backed up to the topographical crest in the center of the other positions. The center position appears to be a command post. The bulk of the structures are oriented to the north and east. The top of the hill is not amenable to digging because it is nearly all fractured rock*

With the preponderance of the evidence that Soaring Hawk is a defensive position, the next question becomes one of its historical origins. While it is possible Native Americans built the site, the condition of the structures and the dry climate would seem to age the pits to the late 1800s to early 1900s, a period of active military maneuvering for U.S. forces in the area.

The site would not have been an effective defensive position for more than twenty people. The dry creek valley could have been a good Indian trail for traveling between the Rosebud Creek and Tongue River drainages. There were four distinct military campaigns in the area that I consider possible origins for this structure, with one being the clear favorite.

The Battle of Wolf Mountain (also known as Battle of the Butte) took place less than ten miles from this site on January 8, 1877. This was an engagement between Colonel Nelson Miles, Crazy Horse's Lakota, and Two Moons' Northern Cheyenne. The battle took place north of the Soaring Hawk site, with Miles' troops originating from Ft. Keogh. Their maneuvers or reconnaissance would not have come this far south with a known hostile force directly in front of them. Also arguing against Soaring Hawk being associated with this engagement is the time of year, namely the harsh Montana winter. It is inconceivable that the hundreds of flat rocks used at Soaring Hawk could be pulled from the frozen, possibly snow-covered ground and placed with such precision.

Another possibility is the site was constructed as a defensive position during the outbreak of the White River Utes in 1906, which I discussed in a previous article (see Chapter 4). The White River Utes had peacefully marched through the general area in their odyssey to the Black Hills but scared many white settlers along the way. There were concerns the Utes would attempt to join the Northern Cheyenne at their reservation. To prevent this, troops were dispatched from Ft. Keogh, Ft. Robinson, and Ft. Mackenzie. While there is evidence that some of these troops had traveled through the area, there is no record of them ever being under such a threat that would cause them to build the structures like those atop Soaring Hawk.

The Battle of the Rosebud took place June 17, 1876, approximately thirty miles to the west of the site in question. In this encounter, a large group of Lakota and Northern Cheyenne under Crazy Horse engaged General George Crook. This battle involved significant levels of soldiers and would have employed scouting parties. Occurring a few weeks before the Battle of the Little Bighorn, General Crook was, at the time, trying to locate a rumored sizeable Indian village. Troop movements for this engagement originated on Goose Creek near present-day Sheridan, Wyoming, and would have approached the subsequent battle from the southwest. Thirty miles further east, the Soaring Hawk site would have been on the extreme practical limits for scouting parties, especially considering that after the battle, General Crook turned around and returned to the shadow of the Bighorn Mountains.

However, after the Custer's disastrous defeat on the Little Bighorn, General Crook was ordered to track down the victorious Indian force. To this end, in late July of 1876, George Crook broke camp on Goose Creek and again entered present-day Montana. It is this effort, I believe, that provides the best explanation for the structures on Soaring Hawk.

Crook's army followed Goose Creek to the Tongue River. His army had several scouts, including Frank Grouard and William F. Cody (Buffalo Bill). According to several accounts, Grouard believed Crazy Horse's band was again on the Rosebud. At a point north of the (present-day) Montana border, Crook's main body moved west from the Tongue River to Rosebud Creek. Given that the area was extremely hilly and rocky, Grouard would have scouted multiple Indian trails to travel between the two drainages. While it is not clear where Crook's main army turned west, I believe the scouting parties may very well have come as far north as the dry creek overlooked by Soaring Hawk.

Contrary to the Army movements in the Ute breakout described above, Crook's troops were under considerable threat during these movements. Crazy Horse and Sitting Bull had separated, and the Indians knew Crook's movements. The Native Americans set several grass fires and harassed Crook's pickets to slow them. The diary of Private William W. Jordan states:

> ***July 30:*** *Moved camp one mile down creek. Indians set fire to the prairie. Entire command out fighting fire until dark.*
>
> ***August 3:*** *Marched all day through smoke of prairie fires. Weather hot. Command suffered for water. Arrived in camp about sundown. Made eighteen miles. . . . The whole country is one sheet of flames, from the valley to the mountan tops. At 8 o'clock p.m. a terrific rainstorm set in. All the tents blown down. I was on picket duty. Indians fire on pickets. Pickets return fire. One Indian killed.*

Such was the environment when Grouard had his scouts deployed looking for an Indian trail to get to the Rosebud from Tongue River. The dry creek of Soaring Hawk was just such a trail, and a scouting party may very well have needed a defensive position with a commanding view of the surrounding country. While there is no direct evidence that this is the origin of Soaring Hawk, it is, in my opinion, the most likely.

NOTES ON CHAPTER 26:

- This article first appeared in the *Powder River Examiner's* February 24, 2022, edition.
- My father wrote his thoughts on this site in a report, which I quoted here and forwarded to the Montana SPHO.

NEWS AROUND HOME.

J. W. Toohey Shot Dead at his Ranch on last Wednesday Afternoon

By Ed. Brown, who comes in and Gives Himself Up—General Local Items.

The headline from the Weekly *Yellowstone Journal* and *Livestock Reporter,* July 10, 1886, issue portrayed the incident at the Birney Post Office.

27

DEATH AT THE BIRNEY POST OFFICE

In 1886, the town of Birney was not located at its present location at the mouth of Hanging Woman Creek. The Birney post office was then located several miles south of present-day Ashland, which was then known as "Strader." The office was located concurrently with a trading store operated by the postmaster, John W. Toohey. Toohey was Birney's second postmaster, the first being trader A.M. Birney, for whom the town was named.

In March 1886, Mary O'Connell, the wife of Custer County Assessor Samuel O'Connell, applied to be postmaster and was approved. There was one problem, however. She had not received notice of her commission from the postal service. Local rancher Edwin Brown, brother of Joseph Taliaferro Brown, who later established the Three Circle Cattle Ranch near Birney, soon learned why. According to the *Yellowstone Journal:*

> *Ed Brown, who claims to have been a friend of Toohey's knowing that Mrs. O'Connell had applied for the position then occupied by Toohey, one day jokingly inquired how long he was going to hold the office, and Toohey said he expected his time was short, at the same time showing Brown an official letter from the department, addressed to Mrs. O'Connell and containing, as Brown inferred, her commission. Brown saw Mrs. O'Connell shortly afterward and told her he thought Toohey had received her commission and was holding it out on her. She repeatedly asked Toohey if any letter from the department had been received addressed to her, and he as often denied that such was the case. Mrs. O'Connell wrote to the department about the matter and the reply was a peremptory order for Toohey to turn over the office to her at once.*

And so it was on July 7, 1886, when Ed Brown entered John Toohey's store to purchase axel grease and a bottle of beer:

I then told him that I wanted to explain to him the matter of the post office packet about which he was kicking, I told him that I had told Mrs. O'Connell that her commission was here with no intention of raising hard feelings and I did not see any cause for the sound abuse he had given me on the Fourth of July. He then said 'If you or anybody else said I had Mrs. O'Connell's commission he is a damned lying son of a bitch.' As he said so he made for his pistol. As he got within reach of it I drew my pistol and held him up. Then he started back where the rifles were, saying as he went "I will kill you as sure as your name is Ed Brown." I threw my pistol on him and said "Mr. Toohey, if you attempt to take one of those rifles, I will kill you."

After some ineffectual maneuvering by both men, Toohey supposedly changed tactics (according to Brown):

He [Toohey] then said, "If you have any manliness about you, you would lay down your pistol and fight me in a fair fight." I said, "to show you, Mr. Toohey, I don't mean to harm you I will go to the field in front of the house away from your guns and I will lay aside my pistol and I will maul the stuffing out of you."

Brown turned to exit the store, with Toohey following. As he entered the field in front of the store, Brown turned to see the postmaster running back into his store, presumably to get a weapon:

I followed him, he slammed the door in my face and held it. When he let go the door I went in and threw my pistol on him just as he was about to take the gun in hand. I prevented his doing so, and he then went behind the counter to where there was a pistol under the shelving. I told him not to attempt to take the pistol if he did I would shoot him. He then began to abuse me and gesticulate with his left hand at the same time with his right he seized the pistol, bringing it up as he did so we both fired. I cannot tell which fired first. I made two or three steps back to the door and fired twice more standing in the door. He, I thought, was firing all the time. When I fired my last shot he was taking aim with both hands. He stooped or dropped behind the counter. I waited in the door, perhaps 30 seconds. I heard a little noise and thinking he was moving towards his other guns, I got in my wagon and drove down to Mr. Wyllie's half a mile distant.

Brown eventually met Wyllie and told him of the incident, not knowing Toohey's condition. Wyllie went down to the store and discovered Toohey had died. Brown then borrowed a horse and rode nearly 100 miles to turn himself in to the authorities. Toohey's body was temporarily stored in an icehouse awaiting the coroner's inquest. One shot had entered Toohey's body under the left armpit and through the body, coming out under the right arm, stopping under the skin of the arm. The killing shot, however, "was near the centre of the forehead, near the left eye."

> *The coroner's jury, after carefully reviewing the body, then went to the store and found a small pool of blood behind the counter where Toohey fell, and his revolver nearby. The weapon was a black gutta percha handled, 38-caliber Colt, self-cocking revolver. The first cartridge had been fired, the next two showed where the hammer had struck but not exploded the cap, but the fourth cartridge was fired, showing that his first and last cartridge had been fired. Two holes were found, one through the glass door and one in the mud chinking between the logs near the door.*

The coroner's jury exonerated Ed Brown on the basis of self-defense. Family and friends of the deceased caused Brown to be re-arrested a few days after the inquest, but Brown was again exonerated. Toohey was remembered fondly by the *Yellowstone Journal:*

> *J. W. Toohey, the deceased, came to this country in the spring of '80 and immediately took up his abode on the upper Tongue River at what was then known as Strader's springs. He has resided there ever since and had built up for himself a good, comfortable trade with the Indians. He was postmaster at Birney for over two years and was exceedingly well known in that part of the country in which he lived. All the old-timers knew J. W. Toohey, the ex-tragedian, over whose untimely death we would wish to draw the manner of charity. "We could have better spared a better man."*

Mary O'Connell took her rightful place as postmaster and moved the post office to Ashland, and so the town has been known ever since. Friends of Toohey claimed he had been murdered. Six months later, a new post office for Birney was established near the confluence of Hanging Woman Creek and the Tongue

River (present-day Birney). Its new postmaster served a few years before moving back to Texas. His name was Edwin Brown.

NOTES ON CHAPTER 27:

- This column first appeared in the April 21, 2022, edition of the *Powder River Examiner.*
- Before his stint as a postmaster, John W. Toohey was known as an actor. His brother Joseph Toohey married my great-great-aunt, Catherine Lynch.

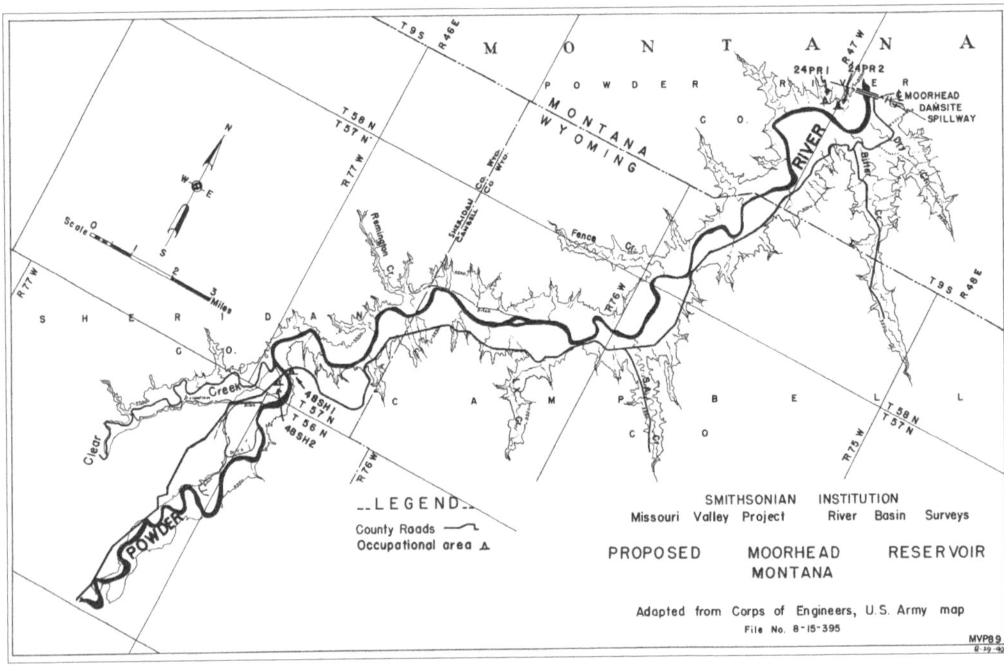

The map pictured here depicts the location and extent of the reservoir created by the Moorhead Dam, originally planned in the late 1940s to dam the Powder River in southern Powder River County; much of the reservoir would be in Wyoming. The project never came to fruition. As a frame of reference, Broadus lies approximately 36 miles northeast of the proposed dam site. MAP PREPARED BY THE MISSOURI VALLEY PROJECT, RIVER BASIN SURVEYS, SMITHSONIAN INSTITUTION.

28

Moorhead, A Struggle by a Dam Site

For good or ill, the Powder River has always been regarded as different from the other tributaries of the Yellowstone. The river's very name originates from the sediment that flows in its water. "A mile wide and an inch deep," with water "too thick to drink and too thin to plow," contrasted with its cousins, the Bighorn River and the Tongue River, both of which are dammed in Montana. These dams allowed their respective rivers to run clear and cold for a portion of their length in Montana, allowing for a trout fishery, standing in stark contrast to the murky, catfish-strewn waters of the Powder. In the twentieth century, these tributaries were the subjects of reclamation projects. The Tongue River was dammed with an earthenware dam in 1937. The Yellowtail Dam on the Bighorn had a much longer and more difficult path to construction, with the concrete arch facility completed in 1967. The Yellowtail Dam's political struggles pale compared to the back-and-forth effort to dam the Powder River at Moorhead between 1947 and 1956. That effort was ultimately unsuccessful, and its supporters have been casting blame for the failure ever since.

Talk of damming the Powder River at Moorhead had been the subject of speculation in the area many years before it first received serious attention from the federal government. One local politician even used the issue for his campaign slogan, "Kelsey for senator by a dam site."

In 1947, Congress appropriated $900,000 to study and begin preliminary development of the Moorhead Project. The dam's site was located south of Moorhead, approximately three miles north of the Wyoming-Montana border. A camp for project workers, engineers, and support staff was constructed at the site, consisting of several buildings and a mess hall. In her book *My Moorhead,* Mary Martha Lawrence Eckhart recalled the dramatic rise in activity near her home:

But not until 1948 did Moorhead hit the headlines. A proposed landfill dam across the Powder River, reportedly the biggest dam of its kind in the country, was to be built not many miles upstream from our place. Engineers, surveyors, government experts, construction crews, and laborers descended on our rural community that, up to now, almost no one in the larger world had heard of. This was good news for my Dad as the store went into full gear to support the families living in the newly-built government homes on the mesa and for workers housed in the pre-fab quarters of the "Camp" thrown up just across the river from the Moorhead Bridge.

Numerous preliminary studies were conducted to determine the project's impact on the local area, with mixed results. The Smithsonian Institution appraised the potential archeological effects of the Moorhead Reservoir. It identified four minor sites "that do not merit excavation, but they furnish definite evidence that the reservoir area was inhabited by aboriginal peoples" and recommended a complete study before the project began. The National Park Service evaluated potential recreational uses of the reservoir, concluding that "due to its isolation, inaccessibility, and the sparse population in the vicinity, no planned recreational development other than minor sanitary facilities, access road, and small parking area appears justified at this time."

The Fish and Wildlife Service concluded the project "would be detrimental to wildlife and beneficial to fish." Even so, it stated, "the future annual fishery value of the proposed reservoir is placed at a low figure because of excessive siltation and light fish pressure anticipated. There is no method for elimination of the silt problem, but it may be possible to encourage greater utilization of the reservoir fishery."

The federal government's lead agency was the Bureau of Reclamation (later called the Bureau of Land Reclamation). It originally planned a multi-purpose earthen dam with a reservoir sized at 300,000 acre-feet. The dam's design would accomplish four primary objectives: flood control, irrigation, storage, and silt control. The proposed dam location near the Wyoming-Montana border meant that two-thirds of the Moorhead Reservoir would be located in the Cowboy State.

Flood and silt control was the primary driver of most efforts to get Moorhead underway. The Bureau of Reclamation had a particular (i.e., congressionally directed) interest in controlling flooding in the entire Missouri-Mississippi

River ecosystem from Montana to Louisiana. Locally, Broadus had experienced a devastating flood in 1923 and numerous smaller ones caused by ice jams or fierce spring runoff. Broadus Mayor Ashton Jones testified before the U.S. Senate:

> *The great flood of 1923 is the gauge by which known damage can be extended to estimate what damage is to be anticipated in future floods. According to the Army engineers, there were 70,000 acre-feet of water being discharged at the Moorhead dam site at the time of this flood which occurred in the fall of the year, not the usual time for floods in the Powder River Valley. A flood of the same magnitude today would cause damage running into millions of dollars in the Powder River Valley.*

Mayor Jones also testified to the recurring drought conditions and the devastating impact of the Powder River's propensity to leave its banks.

> *Many of the other ranchers showed me where the river was cutting into their hay meadows, showed wastes of river bed that were formerly hay meadows. In several cases, notably the Dean Keil ranch on the west side of Powder River, near Powderville, the river has cut into his alfalfa fields. It is only a question of time until his meadow is a sand waste.*

During this period, the primary method of irrigation was flood irrigation which is still in regular use along the Powder today. Sprinkler irrigation systems now standard on the Montana plains were not then in heavy use. In fact, pressure from the Moorhead Project was a key driver prompting the creation of the Greater Yellowstone River Compact between Montana, Wyoming, and North Dakota. This compact governs the distribution of water rights along all the tributaries of the Yellowstone (including the Powder River) to this day. In 2018, the U.S. Supreme Court decided *Montana vs. Wyoming*, a case about whether the Yellowstone Compact had adequately anticipated the impact of technological advances like sprinkler irrigation.

Opposition to the Moorhead Dam was substantial in both Montana and Wyoming. Some Lower Powder River ranchers were unconvinced the project was worth its cost. Others feared the government would impose irrigation districts, limiting them to 160 acres. However, the political dynamic of a dam located in Montana with its associated reservoir located (primarily) in Wyoming caused opposition to the Moorhead Project to have considerably more sway in decision-making.

Ultimately, the perceived lack of popular support doomed the Moorhead Project. The Reclamation Bureau's plans were constantly adjusted as they tried to find a political constituency that could overcome the opposition. The size of the proposed reservoir almost tripled, and projected costs skyrocketed to the alarm of the senators on the Appropriations Committee.

In my next column, I will detail the fierce political infighting that eventually resulted in the demise of the Moorhead Dam project in 1956. In 1957, the mess hall constructed for the dam workers was moved to Broadus for the Lutheran Church. The foundations of the abandoned camp still exist and can be seen from the air. Numerous attempts to resurrect the Moorhead Dam have been made. In the 1970s, a coal gasification company proposed building a smaller Moorhead Dam for industrial purposes. It was the final serious attempt at a dam on the Powder River.

NOTES ON CHAPTER 28:

- This column first appeared in the *Powder River Examiner's* June 30, 2022, edition.

The original caption for this image from the *Denver Post* reads: "SEP 1 1949, Moorhead Dam. The bustling bureau of reclamation construction camp sprang up almost overnight on the banks of the Powder River near the Montana-Wyoming line. Thursday it appeared the camp will become a ghost town with the same rapidity. Workers living there were to construct the controversial Moorhead Dam at a cost of 14 million dollars. But now federal funds have been cut off, to the joy of ranchers fighting the flood-control project. The Bureau of Reclamation says the camp will be boarded up as soon as current work is ended." PHOTOGRAPH FROM THE *DENVER POST* VIA GETTY IMAGES.

29

The Moorhead Opposition Flexes its Muscle

In my most recent column, I described the attempt in the late 1940s and 1950s to construct a dam on the Powder River south of Moorhead, Montana, just north of the border with Wyoming. In 1947, Congress appropriated $900,000 to make initial studies and build a camp for the engineers, staff, and construction workers. This initial appropriation was primarily the work of Wyoming's Senator Joseph C. O'Mahoney, a Democrat occupying an influential seat on the Senate Appropriations Committee. He was assisted in this action by Wyoming's at-large congressman, Frank Barrett. That year, the Truman Administration proposed an aggressive program to control Missouri River Basin flooding. One of the many projects under consideration by the Reclamation Bureau was Moorhead, and O'Mahoney used his considerable influence to make sure that his home state reaped at least some of the financial benefit of the new effort by appropriating the initial money. It would be the last time Senator O'Mahoney actively supported the Moorhead Dam for reasons that will become clear.

By 1949, the initial money had been spent, and the Reclamation Bureau was looking to Congress to appropriate significant amounts for constructing the Moorhead Project. The sum of 23 million dollars was being tossed around. By this time, however, it became apparent that serious opposition to the Moorhead Dam had surfaced.

That opposition was first formed by those landowners whose property would be taken for the reservoir. Most of this land was in Wyoming. It was common for the government's compensation to be viewed as inadequate, and congressmen and senators expected such opposition as a matter of routine politics. Unfortunately for supporters of the Moorhead Dam, this landowner group included one of the most powerful and influential entities in Wyoming, the Kendrick Cattle Company.

At the beginning of the 1900s, John B. Kendrick had established an enormous cattle empire, becoming Wyoming's richest man. This empire included his home ranch (the OW), located along Hanging Woman Creek in Montana. Kendrick also acquired large tracts of land in Wyoming's Sheridan and Campbell Counties, namely the LX Bar and K Ranches near the Montana border. Turning his financial power into a political career, Kendrick became Wyoming's ninth governor in 1915. He was extremely popular in his home state, and in 1916, Kendrick was elected to the U.S. Senate. The "Sagebrush Senator" served in the U.S. Senate for sixteen years and died in office in 1933. The governor appointed Kendrick's former executive secretary to serve the remainder of the term: Joseph C. O'Mahoney.

Wyoming Senator Joseph O'Mahoney, pictured here in 1937. PHOTOGRAPH COURTESY OF THE LIBRARY OF CONGRESS. LC-H22-D-672.

Manville Kendrick succeeded his father as head of the Kendrick Cattle Company. By 1949, Manville Kendrick was powerful in his own right and president of the Wyoming Stockgrowers Association. As initially planned, the Moorhead Project would permanently flood 3,000 acres of Kendrick Cattle Company land.

In testimony before the Senate Appropriations Committee, Manville Kendrick testified:

> *Construction of this dam will destroy the meadows whereupon is raised by far the greatest percentage of Kendrick Cattle Co.'s winter feed and will do substantial permanent damage to our whole ranch unit. Further—to my certain knowledge—it will put several of my neighbors completely out of business, and this, without regard to the compensation which they receive from the government.*

Regarding that government compensation, Kendrick was quick to dismiss the figures discussed:

> *With reference to the claim that $250,000 would be sufficient to purchase the right-of-way for this reservoir, I wish to say that, in my judgment, such a figure would not be a drop in the bucket toward compensating the landowners for their property losses. . . .*
>
> *If the proposed lands are taken, the $250,000 figure would not begin to compensate my company alone for its resulting loss. Naturally, the landowners affected by the taking of this right-of-way will take every effective and legal means to see that they are fairly compensated for the loss.*

A key aspect of Kendrick's appraisal was the presence of large coal and oil deposits under the planned reservoir.

Another group opposing the Moorhead Dam were several ranchers and landowners from Johnson County, Wyoming. This group, the Powder River Water Users Association, advocated for an alternative plan for flood control of the Powder River. This plan would build several (up to seven) smaller dams on the Powder's tributary streams in the foothills of the Bighorns. They argued that flooding that plagued the lower Powder River could be fixed at its source (i.e., the spring runoff in the mountains). This plan not only solved the lower flooding, but these dams would also be relatively free of the silt the Powder River accumulated once it left the higher ranges for the plains.

The Johnson County group's goal was simple and obvious: to control the water near their land and use the smaller reservoirs to improve the productivity of their property. The Moorhead Dam's looming presence threatened this practically and legally. They feared that the construction of Moorhead would create a water right for those downriver that would be prioritized over their own claims.

Western water law is a complex patchwork of federal, state, and tribal laws that allocate water rights and is different from the water laws of the eastern United States. The east that was settled by white men before moving west had more precipitation, and thus less need for water diversion. The eastern system is based on "riparian water rights." In the West, we use a system based on "appropriative water rights." Law Professor Gary Libcamp recently explained that:

> *Under the prior appropriation doctrine, there is a ladder of water rights on each stream that range from highest to lowest priority, and the highest priority claim gets first access to the water. Relative to junior priority rights, then, senior water right holders are more certain to receive water*

> *delivery, are more valuable, and thus provide more incentive to invest in water infrastructure.*

The alternative proposal had several features that allowed the opposition to the Moorhead Dam to comingle their personal interests in the water with the overall goals of the Reclamation Bureau. The opposition's political allies, like Senator O'Mahoney, could thus argue that they were not against necessary flood control in the lower Powder River but that it could be done more easily, cheaply, and effectively in Wyoming. Moorhead advocates in Montana had claimed, "we only want the water that Wyoming wastes." At one point, O'Mahoney even suggested that both the smaller reservoir plan and Moorhead be funded, with the caveat that the small reservoir plan be started first to establish his constituency's water rights.

Another issue that was, at the time, causing considerable mischief was the status of a water compact between Montana, Wyoming, and North Dakota. Congress had authorized such a compact in 1933. After negotiation, the compact would need to be approved by each state legislature and then by the U.S. Congress. These negotiations had failed several times in the intervening years. The Wyoming State Engineer supported the construction of Moorhead on its merits but refused to sign off on the plan until the compact was enacted. "I do not believe there would be many that would oppose the Moorhead development," he wrote, "if we can come to an agreement on the division of water." After several stops and starts, the compact finally came into being in late 1950 after the best chance to fund the Moorhead Dam had died.

Arvada Rancher Clark W. Ritchie testified to a House Committee regarding the silt problem:

> *The cost of Moorhead Dam, 25 millions of dollars or somewhere thereabouts in round figures, is a lot of money. You could do a lot of good with it before you get into Powder River, and you can create a mudhole with it after you get it into Powder River.*

Perhaps the final straw was the changing scope and accompanying price tag of the Moorhead Dam. Initially planned as a flood and silt control dam with a 300,000 acre-foot reservoir, the Reclamation Bureau soon adjusted the plan to 800,000 acre-feet to include irrigation capabilities. This created even more problems and more arrows in the opposition's quiver. The newly elevated price tag alarmed the appropriators. The prospect of new irrigation districts capped at 160 acres persuaded several Montana Powder River landowners to sign a petition opposing Moorhead.

Senator O'Mahoney, like his former boss John B. Kendrick, was popular in the Cowboy State, being elected in his own right in 1934. By 1949, O'Mahoney was well into his third term in office and had a significant change of heart concerning Moorhead. While that change of heart may have been initially motivated by his personal association with the Kendricks, it became clear that it was not in Wyoming's interest for the Moorhead Dam to be built. Such a dam may have been in Montana's interest, but the Treasure State did not have a seat on the Appropriations Committee. O'Mahoney skillfully led these various opposition groups and prevented further appropriations to the project. Within a few years, the camp constructed at the site was torn down, with only foundations and some bitter memories remaining.

The empty foundations pictured in the foreground tell a tale of a project which never came to fruition—the Moorhead Dam. The foundations were poured for structures in anticipation of a dam access across the Powder River, which if approved would have spanned the river between the plateau on which the foundations are pictured across to the timbered bluffs on the far bank, approximately in the center if the image. PHOTOGRAPH COURTESY OF BILLY STUVER.

NOTES ON CHAPTER 29:

- This column first appeared in the July 14, 2022, edition of the *Powder River Examiner.*

Grant Dunning, his cowboys, and the Moncreiffe Brothers at Bovino, February/March 1902. Grant Dunning (front row, third from left) and his cowboys pose for a picture at the Bovino Stockyards of Grand Junction, Colorado. Also pictured are Moncreiffe Brothers Malcolm (front row, first from left, wearing a Scottish bunnett) and William (back row, sixth from left, wearing a Scottish bunnett). Horses intended for use by the British Empire in the Boer War are pictured in the background.
PHOTOGRAPH COURTESY OF THE CHARLIE DUNNING FAMILY.

30

The Last of the Boer War Horses

A year ago, my cousin showed me an old, sepia-colored family photograph of several cowboys in a corral. The picture's owner (my cousin) challenged me to see what I could find of the image's backstory. Included in the picture was my great-great-grandfather, Grant Dunning. An additional photo, obviously taken the same day, had a few bits of information written on the back:

> *Picture of Grant Dunning Cowboys. Guys in back are contractors William and Malcolm Moncreiffe. Bought horses and sold them to British. British sold them to the Boer War. Picture taken at Grand Junction Stockyard, 1900–1905.*

The Boer War (technically, the Second Boer War) was fought from October 1899 to May 1902. It was a conflict in Southern Africa between the British Empire and two Boer Republics (Afrikaners). As part of the war effort, the British government contracted with the Moncreiffe Brothers of Big Horn, Wyoming, to supply horses to the military. The Moncreiffes were the younger sons of Scottish nobility and had contacts with the British government.

Grant Dunning and his younger brother Luther were well-known stockmen and pioneers in southeastern Montana. In 1897, English nobleman (and notorious playboy) Sydney Paget deeded his ranch on Otter Creek to the Dunning brothers when he left Montana. Their brother, Bill Dunning, was a well-known stock inspector in Sheridan.

With the two photographs came an oral history hinting at a remarkable achievement: Grant and his cowboys had trailed several hundred horses from Sheridan to Grand Junction, Colorado. My research began with this framework. I could not proceed further without verifying, at least in some respects, the information on the back of the second picture. Was Grant Dunning ever in

Grand Junction with a group of cowboys, and when did this occur? I searched in vain for newspaper accounts of some grand horse herd traversing the Wyoming plain. Fortunately, cowboys on trail rides are known not only for their exploits on the prairie but also for rabble-rousing. In the March 22, 1902, edition of Grand Junction's *Daily Sentinel*, I found the following article under the headline "A Vile Attack":

> *An assault was committed upon H.G. Bedwell at the Bovino stock yards yesterday afternoon about 3 o'clock which, from all accounts that can be obtained, was entirely unwarranted and unprovoked, so far as Mr. Bedwell was concerned.*
>
> *The attack was made by two of the cowboys who are engaged at the stockyards and in the one-sided fight Mr. Bedwell was knocked down several times and was struck twice in the head with a quirt. Both of the cowmen were very large fellows and everyone who knows Mr. Bedwell will see at once that, even had he been given a fair show, he could not have gained anything from the fight. . . .*
>
> *The beginning of the trouble occurred about a week ago, when Grant Dunning, one of the cowmen, was arrested in this city for creating a disturbance on the "row" on Colorado avenue. Some parties had informed the men that Mr. Bedwell was responsible for Dunning's arrest. His companions decided to punish Mr. Bedwell for his interference. They, however, in yesterday's affair did not allow that gentleman time to explain that he was not the man who complained against Dunning.*

This story confirmed many items written on the photograph. Grant was indeed in Grand Junction with some cowboys and had a relationship with the stockyards there. Most importantly, it fixed the date to March 1902. This date was a critical marker in determining more precisely why my great-great-grandfather was in western Colorado and what he was doing (when he wasn't getting arrested, that is).

While the story of the Moncreiffe's Boer War effort is well known, there are surprisingly few primary sources for details. The best source is Floyd Bard's book *Horse Wrangler: Sixty Years in the Saddle in Wyoming and Montana.* In that book, Bard describes how the Moncreiffe's horse operation flooded Sheridan with money, and Grant and Luther Dunning led their efforts:

Ten of Grant Dunning's cowboys, with the Moncreiffe Brothers at Bovino (1902). Cowboys who worked for Grant Dunning processing the last of the Boer War horses pose for a picture. Also pictured behind the cowboys are Malcolm Moncreiffe (left) and William Moncreiffe (right). The date of this photo is probably February/March of 1902 at the Bovino Stockyards near Grand Junction. According to the handwriting on the back: "Left of picture: Bert Arison, Ore Brown, Harry Bringon, Ed Thorp."

> *Late in the fall of 1901, the company moved their inspection outfit to Grand Junction, Colorado. During that winter the company held regular inspections the same as they held at the Moncreiffe ranch. By the following spring, 1902, the horse business was over. The company shipped their outfit back to Sheridan, then on to their Big Horn ranch.*

Grand Junction had been one location for several inspection stations for the Moncreiffe's horse operations. Railroads shipped the horses to New Orleans, where they were eventually placed on ships and sent to South Africa. Many of the horses did not survive the trip. Those that did were not expected to survive more than four months in the grueling South African sun.

By the time of the photographs, the conflict was winding down. A war characterized early on by glorious offensives and hard-fought sieges had, by 1900, turned into a guerilla war. The British countered the Boer tactics with scorched earth policies and concentration camps. By 1901, peace negotiations were underway, and time was running out for the Boer insurgents. The war effort's need for American horses wound down along with the Boer military's prospects. The consolidation of operations from distant posts (like Sheridan) to the more centrally located Grand Junction brought these Montana and Wyoming cowboys to the western slopes of Colorado in the late winter. The *Wyoming Industrial Journal* reported in its February 1, 1902, edition:

> *The Moncrieffe Brothers of Big Horn, Wyoming are holding a band of 500 unbroken Oregon horses at Bovino, near Grand Junction. The band is being broken by some cowboys and after the obsequies are over the stuff will be sent east to fill an army contract with the British government.*

The presence of the Moncreiffe Brothers (William and Malcolm) in the picture demonstrates that they were personally overseeing the winddown of operations. Grant and Luther Dunning's close relationship with the Scottish noblemen probably demanded their presence in Grand Junction as well. I speculate that Grant and Luther, with a group of trusted broncobusters, did indeed drive a last herd of horses from Sheridan to Grand Junction. They had, likely, paid $40 each for them, and the only way they could get paid was to get them to the inspectors. Thankfully, one can trail horses much faster than cattle. While it is possible the horses were sent by train from Sheridan to Grand Junction, such an effort would have been expensive and just as dangerous for the health of the horses, who needed to pass a health inspection to be purchased.

I was initially skeptical that such a trail drive was advisable or financially feasible. Grant's presence in Colorado in February/March 1902 meant they would have had to drive this horse herd south in the dead of winter past the Big Horn Mountains, crossing the Continental Divide through South Pass, and down into Colorado. I have since learned that this challenging feat may not have been as formidable as I first imagined. Indeed, the mountain valleys in northern Colorado's Moffat County were well-established winter grazing sites. Heading south from the pass and into Colorado via Savery Creek (near Baggs, Wyoming) would have brought them down into the western slopes of the Colorado Rockies.

While he was not present for either picture, it is clear that Luther Dunning was also in Colorado at this time. Newspaper accounts show him in nearby Craig, Colorado, on March 1, buying Boer War horses for the Moncreiffes. For those curious, Luther's descendants are the Dunnings who presently live along Otter Creek.

While the Boer War horse enterprise ended in 1902, it would not be long before Grant and Luther were once again engaged in the great enterprise of supplying military horses. The outbreak of World War One started it up again for both the British and American forces. Finally, the remount program of the U.S. Army was the third and last profitable effort to provide Montana and Wyoming horsepower to the military up to the pre-World War Two period.

These two photographs represent the end of a significant era in the American West: the last of the Boer War Horses. I am grateful to be able to give these great images their due on these pages.

NOTES ON CHAPTER 30:

- This column first appeared in the *Powder River Examiner's* September 29, 2022, edition.
- After further research, I believe Luther Dunning is indeed in the first photograph (front row, second from left). This cowboy is not present in the second "Grant Dunning's cowboys" photograph. This makes me think the setting prompted some reason for this cowboy's removal. The only other rider missing from the second image was Grant, which implies an association with the leader. Also, the fact that this cowboy superficially resembles Luther further grounds my suspicion.

Rosebud County Sheriff Billy Moses, prior to his death in 1914. PHOTOGRAPH COURTESY OF ROSEBUD COUNTY.

31

Two Powder Kegs and a Spark

According to the precise definition, Rosebud County Sheriff Billy Moses died in the line of duty. On January 14, 1914, Sheriff Moses arrived at the Rosebud (the town) residence of Johnnie Burgess to serve a misdemeanor warrant for disturbance. Moses was dead only a few minutes later, shot in the chest and the neck. Law enforcement officers face terrible uncertainty, never knowing what awaits them, even in the most routine of duties. However, this was in no way a routine service of a warrant, and Billy Moses knew this.

Originally from Texas, William Moses came to the northern plains working the trail herds. In 1900, he was elected sheriff of Butte County, South Dakota. Its county seat, Belle Fourche, was a rough and tumble town on the crossroads of three states. Moses was a successful sheriff and was re-elected several times. In 1906, tragedy struck when his wife, Nellie, died unexpectedly.

He went seeking new surroundings and found it as a livestock inspector in northern Wyoming and southeast Montana. Livestock rustling was a chronic problem in the area, and Moses' reputation as a dogged enforcer of the law attracted the attention of some large cattlemen in the area. John B. Kendrick and the Spear Brothers helped to recruit the former Butte County Sheriff to relocate a few clicks west. He was an effective livestock inspector, and within a few years, he settled down enough to marry twenty-one-year-old Dora Wright. In 1912, Billy Moses ran for sheriff of Rosebud County and won.

Johnnie H. Burgess had been a long-term resident of the territory between the Tongue and Powder Rivers. He had a successful career as the trail boss of the SH Cattle ranch on Powder River. He married Martha Bowles (widow of William Bowles) and settled down in the town of Rosebud. Johnnie Burgess seriously considered running for Rosebud County Sheriff in 1912 but declined in order to support the candidacy of his good friend, Billy Moses. One of Sheriff Moses' first acts was the appointment of Johnnie Burgess as

Johnnie Burgess. PHOTOGRAPH COURTESY OF THE RANGE RIDERS MUSEUM, MILES CITY, MT.

deputy. Only two years later, their relationship radically changed. A local newspaper explained:

> *There has been a bitter feeling between the two men which arose less than six weeks ago, when the sheriff's wife left him because of brutal and inhuman treatment and came to the Burgess home and asked if she might stay there. . . .*
>
> *Mrs. Burgess had conferred a number of favors on Mrs. Moses before and they were very good friends and naturally, in her hour of trouble,*

> *Mrs. [Moses] came to Mrs. Burgess for help and consolation. Mrs. Moses told them how she had been beat and choked by Mr. Moses and that she could no longer stand his brutal and inhuman treatment and that she had left him for good and was going to secure a divorce and asked Mrs. Burgess if she could stay there until she could get her divorce and set up some business matters. She told them she did not have sufficient funds to go to a hotel. Mrs. Burgess told her that she could.*

Sheriff Moses deeply resented what he viewed as Burgess' interference in his personal affairs. "The sheriff, it is said, had determined to fight the matter [the divorce] to the utmost." Johnnie Burgess resigned his position as a deputy in early January 1914. Days later, the two got into a physical altercation in the streets of Forsyth. In fear of his life, Burgess received the written permission of Rosebud County Judge Crum to carry a pistol specifically for the purpose of self-protection from Moses.

Such was the situation when Billy Moses traveled to Rosebud for a sheriff's sale. After this routine business was concluded, he was handed an arrest warrant against John Burgess. The previous day, Burgess had caused a disruption in a local saloon, displaying a gun in the process. Anticipating trouble, Moses hired a local man, William Finch, to drive him up to the Burgess house in his wagon and to witness any subsequent events.

The Forsyth paper stated: "It was as though two kegs of powder stood side by side only awaiting a spark to cause an explosion." When Moses exited the wagon and walked up to the Burgess residence, he was met at the door by Martha Burgess, holding a Winchester rifle. Mrs. Burgess testified:

> *"Don't come in," she told the sheriff.*
>
> *"Madam, I'm an officer of the law, and go where I please," was the sheriff's reply.*
>
> *"You ordered me out of your house, now you stay out of mine," she replied.*
>
> *"You put down that gun," said the sheriff.*
>
> *"You have threatened to kill Johnnie and me both," she said.*
>
> *"Yes, and I will," she testified the sheriff replied.*

The sheriff then told her he had a paper to serve on her husband, and she answered: "All right, Johnnie will come to the door." She testified to having told Bill Bailey [a family friend who was staying at the house] to call her husband, who came to the door.

"What is it Bill?" said Burgess when he reached the porch.

"I have a warrant for you," said the sheriff.

"All right, I'll get my coat and hat."

"It's a misdemeanor," said the sheriff.

"All right, I'll go," answered Burgess.

Mrs. Burgess testified to putting on her sweater and preparing to accompany them when the sheriff said to her: "You're not going."

"Yes, I am," she said and instructed Bill Bailey to go with them also.

At this moment, Mrs. Burgess testified, her Winchester went off accidentally, the bullet going through the toe sole of her shoe and into the porch. She exhibited the shoe with the tear in the sole.

"That was an accident, Billy," she said she told the sheriff.

"What do you mean? Give me that gun, God damn you," said the sheriff, stepping toward her and grabbing her right arm with his left hand but keeping his right hand out of her sight.

Then the sheriff fired a shot, followed by a shot from [Johnnie] Burgess and then more firing. Finally, Moses fell and Burgess ceased firing.

During the struggle, Martha received a gunshot wound in her shoulder. Thus the "accidental explosion of the gun held by Mrs. Burgess furnished the spark to the powder," as the Forsyth paper continued its metaphor.

Testifying that he knew Moses was dead, Johnnie Burgess and Bill Finch drove the wagon to fetch the doctor. Burgess surrendered to the authorities after ensuring his wife's medical attention. He was quickly transferred to the Rosebud County jail in Forsyth. Martha was treated for a broken collarbone.

The trial of Johnnie and Martha Burgess was moved to Custer County in Miles City, providing virtually all of the eastern Montana papers with its salacious details. Judge C.C. Hurley made several important rulings that greatly impacted the trial. Murder charges against Martha Burgess were dropped. Testimony regarding Moses' marital issues was excluded. Most importantly, testimony regarding Moses' threats to Burgess was also disallowed unless the defense could demonstrate that the sheriff actually intended to carry out those specific threats. Overall, the trial was characterized by wildly conflicting witness testimony and uncertainty as to who shot who and when.

Moses had several family members who tried to get involved in the trial. Dayton Moses, one of Billy Moses' younger half-brothers, was an influential lawyer in Texas and was not impressed with the prosecution team. He urged powerful cattle baron John B. Kendrick (then a Wyoming state senator) to use his political influence to have himself added to the prosecution.

The prosecution was expanded but did not include Dayton Moses or any of his suggested alternatives because the younger Moses "had entirely too much feeling in the matter to allow us to participate in the trial."

Prosecutors argued that four shots were fired after Martha's accidental Winchester discharge. They claimed that Burgess had fired first, quickly followed by one shot from Moses, with Burgess firing a final two. The doctor testified that either of Moses' two wounds would have produced his almost instantaneous death. The defense claimed self-defense and that Moses had shot first. Both sides seem to agree that both Moses' and Johnnie Burgess' first shots were fired nearly simultaneously.

Then the mudslinging began. Each side presented several witnesses who heard Moses threaten Burgess' life and vice versa. The defense then presented multiple witnesses who claimed Moses had a reputation for being a violent and quarrelsome man. Other witnesses testified to Moses violently abusing his official powers as sheriff in Montana and South Dakota. Apparently, Moses' effectiveness had won him several enemies willing to disparage the dead man's reputation.

To counter this, the prosecution also produced their own slate of witnesses confirming Billy Moses' reputation as an effective lawman with a good reputation. These witnesses included former Rosebud Sheriff Robert Guy and several colleagues from Belle Fourche and Forsyth.

On May 27, after four hours of deliberations, the Custer County jury found Johnnie Burgess not guilty. Friends of the accused were naturally elated, while those close to Moses were despondent. Johnnie and Martha Burgess continued to live in Rosebud well into old age.

Embittered, Dayton Moses returned to Texas, but not without lambasting anyone remotely involved in his brother's career in Montana. He wrote John B. Kendrick:

> *I feel that, to a large extent, Spear Brothers & Kendrick are responsible for Billy Moses moving to Rosebud County. I think you will agree that during his stay in the County the custom of stealing cattle belonging to you gentlemen has ceased and that this condition is due to the activity of my late brother and the fear he instilled into the minds of cattle rustlers in the vicinity of your ranches, thus saving you gentlemen many times over the salary you paid him as inspector. I feel that it is also true that [the] many enemies [my] brother had in Rosebud County were made by his devotion to duty in guarding your interests and his personal loyalty to yourself as an old-time friend. I feel that I know if conditions were different, and after losing all of your property you, instead of Billy Moses, had been murdered, he would have gone to the limit in time and money to assist, in so far as was possible, the conviction of your murderer. . . .*
>
> *I am going home, trusting it will never become necessary for me to return to the State of Montana. I am so thoroughly disgusted with the judicial proceedings in this State that I hope I may be able to spend the remainder of my life in a State in whose judiciary I have confidence.*

Notes on Chapter 30:

— This article first appeared in the December 1, 2022, issue of the *Powder River Examiner.* ←

Remains of the christening bottle of the Liberty Ship *William Bradford,* christened by Mary Bradford in 1942. This heirloom eventually came west to Bradford's home in Wyoming. It resided on her mantelpiece for years and eventually passed to her eldest son, Forest Dunning. The bottle has been honored on Dunning's mantelpiece ever since. PHOTOGRAPH BY SHANE DUNNING, BRADFORD'S GRANDSON.

32

In Defense of the Mantelpiece

One holiday tradition I remember as a youngster was going to my grandmother's house for Christmas in Big Horn, Wyoming. These occasions usually gathered a host of aunts, uncles, cousins, and family friends. The house's social center (even during non-holidays) was the kitchen. Most visitors would be found visiting with my grandmother, my step-grandfather, or both. Only when large groups of visitors were present would the living room see significant traffic, such as our Christmas gatherings. The living room was not large, and because its only two windows were semi-covered by trees, it was not well-lit. A large flagstone fireplace with an insert stove dominated the room. Along the top of the fireplace was a shelf I could barely reach as a curious youngster. On this shelf was a small wooden box, about a foot long and six inches in height and width. A long glass plate served as the box's top panel.

This box always fascinated me during our visits. It was a struggle to get up to it, and the room's poor lighting conditions made it almost impossible to determine what was inside. To make things worse, I was told the box was not a plaything, making its study an exercise in childhood duplicity. When I finally got the box off the shelf, to my horror, I heard the distinctive sound of broken glass. Convinced that I had somehow damaged it, the box was quickly but gingerly returned to the mantel.

This incident was the primary reason I did not call attention to the box by asking my grandmother about its contents. When our annual Christmas gatherings brought me back to the living room, I often glanced up to confirm that the box still held its usual place.

Eventually, I grew tall enough to reach the box easily, confident I needed no further subterfuge to examine it. Looking through the glass plane, I could see colorful pieces of cloth in what seemed to be the shape of a bottle. On a small descriptive plate on the side of the box were words:

CHRISTENING BOTTLE
S.S. "WILLIAM BRADFORD"
MISS MARY F. BRADFORD
SPONSOR
NOVEMBER 14, 1942
SOUTH PORTLAND SHIPBUILDING CORP.
SOUTH PORTLAND MAINE

I was relieved to learn I had not damaged the box as a child. The broken glass I had heard was the sound of the damaged christening bottle as it shifted inside. Mary Bradford was my grandmother's maiden name. I knew she was originally from Massachusetts (she never lost the accent) and a direct descendant of William Bradford, the Governor of Plymouth Colony and signer of the Mayflower Compact. It was this group of colonists that participated in the original Thanksgiving story. For years, I had heard about this particular heritage, but I didn't recall stories about a ship other than the *Mayflower*. I took the information etched on the box as it was. As a stupid teenager with equally stupid things on my mind, I never thought to ask my grandmother about it.

I went away to college, and eventually, both my grandparents passed away. As the eldest son, the christening bottle came to my father, who immediately placed the box in a place of honor on his own mantel. From him, I learned that the SS *William Bradford* was not some run-of-the-mill sea vessel. It was a "Liberty ship."

Liberty ships were a particular class of cargo ships built during World War Two under the Emergency Shipbuilding Program. Between 1941 and 1945, eighteen American shipyards built 2,710 Liberty ships on both shores. Members of the U.S. Merchant Marine crewed these ships. Liberty ships used a standard design to facilitate their construction and repair. On average, three Liberty ships were launched every two days during the war, an extraordinary display of American industrial capability.

Many Liberty ships were named after famous figures in American history, starting with the men who signed the Declaration of Independence. Because she was a direct descendant of William Bradford, the South Portland Shipbuilding Corporation wrote twenty-year-old Mary Faith Bradford, asking her to be the new ship's sponsor.

Launching of the SS *William Bradford* on November 14, 1942. The launch occurred at the South Portland Shipyards in South Portland, Maine. While the photo is unattributed, it is believed to be from the Associated Press, which covered the launching. PHOTOGRAPH COURTESY OF THE MARY BRADFORD MORELAND FAMILY.

This company expects to launch the S.S. "William Bradford," which is being built for the United States Maritime Commission, on November 8th, 1942.

The South Portland Shipbuilding Corporation and the United States Maritime Commission would feel highly honored if you would consent to sponsor this ship.

Another view of the SS *William Bradford's* launch. Liberty Ships such as the Bradford carried 75 percent of the cargo needed to win WWII.

As the sponsor, my grandmother served the traditional role of the "godmother." The godmother makes a sacrifice to celebrate the ship's launch, and in modern times this "sacrifice" is a bottle of champagne broken on the bow of the vessel. The sacrifice invites good fortune and safe travels on the ship about to be launched. On November 14th, my grandmother christened the boat with a champagne bottle wrapped in red, white, and blue cloth. The remains of the bottle stayed in the wrapping, allowing the young Bradford to keep it as a souvenir.

Liberty ships weren't noted for their beauty. President Franklin Roosevelt famously called them "a dreadful looking object," an opinion that resulted in the entire class being known as "Ugly Ducklings." They were 441 feet long, displacing 10,685 long tons. In addition to anti-aircraft guns, the stern mounted a 4-inch deck gun for use against surface ships, particularly submarines. The first Liberty ship (the SS *Patrick Henry*) was named after the famed American revolutionary, and FDR's speech on its launch gave the class its name:

> *We propose that these ships sail the seas as they are intended to. We propose, to the best of our ability, to protect them from torpedo, from shell or from bomb.*
>
> *The Patrick Henry, as one of the Liberty ships launched today, renews that great patriot's stirring demand: "Give me liberty or give me death."*
>
> *There shall be no death for America, for democracy, for freedom! There must be liberty, worldwide and eternal. That is our prayer—our pledge to all mankind.*

It is estimated that Liberty ships carried 75 percent of the cargo used in the war. Many of the construction crews were staffed by women.

The SS *William Bradford* launched on November 14, 1942; the tenth Liberty ship launched from the South Portland Shipyards. One of its crew members, Ensign Dae Baird, Jr. (the ship's purser), recalled sailing from Norfolk, Virginia, in a convoy of 131 ships escorted by three destroyers and six destroyer escorts. The *Bradford* carried ammunition and crated airplane engines to be unloaded at Bandar Shahpur in Iran. This cargo was then shipped to our Soviet allies via the Trans-Iranian Railroad. The importance of this resupply effort to the Soviets resulted in Ensign Baird receiving a medal from the Russian government fifty years later, with a certificate signed by President Boris Yeltsin. Despite being strafed in the Mediterranean at least once, the Bradford survived the war and was eventually scrapped in 1960.

World War Two has often been called a resource war in that the industrial capacity of the United States proved to be the critical advantage resulting in the Allied victory. As memories of WWII fade, what remains is often the "sexy" aspects of the American effort, such as the war's scientific advancements, grand strategy, and weaponry. These things are indeed important and often fascinating. However, the American workforce's extraordinary effort in supporting the Allied effort was equally important and worthy of our highest honors.

That sentiment brings me back to the importance of mantelpieces. My purpose in telling this story is not necessarily to brag about my own family's history. Rather, I hope this story encourages you and your family to preserve the three-dimensional remnants of your history and that of your family. If, before reading this, you were unaware of Liberty ships and their importance, then you can thank a mantelpiece. If you were previously aware of Liberty ships and this piece allows you to pass on your knowledge, then you can also thank a mantelpiece. If your family is lucky enough to have a mantelpiece, please make the most of the opportunity to honor yourself and those who came before you.

NOTES ON CHAPTER 32:

- This article first appeared in the December 22, 2022, edition of the *Powder River Examiner.* ←

Winnie Brown was traveling this road when Richard Dixon ambushed and shot him. Dixon confessed and implicated George and Regina Geddes and Tom Welch as co-conspirators. Their trials illustrated complex views on race, criminality, and gender roles at the end of the nineteenth century. PHOTOGRAPH BY SHANE DUNNING.

33

The Geddes Murder Trials: Gender, Race, and Murder-for-Hire in Eastern Montana's Criminal Justice System

Armed with a rifle and wearing a dark mask, Richard Dixon, an African American, rode hard toward three white men traveling with a lumber wagon loaded with vegetables. It was a cold November day in 1897 near the Tongue River in southeastern Montana. Clemence "Winnie" Brown and his brother Clarence were driving the wagon, with another brother, Hersey, following on horseback. Hidden in a nearby coulee, the masked gunman had waited for the wagon to pass before putting the spurs to his horse. Overtaking the wagon, Dixon shot Winnie in the lower back through his gut, sending him toppling to the ground. Both brothers stopped to aid their wounded sibling while Dixon passed them and climbed to a nearby hill. Clarence fired off one shot at the assassin and received two wayward shots in return as Dixon fled on his horse. His brothers took the severely wounded Winnie to the nearby ranch of their brother-in-law. It took several painful hours for Winnie to die, and he begged multiple times to be put out of his misery. Despite the mask, Winnie had recognized his killer. Before dying in the early morning hours of November 5, 1897, Winnie signed a statement identifying Richard Dixon as the man who shot him.[1]

Hours after the crime, Custer County special deputy Johnnie Stafford found two empty .30 caliber shells at the top of the hill near the crime scene and followed the trail of the shooter's horse to the nearby ranch owned by George Geddes and his wife, Regina. Deputies arrested Dixon in the company of Regina Geddes within days, although Regina had told the deputy her employee had been ironing clothes with her all day on November 4. After several days

[1] *Inquest of Clemence Winifred Brown,* Nov. 8, 1897, Custer County Courthouse, Miles City. Brown's dying statement misspelled Dixon's name as "Dick Richardson." For Brown's dying declaration, see *State of Montana v. George Geddes,* Case 1308, Montana Supreme Court Records, 1868-1938, SMFICHE 18, MHS.

in jail, Richard Dixon admitted to being the gunman and revealed a much larger conspiracy to kill Winnie Brown. Investigators found more shells inside a tomato can buried in a manure pile based on Dixon's confession, as well as George Geddes' Winchester rifle in the bedroom closet. Deputies also found a horse matching the Brown brothers' description of the assassin's mount in the Geddes' barn. With the killer's testimony in hand, Custer County prosecutor Thomas J. Porter charged George Geddes, his wife Regina, and Thomas Welch, a family friend, with first-degree murder. These charges were based on the legal principle that conspiracy to commit murder is the same crime as the act of killing itself.[2]

Nearly six months after the crime, on April 11, 1898, twenty-eight-year-old Regina Geddes walked through the doors of the Yellowstone County Courthouse in Billings to begin her trial for first-degree murder. She stood accused of conspiring to kill Winnie Brown. As the third member of the alleged cabal to face trial, she had reason to be concerned. Juries had convicted two other members of the murder plot, George Geddes and Tom Welch, of second-degree murder in a Miles City courthouse on January 12 and February 11, respectively. At her lawyer's request, Regina's trial was moved to Billings, but the proceeding would occur before the same judge with the same prosecutors and defense attorneys as the previous two trials. The evidence, while focusing on her individual actions during the conspiracy, was essentially the same as for her co-defendants.[3]

The first to stand trial, George Geddes had brutally assaulted Winnie Brown six months before the killing and supplied the conspiracy's primary motive. These aspects undoubtedly caused the jury to sentence him to an

---

[2] *State v. George Geddes.*

[3] While the history of women in the western American frontier has been a source of impressive scholarship, a great deal of this work has focused on more positive aspects and accomplishments. Sociologist Elizabeth Maret, for example, explored the role of women in shaping the Texas cattle industry. She found that "given the particularly legendary character of the Texas cattle industry, women's part in this great and historic activity can most accurately be described as invisible." Elizabeth Maret, *Women of the Range: Women's Roles in the Texas Beef Cattle Industry* (College Station: *Texas A&M Univ. Press, 1993), 12-13.* Sue Armitage, "Western Women: Beginning to Come into Focus," *Montana* 32:3 (Summer 1982): 2-9, describes the struggle to chronicle women's contribution to Montana society and culture. Karen Anderson, "Work, Gender, and Power in the American West," *Pacific Historical Review* 61:4 (Nov. 1992): 481-99, explores how women workers impacted the frontier West. Those interested in women's experiences along the Tongue River during the same period as this narrative should read Nanie Alderson's (with Helena Huntington Smith) classic, *A Bride Goes West* (Lincoln: Univ. of Nebraska Press, 1942), as well as Margaret Bailey Broadus, *Through the Rosebuds: A Tale of Rosebud Creek, Montana* (Centennial, CO: CGI Books, 1987).

almost then-unheard-of ninety-nine years. Tom Welch received a sentence of twenty years. Publicity had been extensive and escalated in the furor of the first two trials. Importantly, however, the two male conspirators were treated quite differently than Regina. Those differences broke down along gender lines, a point that established the Geddes trials as a useful case study on the treatment of women accused of serious crimes in frontier America. Analysis shows that Regina Geddes exploited a male-dominated legal system and public opinion, with its accompanying mindsets, resulting in her overall legal triumph in this unusual case. When her trial finally ended, Regina Geddes walked out of the Yellowstone County Courthouse a free woman.

The events around Winnie Brown's murder expose the multiple Victorian-era influences on Montana's emerging society. While the trials resolved along the lines of gender, both the underlying facts of the crime and the behavior of the trial participants revealed how assumptions about race, class, and sexuality permeated the most rural parts of Montana.

Despite prior efforts to kill Winnie Brown, the act was ultimately performed by an African American in the employ of an affluent white man. The killer, Richard Dixon, was directed by a social-climbing woman of considerable charm and determination. Under pressure, he confessed and served more than a decade in prison. Tom Welch, a multiracial cowboy who had killed before, tried and failed to put Winnie out of the way after he had angered George Geddes by openly questioning the sexual habits of his wife. Those habits may have included the cowpuncher and the African American laborer, all with the knowing assent of Geddes, a self-destructive man consumed with protecting his legacy from his own mistakes. The spectacle of the murder trial engulfed Montana's press, its legal system, and the public at large.

Women accused of serious crimes in the Victorian era were often treated differently than men due to the gendered presumption that sane, white women were almost incapable of violent crime, whereas men, due to their baser nature, often acted violently. The *Geddes* cases highlight those distinctions, as three defendants, two men and one woman, each stood accused of conspiracy. None of the three was the actual killer of Winnie Brown. The assassin, Richard Dixon, was a twenty-two-year-old African American laborer. He had worked for George and Regina Geddes off and on for two years and was in their employ the day he shot Winnie Brown. Identified as the shooter, Dixon confessed to the conspiracy after a brief resistence. The confession immediately changed the nature of the case. Dixon informed prosecutors his actions were the closing act of a determined conspiracy to silence Winnie Brown by orchestrating his death. The confession created a sensation that quickly spread across Montana's newspapers.[4]

Dixon claimed that he killed Winnie Brown at Regina Geddes' insistence. Mrs. Geddes had observed the Brown boys on their way to Miles City and offered Dixon fifty dollars "for you and anyone else that will get away with that Brown boy." Observing the Tongue River Road from her house, she identified Winnie driving the wagon on their return trip. Dixon testified to this role in the murder:

---

[4] "Killed Clarence Brown," *Helena Independent,* Nov. 8, 1897, 1. For years before the Brown killing, Dixon was known in the area by a racist epithet, which was reprinted broadly. The nature of the Geddes case partially controls for complicating factors nearly always present when comparing criminal justice out-comes. Even when a single case can be found with multiple defendants of different gender, considerations such as different lawyers, judges, and law enforcement, as well as variable levels of criminal involvement necessarily obscure comparisons between participants. In the late Victorian era, views on female criminality were in a period of change. According to Lucia Zedner, "up to the mid-nineteenth century, the predominant approach to women's criminality was moralistic. Women criminals were judged against a highly artificial notion of the ideal woman—an exemplary moral being." In this sense, the commission of serious crimes reinforced some gender roles and obfuscated others. "Men who committed many of the less serious forms of crime could be seen as displaying attributes not too far removed from Victorian notions of masculinity: entrepreneurial drive, initiative, courage, physical vigor, and agility were all thought to be appropriate male traits. Although male criminals undoubtedly broke the law, they did not necessarily deviate from accepted notions of 'manliness.' By contrast, the literature . . . suggests criminal women were seen to repudiate revered qualities of femininity. In doing so, they offended not only the law but against their ascribed social and moral roles." Lucia Zedner, "Women, Crime, and Penal Responses: A Historical Account," *Crime and Justice* 14 (1991): 307-62, 320. This mindset explains why the accusation of serious crime—notwithstanding conviction and punishment—against women was so tricky in Victorian societies. An allegation against a woman would destroy her if false and could destroy society if true. As the 1800s ended, the supposed inability of women to commit serious crimes began to be explained in less moralistic and more pseudoscientific terms. Female criminality resulted from irregularities with menstrual cycles or women's innate irrationality. Dorie Klein called these distinctions "taking a moral position that often masquerades as a scientific distinction." Dorie Klein, "The Etiology of Female Crime: A Review of the Literature" in *The Female Offender,* ed. Laura Crites (Lexington, MA: DC Heath & Company, 1976), 5-31. Klein's article was originally published in *Issues in Criminology* 8:2 (Fall 1973): 3-30. Documentation of serious criminal activity by women, especially white women, in the American West is more difficult to find. Stories of prostitution and related events are the most common examples of female criminality. Ellen Baumler documented the stories of the few women sent to Montana's prison at Deer Lodge. Many of the cases Baumler presented intertwined with her subjects' class and racial origins, factors that complicate any comparative study of criminal activity between men and women. Ellen Baumler, "Justice as an Afterthought: Women and the Montana Prison System," *Montana* 58:2 (Summer 2008): 41-59, 97-99. Anne Butler also explored female criminality and its impact on western state penitentiaries from 1865 to 1915. Anne M. Butler, *Gendered Justice in the American West: Women Prisoners in Men's Penitentiaries* (Urbana and Chicago: Univ. of Illinois Press, 1997). Gordon Morris Bakken and Brenda Farrington, *Women Who Kill Men: California Courts, Gender, and the Press* (Lincoln: Univ. of Nebraska Press, 2009), 1-16, is a more recent resource, providing examples from California that closely dovetail with many aspects of the *Geddes* trials.

This portrait of Regina Geddes was found on the person of Tom Welch at the time of his arrest and is the only known photo of any of the conspirators. Welch's possession of this photograph indicates that some of Winnie Brown's rumormongering was based in truth, or close enough to the truth to be uncomfortable. The Geddesses and Welch feared Winnie's gossip might ruin their reputations and impact an expected inheritance; death seemed the only way to silence him. PHOTOGRAPH FROM *STATE VS WELCH,* CASE 1329, MONTANA SUPREME COURT RECORDS, 1868-1938. SMFICHE 18. MONTANA HISTORICAL SOCIETY RESEARCH CENTER.

Thursday, when I killed the boy, about two o'clock, Mrs. Geddes was ironing in the kitchen; and she went into the front room and took field glasses and looked out and she says, "Dick, there comes the Brown boys." And she came back into the kitchen and wanted to know if I was not going to do that for George Geddes, and I told her "no" and she says "go on and kill him," so he would not go on the witness stand and swear against George Geddes, and I went and got the gun and got on my horse and went up the river, inside the fence and the irrigating ditch and went to the mouth of Lay Creek and stayed there in a canyon and waited for the boys to come past. I shot and ran around a big butte. When I got to the ranch, I says "Mrs. Geddes, I done it," and she says "I am not a damn bit sorry. He put us to a lot of trouble." I said, "I have done something I am sorry for, Mrs. Geddes," and she said, "I am not."[5]

[5] *State v. George Geddes,* Opinion 1308 of the Montana Supreme Court, Dec. 1899, *Reports of Cases Argued and Determined in the Supreme Court of the State of Montana from December 2, 1898 to May 29, 1899,* 22:68-92. Various elements of Dixon's testimony were summarized by the court in its opinion and are quoted here as printed in that document. Dixon's testimony in Tom Welch's trial is slightly different. In that trial, Regina Geddes was alleged to have said that "the son-of-a-bitch put us to a lot of trouble." *State v. Welch,* case 1329, Montana Supereme Court Records, 1868-1938, SMFICHE 18, MHS.

The motive—the "lot of trouble" to which Regina Geddes allegedly referred—was criminal first degree assault charges and an associated civil lawsuit pending in Custer County brought by Winnie Brown against George Geddes earlier that year.

In June 1897, George Geddes lured Winnie Brown to his ranch with an offer of work. He then forced Winnie to strip to his waist at the point of a revolver and tied his hands and feet. Geddes then hung Brown by his body a foot off the ground and beat the young man with a black snake whip—tipped with wire—for fifteen long minutes. It was a severe beating. He threatened to kill Brown multiple times with the revolver in his hand. Winnie went to the authorities when he was released, and soon Geddes was facing criminal charges and a lawsuit seeking $1,500 in damages.[6]

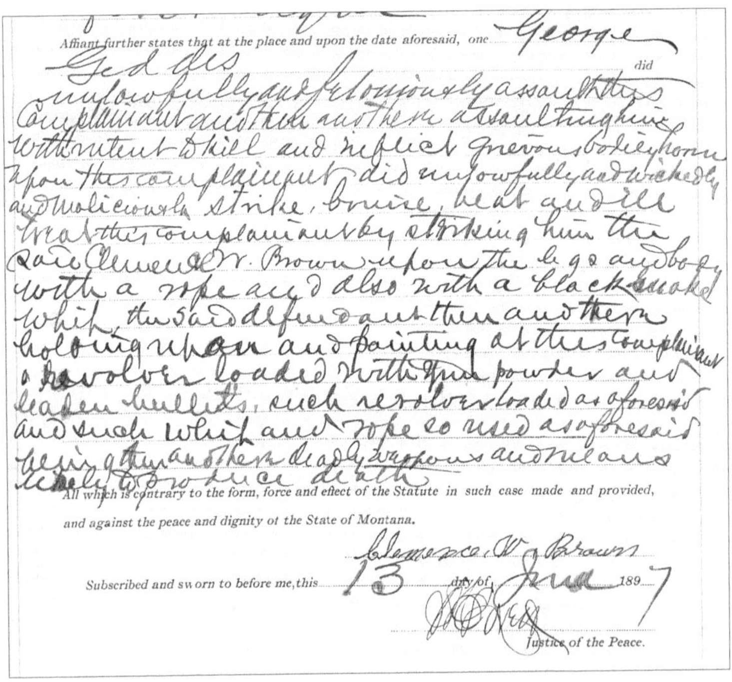
Affiant further states that at the place and upon the date aforesaid, one George Geddes did unlawfully and feloniously assault this complainant and then and there assaulting him with intent to kill and inflict grievous bodily harm upon this complainant did unlawfully and wickedly and maliciously strike, bruise, beat and ill treat this complainant by striking him the said Clemence W. Brown upon the legs and body with a rope and also with a black snake whip, the said defendant then and there holding upon and pointing at this complainant a revolver loaded with gun powder and leaden bullets, such revolver loaded as aforesaid and such whip and rope so used as aforesaid being then and there deadly weapons and means likely to produce death

All which is contrary to the form, force and effect of the Statute in such case made and provided, and against the peace and dignity of the State of Montana.

Clemence W. Brown

Subscribed and sworn to before me, this 13 day of June 1897

Justice of the Peace.

This June 13, 1897, assault complaint against George Geddes cost Clemence "Winnie" Brown his life. This image and caption were not included in the original *MMWH* article.

[6] *State v. George Geddes,* Charged with Assault, case 170, Jun. 13, 1897, Custer County Courthouse, Miles City. Geddes allegedly told Dixon he paused for a moment in his beating of Brown, "then he set down on the sill of the barn and rolled a cigarette, and took a little rest and said, 'as soon as I smoke I will whip you some more.'" This quote is from Dixon's testimony in the *George Geddes* murder case.

George Geddes whipped Winnie Brown to punish the young man for making scandalous comments about his family. John C. "Kid" Anderson, a trial witness, testified to a conversation with George after the county attorney filed the assault case:

> *That he asked [Geddes] how he was getting on with the case in regard to whipping Brown and [Geddes] said he had got it put off until the next term of court; that he had not presented his side of the case yet and, when he had, it would show up in a different light; that Brown had been talking about his famiy and that this talk had got to stop; that if it did not there would be something happen or words to that effect. In talking about the whipping of Brown, he said he was sorry he did not kill him; that, if he had to do it over again, he would. He said Winnie had been talking about his family, and he did not know why people did not leave his business alone, as he did not interfere with anybody else and that if this talk did not stop there would be something happen, or words to that effect.*[7]

According to Dixon, George Geddes was incensed by rumors spread by Winnie Brown and others that the Geddes' youngest child, born earlier that year, had a parentage that did not include him. Two candidates, it had been speculated, could be the natural father: Tom Welch and Dixon himself. Dixon testified to several conversations where George Geddes explicitly stated his intent to kill Brown after the whipping. In a buggy ride to Rosebud, Geddes told Dixon, "It's a good thing my arm is hurt. I was just getting so that I could ride, or I would have killed [Brown] long ago. I intended to kill him and roll him up in a canvas and throw him in a burning coal bank."[8]

Dixon described Tom Welch's participation in the plot. The shooter testified that George Geddes told him "If Tom Welch ever caught [Brown] in the hills, he would kill him, and nobody would know what had become of him." Welch was a twenty-nine-year-old cowpuncher who had worked on

[7] Various elements of Anderson's testimony were summarized by the supreme court in its opinion and are quoted here as printed in that document. *State v. George Geddes.*

[8] "A Black Fiend's Crime," *Billings Weekly Gazette,* Apr. 19, 1898. In the newspaper report of J.C. Anderson's testimony in Regina Geddes' trial, he related his conversation with George Geddes more specifically: "That Brown boy has done a whole lot of talking about my wife and has told around that [Dixon] is the father of my baby. I ought to have killed him, and if I had it to do over again I would." The identification of Welch as the baby's potential father was in Dixon's testimony in the Welch case. *State v. Welch; State v. George Geddes.*

ranches throughout Custer County. He was the son of a Scottish immigrant and a half-Indian mother from Washington. In 1888, Welch killed a man in Pennsylvania and successfully argued self-defense. Dixon testified that Regina Geddes quoted Welch as saying, "if a man had killed, another doesn't amount to anything."[9]

Dixon gave context to one of the prosecution's few pieces of physical evidence: a letter Welch wrote to Winnie Brown in August 1897. Two surviving Brown brothers testified how Welch had arrived at their ranch in the middle of the night, inquiring after Winnie. Upon learning Winnie was not present, Welch left the following letter and five dollars:

> *Lay Creek, Mont. August 15th, 1897*
> *Winifred Brown*
>
> *Friend Winnie:*
> *I wish you would come up to the OW ranch, be there Saturday, 21st. I want to see you on some important business. I will depend on you to be there as a friend. I will pay you well for your trouble. I will leave $5.00 for pocket money. The way to go to the OW is to go up the Tongue River to the mouth of Hanging Woman and up Hanging.*
> *Will depend on you to come.*
>
> *I remain as ever your friend.*
> *Tom Welch*[10]

Winnie Brown was suspicious of this offer and did not go to the OW. Jack Donahue, manager of the OW Ranch on Hanging Woman Creek, testified that Welch arrived one day in August, waiting all day for someone to arrive. Dixon testified that Regina Geddes told him Welch "had laid eighteen hours for the purpose of killing him." Tellingly, she informed Dixon about Welch's letter to

---

[9] In a case full of parallels to the Brown case, Welch had openly begun a romantic relationship with a white woman of dubious reputation while in Pennsylvania. She was the common-law wife of an African American man named Diggs Little, whose reputation was equally questionable. When Little confronted the couple in the street, Welch shot and killed Little. Little's dying declaration asserted that Welch was encouraged to shoot by his wife. "An Acquittal: The Montana Cowboy Who Killed a Man in Pennsylvania is Cleared by Jury." *Daily Yellowstone Journal*, Dec. 18, 1888, 1. "Not Guilty: Westward Now He Goes," *Valley Spirit* (Chambersburg, PA), Dec. 13, 1888, 3; *State v. Welch*.

[10] *State v. Welch*.

Winnie Brown, and that if Brown had met Welch, "he would have never come back." After the murder, this letter found its way to the prosecutor's desk.[11]

Furtermore, Dixon detailed the role of Regina Geddes in the conspiracy, including abetting and destroying evidence:

> *I wore a black silk handkerchief over my face. I cut two holes in it, so I could see, with a pen knife. When I got back to the ranch and showed Mrs. Geddes the handkerchief, she took it and burned it up in the kitchen stove—in the range. That was just after I got back from killing the boy. When I got back in the house first, I cleaned the gun and set it in the closet; and Mrs. Geddes went and got the gun and put it in the case and put it up between the ceiling and the stair landing.*[12]

Tom Welch was at least fifteen miles away when Dixon shot Winnie Brown, working a roundup for the Circle Bar Ranch on Otter Creek. At the same time, George Geddes was in Chicago for surgery on a disclocated arm.[13]

A few days after the killing, Tom Welch received a letter from Regina Geddes, which he burned after reading. Welch then informed his employer, Gus Howes of the Circle Bar Ranch, that he intended to leave the roundup even if it meant quitting. He requested that Howes cut an immediate check for fifty dollars in wages. Welch soon delivered that check to Regina Geddes, endorsing it to her. The two cashed the check at a Miles City bank, likely to pay Dixon. The sheriff's department arrested both of them soon after. A portrait of Regina Geddes was found on Welch's person when he was arrested.[14]

Murder conspiracies were nothing new to the northern plains, but an elaborate conspiracy involving an attractive young mother was. Initial newspaper reports immediately compared the Geddes cases to the Harry Hayward murder conspiracy. In 1894, Hayward, the "Minneapolis Svengali," used his

---

[11] Apparently, Welch's plan was to ambush Brown while alone on the prairie. Welch took special pains to offer Brown a particular horse, owned by George Geddes, to ride to the OW, as Brown did not have his own horse. Testimony in the *Welch* case claimed the horse was known to spook violently if it saw a rope near its feet. Welch denied the horse had this characteristic, and that the horse was a favorite of Brown's and was offered to him as part of a settlement. Winnie sent the note to Charles Brown (unknown if related, but not a sibling) with instructions to give it to the county attorney. *State v. Welch.*

[12] *State v. George Geddes.* Various elements of Dixon's testimony were summarized by the court in its opinion and are quoted here as printed in that document.

[13] *State v. George Geddes.*

[14] *State v. Welch.*

charm—and purportedly hypnosis—to have one of his lovers killed by a hired thug to collect on an insurance policy. Perhaps the most infamous example of female participation in nineteenth-century murder conspiracies was the case of Mary Surratt, who was convicted of involvement in Abraham Lincoln's assassination by a military commission in 1865 and given a death sentence. Mary Surratt joined three other conspirators hanged on July 7, 1865, the first woman executed by the federal government.[15]

Newspaper accounts of criminal activity by white women in the United States were often restricted to tragedies ascribed to mental health disorders. Lizzy Borden, infamous for the 1892 "forty whacks" axe killing of her father and stepmother—memorialized in a children's rhyme—exemplified how gender stereotypes played into explanations of violent crimes. Borden was exonerated based on the belief that she had either committed the crime in a fugue state brought on by abuse by her parents or else was not capable of doing it over doubts that a woman could produce the wounds. Jean Filetti observed that Borden's successful defense was "determined by the degree to which the 'victimized' woman demonstrates her feminity." The active participation of a white woman such as Regina Geddes in a conspiracy to murder a young man, especially one she did not seem to have a romantic attachment to, did not fit the mold.[16]

Winnie Brown's death resulted in three separate criminal trials and a formal proceeding where Dixon pleaded guilty to second-degree murder. George Geddes

---

15 "Dickinson Tells it All," *Anaconda Standard*, Nov. 9, 1897, 1. Quoting the first sentence of the article: "The Brown murder case has taken a new turn and Montana has a Harry Hayward case with all the embellishments." Shawn Francis Peters, *The Infamous Harry Hayward: A True Account of Murder and Mesmerism in Gilded Age Minneapolis* (Minneapolis: Univ. of Minnesota Press, 2018), 1-49. Hayward's murder victim was Catherine Ging, a dressmaker. Notably, the conspiracy to assassinate President Lincoln and other high government members was initially a kidnapping plot. There was little evidence to suggest Mary Surratt knew the conspiracy leaders' late change in plan. Surratt's involvement was seemingly limited to providing a meeting place and knowledge of the initial plot. Even with the patriotic zeal to avenge the killing of Lincoln, the military commission still faced difficulty sentencing a woman to hang. Fred L. Borch, "'Let the stain of innocent blood be removed from the land': The Trial of the Lincoln Assassination Conspirators by Military Commission," *Army History* 86 (Winter 2013): 6-19. The lower evidence standards of a military commission, as compared to a civilian court, facilitated Mary Surratt's conviction, and she was given a death sentence. A majority of the commission compromised by pronouncing the death sentence and at the same time appealing to President Andrew Johnson for commutation of the same. Controversially, Johnson claimed he never received the appeal in time. John W. Clampitt, "the Trial of Mrs. Surratt," *North American Review* 131:286 (Sep. 1880): 223-40.

16 The phrase comes from a well-known children's rhyme about the Borden killings: "Lizzie Borden had an axe. She gave her mother 40 whacks. When she saw what she had done, she gave her father 41." Jean S. Filetti, "Lizzie Borden to Lorena Bobbitt: Violent Women and Gendered Justice," *Journal of American Studies* 35:3 (Dec. 2001): 471-84. See also Joseph A. Conforti, *Lizzie Borden on Trial: Murder, Ethnicity, and Gender* (Lawrence: Univ. of Kansas, 2015).

The Custer County Courthouse, circa 1884. Located in Miles City, the courthouse hosted the trials of both George Geddes and Tom Welch. The amount of publicity and overall spectacle of these trials convinced Judge Charles Loud to approve Regina Geddes' request to have her trial moved to Billings in hopes of finding a more impartial jury. PHOTOGRAPH BY W.E. SAVAGE, COURTESY OF THE MONTANA HISTORICAL SOCIETY, 949-272.

was first to the criminal bar, followed by Tom Welch and Regina Geddes. Unlike Dixon, the others charged with Brown's murder were accused as members of the same conspiracy, only legally distinguishable by their individual participation in the plot and the evidence presented. Chief among that evidence was the testimony of the actual killer, who, during the conspirators' trials, had yet to face his own hearing. The prosecution was aided by the temporary services of Jason W. Strevell, a well-known litigator, former judge, rancher, and personal friend of Abraham Lincoln. The ex-judge provided such oratorical skill and reputational heft that the Geddes defense claimed in later filings that Strevell exerted "undue influence over the jurors in Custer County." Attorney Charles H. Loud was the trial judge and also a Custer County rancher who had been a delegate to Montana's 1889 constitutional convention.[17]

[17] Affidavits for Change of Venue by the Defense, Mar. 1898, *State v. Regina Geddes,* Case 179, 1897-1898, Custer County Courthouse, Miles City; *State v. Regina Geddes,* 1898, Yellowstone County Courthouse, Billings. Range Rider Reps, *Fanning the Embers* (Billings: Gazette Printing and Lithography, 1971), 252-53. Complicating matters for the Custer County prosecutor was another well-publicized set of trials handled by his office: the "Little Whirlwind" cases. Sheepherder John Hoover was murdered by members of the Northern Cheyenne four months before and within a few miles of Winnie Brown's killing. Immediately after Hoover's killing, many white settlers evacuated their homes for fear of the "Cheyenne Outbreak of 1897." These tensions eased when the Cheyennes turned over the alleged killer and his accomplices. The trials of these two high-profile murders coinciding put immense pressure on the prosecutor. Regarding the *Little Whirlwind* cases, see Orlan J. Svingen, *The Northern Cheyenne Indian Reservation, 1877–1900* (Niwot: Univ. Press of Colorado, 19930, 113-29). For Strevell's biography, see Charles Nettleton Strevell, As I Recall Them (Salt Lake City: Stevens and Wallis Company, 1943), 11-26, 43-123.

Regina Geddes faced the most difficult legal headwinds of the three conspirators. All faced first-degree murder charges, but neither George Geddes nor Tom Welch were present when Dixon killed Brown, nor in the immediate aftermath. According to Dixon, Regina Geddes ordered the killing that day, concealed and destroyed evidence, and provided the assassin with a false alibi. Given these circumstances, the different verdicts handed down suggest that there was something other than the law, the facts, or the lawyers that drove each jury's decision-making. The gender of each defendant materially impacted the behavior of law enforcement, the court system, and the press, which resulted in a verdict that freed Regina Geddes.

In 1897, Custer County was sparsely populated and covered much of eastern Montana south of the Yellowstone River. Law enforcement was centered in Miles City, the county seat. The Custer County Sheriff's Office's first encounter with the Winnie Brown shooting was Special Deputy Johnnie Stafford from nearby Ashland. Stafford followed the tracks of Dixon's horse to the Geddes ranch. During the trial, Stafford admitted under cross-examination that if he

A view of Ashland, circa 1908. Deputy Johnnie Stafford from Ashland conducted the initial investigation due to proximity to the murder site. In 1900, the town relocated six miles to the confluence of the Tongue River and Otter Creek in order to be outside the boundaries of the newly expanded Northern Cheyenne Indian Reservation. PHOTOGRAPH BY L.A. HUFFMAN, MONTANA HISTORICAL SOCIETY, 981-1164.

"had the deciding of the case, he would turn Mrs. Geddes loose, even though he knew she was guilty."[18]

After his arrest, Dixon initially kept quiet. Sheriff John Gibb and county attorney T.J. Porter wore the suspected shooter down, and Dixon initially identified Tom Welch as the shooter. The sheriff informed Dixon about Welch's airtight alibi, but it was only when Dixon heard Welch quoted as saying "the black son-of-a-bitch ought to hang for it" that Dixon started talking in earnest. Dixon's rumored cooperation caused Regina Geddes to write the killer, an act somehow allowed by Sheriff Gibb. This letter titillated trial onlookers and may have shifted Dixon's attittude toward confessing.[19]

The *Yellowstone Journal* described the letter's impact on public perception:

> *During [Dixon's] examination, a large number of women, attracted out of curiosity, occupied seats in the court room and seemed to take delight in listening to the tale of murder, but they hid their faces when the negro told about a certain letter that he said he received from Mrs. Geddes. That letter, however, didn't show that the defendant was other than a virtuous woman but simply demanded to know if the negro had made certain statements reflecting on the chastity of herself and two sisters. The language of the letter was its worst feature and would not look nice in cold type.*[20]

Allowing the defendants to communicate before the trial did not seem to concern Custer County's law enforcement officials either. George Geddes and Tom Welch were housed in adjoining cells. George Geddes had not offered any alternative explanations for his action during his own trial. At the subsequent proceedings against Tom Welch, the defense claimed Welch's efforts to communicate with Brown were actually a good faith attempt by Geddes to settle Brown's lawsuit. The prosecution directed the jury's attention to the probability of collusion between the two defendants housed in adjoining cells.[21]

---

[18] "The Geddes Trial," *Billings Semi-Weekly Gazette*, Apr. 22, 1898, 5.

[19] The letter and Welch's comment that Dixon should hang angered the killer into full cooperation. Dixon's first statement as a cooperating witness claimed that Welch was the shooter. *State v. Welch*. Dixon had reason to fear extra-legal violence, given the history of lynching in the region and the United States. See Michael J. Pfeifer, *Rough Justice: Lynching and American Society 1874–1947* (Urbana: Univ. of Illinois Press, 2004).

[20] *Yellowstone Journal*, May 12, 1898, 3.

[21] *State v. Welch*.

While unsupervised communications between jailed male defendants was not a problem for the court, Regina's motherhood was. Locking up the mother of three children (aged five, three, and six months) for an extended period caused the court considerable angst. When Regina was jailed in Miles City during her husband's and Welch's trials, the court ensured the young mother had supervised visitation with her children for an hour up to two times a week. George Geddes received no such consideration.[22]

The trial judge for the murder trials, Charles H. Loud (pictured ca. 1915) was a well-known rancher and lawyer. It was his decision to move Regina's trial to Billings—a move he likely regretted once her trial gained even greater publicity from the *Billings Gazette*. After the jury hung 11-1 on acquitting Regina, Loud refused to move the location for a possible retrial, and the combination of drained public finances and a hostile environment for the prosecution meant that Regina kept her freedom once and for all. PHOTOGRAPH BY E.G. WILLIAMS & BRO., MONTANA HISTORICAL SOCIETY, PAC 2010-32.05.

Due to enormous publicity and a shrinking jury pool, Judge Loud moved Regina Geddes' trial to Billings at her lawyer's request. Yellowstone County sheriff George Berky then became embroiled in controversy regarding his unusual treatment of the now-infamous Mrs. Geddes. The prosecution complained that the sheriff "sought to enlist the sympathy of the community on behalf of the defendant by parading her on the public streets and taking her to dinner in a public place and that he was unfriendly toward the prosecution." Sheriff Berky hotly denied giving Geddes special treatment. He admitted he had taken the defendant to a millinery store and to a restaurant on separate occasions. During the restaurant trip, they had

[22] "Order of Judge C.H. Loud to the Sheriff of Custer County," Nov. 19, 1897, *State v. Regina Geddes*, Custer County Courthouse. Quoting the order: "The sheriff of this County place the said Mrs. George S. Geddes in the charge of some trusted deputy, as often as twice a week, until further order of this court, for the purpose of taking her to the said place where her infant children are, whose duty it shall be to permit her to visit her children on each occasion for the period of one hour, during all of which time she is to be under the immediate charge of such officer, whose duty it shall be to return her to the said jail."

taken their supper in a private room in the company of the sheriff's wife and children. Fresh painting and wallpapering in the sheriff's office had closed the kitchen that day, forcing Berky to make those arrangements. It is noteworthy that the sheriff laundered the spectacle with the presence of his own family.[23]

At the trials, too, the question of motive held gendered implications. George Geddes' brutal assault on Brown was understood to have been a masculine defense against Brown's alleged rumormongering. If he lost the resulting criminal and civil cases, Geddes would be liable for damages. That uncomplicated motive was as far as Richard Dixon's testimony could take the prosecution, and the jury found it adequate for conviction. By this motive, George had unlawfully defended his honor by whipping Winnie. The resulting lawsuits threatened George's status as an adequate provider for his family and his fragile reputation as a monied man. Regina's motive for directing the murder was similarly straightforward and as feminine as her husband's was masculine. Her directing of Winnie's killing was to support her husband and in defense of her reputation. The juries understood these gender norms.[24]

The prosecution team's presentation of George and Regina Geddes' motives fit late nineteenth-century concepts of how men and women might behave under such circumstances. However, these motives do not account for the extraordinary efforts made to silence Winnie Brown that a more thorough examination would have revealed: the sexual practices and financial realities of the Geddes family. It is doubtful the trial judge would have allowed such inflammatory evidence. Still, the prosecution did carefully imply some of these delicate matters, particularly in the Tom Welch trial. This attempt backfired on prosecutors Porter and Strevell, though, when the *Welch* case came before the Montana Supreme Court.[25]

---

[23] Affidavits for Change of Venue by the State, Jun. 1898, *State v. Regina* Geddes, Yellowstone County Courthouse, Billings, MT.

[24] Since he was already convicted, George was able to testify for the defense in Welch's trial. When questioned about his whipping of Brown, Geddes testified, "I tell this jury that in whipping that boy I didn't consider myself in the wrong. I considered that I was doing right. I suppose it is a right any man has. Under sufficient provocation, it is a right that any man has to best another." *State v. Welch.* For a discussion of women's criminality in the West, see Bakken and Farrington, *Women Who Kill Men,* 1-5, 55-80.

[25] Quoting the Montana Supreme Court's opinion: "The sole purpose the State could have had in using the picture before the jury was that they might be afforded the priviledge of inferring an intimacy, possibly criminal in its nature, between Welch and the wife of George Geddes." *State v. Welch,* Case 1329, Montana Supreme Court Opinion, Reports of Cases Argued and Determined in the Supreme Court of the State of Montana from December 12, 1898 to May 29, 1899, 22:92-99.

The prosecution hired attorney Jason W. Strevell to assist them during the Geddes and Welch trials. His oratorical skills were well known, and his talents were said to have unfairly swayed the jury. Strevell, a politician and lawyer, had gained experience in the lower house of the Illinois legislature before moving to Montana. PHOTOGRAPH COURTESY OF THE RANGE RIDERS MUSEUM, MILES CITY.

The prosecution implied that the "friendship" between the Geddesses and Tom Welch was more than platonic. Trial testimony stated that Welch was unusually welcome at the Geddes ranch, no matter the time, always arriving alone. Phillip White, a former employee, testified about a particular night at the Geddes home. Tom Welch arrived around eleven o'clock at night and went directly to the master bedroom, where both Geddeses were present. White testified that he heard Welch welcomed into the room by Regina. The prosecution evoked Dixon's testimony regarding the possible parentage of the youngest Geddes child. Bolstering this implication, the prosecution revealed the existence of a secret and lengthy written correspondence between Welch and Regina Geddes. Welch admitted to destroying his correspondence with George and Regina Geddes and denied they contained anything indecent. Finally, the prosecution showed the jury the portrait of Regina Geddes found on Welch during his arrest. George admitted knowing Welch had the image and claimed Welch also possessed pictures of the Geddes children.[26]

[26] Dixon testified that Regina Geddes read one of her Welch letters to him before having Dixon deliver the letter to the post office. The contents of this letter warned Welch that his OW letter to Brown was in the possession of the county attorney. Dixon also testified that Regina wrote in the note that she "couldn't write to him what she wanted to tell him." In addition, Dixon stated under oath that Regina never asked him to deliver letters addressed to Welch when George was present. Regina's actions may have been an attempt to manipulate Dixon into committing the crime by exacerbating the rivalry between Dixon and Welch. Welch himself testified that the letter he burned at the roundup was a request from Regina to borrow fifty dollars. He did not state a reason for the request. *State v. Welch.*

George's seeming acquiescence—if not participation—in these behaviors between his friend and his spouse is inconsistent with his supposed motive for harming Winnie Brown. Geddes insisted that when he told his side of the assault case, "it would show up in a different light." As a white man in the Victorian Era, George Geddes could avail himself of numerous legal remedies if his wife were simply unfaithful. Historian Hendrick Hartog described the "Unwritten Law" of the time that allowed a cuckolded husband to kill his wife's lover, but only if they were caught in the act and the husband acted immediately. Yet Winnie Brown was not Regina's lover, and George's attack was premeditated. The whipping was an obvious crime that George Geddes could not legally justify as a wronged husband. Given this, another explanation more squarely fits Geddes' behavior: at least some aspect of Brown's rumormongering was true, and Geddes was willing to risk imprisonment to quash these stories.[27]

George Geddes was a figure known in the American West as a "remittance man." This term described a young man, usually the son of European nobles or wealthy eastern Americans, who came west to play cowboy but depended on regular family remittances to maintain their lifestyle. Apparently, George was also a heavy drinker:[28]

> *Peter Geddes, a multi-millionaire of New York City, bought a big cattle ranch on Tongue River for his son George . . . [George] never stayed at the ranch, spent his time in Miles City soaked to the gills. One day he loaded up on the remedy for snake bites, got on his horse, rode down to the depot and roped the smokestack of a freight engine. When the train was ready to pull out the engineer told him to take his rope off. George said he would not do it [as] he intended to hold the train until he got ready for them to go. The engineer threw in the throttle. George set back on his horse. Faster and faster they went until the horse was jerked off his feet and dragged. It should have been curtains but the rope broke. When George got up [he] had left part of his hide mingled with the cinders and for once in his life he was duly sober.*[29]

---

[27] *State v. George Geddes*. Hendrick Hartog, "Lawyering, Husband's Rights, and 'the Unwritten Law' in Nineteenth-Century America," *Journal of American History* 84:1 (Junc. 1997): 67-96.

[28] Wally McRae, "Regina Geddes." *It's Just Grass and Water* (Spokane: The Oxalis Group, 1986)

[29] Mark H. Brown and W.R. Felton, *The Frontier Years: L.A. Huffman, Photographer of the Plains* (New York: Henry Holt and Company, 1955), 155.

Peter Geddes was a Scottish immigrant and the American representative of one of the world's wealthiest men, George "Chicago" Smith. Smith, also from Scotland, invested much of his considerable fortune in railroads. As Smith's American agent, Peter Geddes was a long-serving member of the Chicago, Milwaukee, and St. Paul Railroad Board of Directors and himself a man of considerable wealth.[30]

George Smith Geddes bore the name of his father's patron and may have been Smith's godson. At the time of Brown's murder, Smith was living a secluded London retirement and in failing health—he died in 1899. After the trials, the prosecutors speculated that George Geddes' assault on Winnie Brown threatened an anticipated inheritance from Smith. By 1897, Geddes was financially struggling. His cattle ranch had found only minor success. His other independent income source was his position as postmaster of the Geddes, Montana, post office—named after himself—which closed days before the Brown murder due to small volume. The nature of George Geddes' inheritance was not certain or widely known. Therefore, George could credibly assert that Brown's $1,500 damage claim represented a real financial threat to him even as other, more dire reasons were kept hidden. These hidden

A portrait of George Smith, a Scottish investor and financier. Among the wealthiest individuals in the world at the time, Smith invested heavily in railroads in the United States. Peter Geddes, George Geddes' father, was a business associate of Smith and received a bequest upon Smith's death in 1899. Peter Geddes financed the defense of George, Regina, and Tom Welch, and passed along some of George Smith's money after the Montana Supreme Court overturned George's conviction, making him a free man. PHOTOGRAPH COURTESY OF THE WISCONSIN HISTORICAL SOCIETY, WHI105161.

[30] Alice E. Smith, *George Smith's Money: A Scottish Investor in America* (Stevens Point, WI: Worzalla Publishing/The State Historical Society of Wisconsin, 1966), 149-59.

motives far better explain a tight-knit and elaborate murder plot involving four conspirators over six months.[31]

Geddes differed from other remittance men of that area in both agricultural success and local reputation. He felt disdain for working people like Winnie Brown, enough that he felt entitled to savagely whip the young man. "I myself was the judge of the provocation," Geddes testified. "That is the rule that I expect to set upon with that particular class of folks." This classist contempt for Winnie Brown and his family was shared by Tom Welch, who testified that "everyone who is well acquantied with them [the Browns] speak of their being shy, that they are backward."[32]

Regina Geddes was aware of the possible financial legacy from Peter Geddes or George Smith and that her husband's recklessness threatened this inheritance. She came from a hardscrabble home—her widowed mother ran a Unionville boardinghouse. Regina and George had three chidren, only one whose paternity was in question. Peter Geddes' estate acknowledged all three children when the elder Geddes died in 1913. Winnie Brown's lawsuit threatened the financial security provided by Regina's marriage and embodied in her three children, offering a strong motive for Mrs. Geddes to ensure the boy's permanent silence.[33]

---

[31] *Ravalli Republic* (Hamilton), Jun. 7, 1901, 3; "Recalls an Almost Forgotten Tragedy," *Anaconda Standard*, May 30, 1901, 11. *State v. George Geddes.* George Smith's will became the subject of considerable public angst after his death, with several anticipated beneficiaries being disappointed. "George Smith's Will," *Chicago Tribune*, Nov. 8, 1899, 1. While George Geddes' wealth at the time of Brown's murder cannot be determined, it is known that his father funded the legal defense. "20 Years for Welsh," *Helena Independent*, Feb. 5, 1898, 5.

[32] Two similar remittance men, Sidney Paget and Oliver Wallop, both had reputations as horse breeders and honorable employers, even if their morals were sometimes questionable. Paget in particular was notable as a playboy who publicly associated with Connie Huffman, to whom he was not married. For information on Oliver Wallop, see Floyd C. Bard, *Horse Wrangler* (Norman: Univ. of Oklahoma Press, 1960); and Gerard Wallop, *A Knot of Roots* (New York: New American Library, 1965). For Sidney Paget, see Mark Brown and W.R. Felton, *The Frontier Years* (New York: Henry Holt, 1955.) For Connie Huffman, see Milton F. Ayers, "Connie Huffman: Early Day Character of Eastern Montana and Intimate Friend of Many Early Day Stock Men," Item #31, *Federal Writers Project Collection* (Montana, Custer County), Custer County Library Montana Room, Miles City. *State v. Welch.* For detailed discussions of class-based violence in the American West, see *Clare v. McKanna Jr., Homicide, Race and Justice in the American West, 1899–1920* (Tuscon: Univ. of Arizona Press, 1997), 84-98; and Marilynn S. Johnson, *Violence in the West: The Johnson County War and the Ludlow Massacre* (Long Grove, IL: Waveland Press, 2009), 18–33.

[33] Regina Geddes to the *Helena Independent*, Aug. 8, 1951, bx 1, fldr 49, Collection 3, MHS. Probate Records of Peter Geddes, Mar. 4, 1914; Catherine Downey to Joseph Tanzer, 1914, Probate Administration Records, Probate Place, New York Surrogate's Court, Kings County, New York. *Marriage Record of Emily Geddes Bailey, Feb. 5, 1913,* Oregon Marriage Records, 1906-1910, 1946-1966, Salem Oregon, Oregon State Archives.

Winnie's loose talk was a major issue for Regina. Similar aspersions regarding her fidelity led her to admonish Richard Dixon in writing while he was in jail. However, the truth of her and her husband's sexual habits may have left her scant legal recourse concerning these rumors. Included among these may have been that George's participation in Regina's escapades was due to sexual dysfunction, which may result from long-term alcohol abuse. Other explanations for George's alleged assent to his wife's behavior, including a ménage à trois, are also possible. In any event, Regina's motivations seem much more nuanced than the gender-laden trope of a wronged woman having her honor defended by a man.

The Brown murder conspiracy garnered considerable attention in Montana newspapers and from the public. Spectators packed the courtrooms. The rhetoric of the *Yellowstone Journal* and the *Billings Gazette* was so inflammatory that, on separate occasions, both the prosecution and the defense requested changes of venue based in no small part on the news coverage. That sensationalism employed familiar tropes around gender and race. The *Yellowstone Journal* described the African American gunman as "anything but prepossessing in appearance and in a beauty contest would not even receive mention among others that contested." The Miles City paper added an innuendo-filled preview of the forthcoming trials when George was sentenced: "Geddes continues to take his sentence of 99 years with [the] same sang froid and reckless indifference that marked his behavior when he first heard the verdict read." In contrast, that same article emphasized Regina's femininity and sexuality: "Mrs. Geddes requested Sheriff Gibb yesterday to be permitted to spend the night in her husband's cell. The request was refused. She is now engaged in preparing an elaborate costume to wear during the trial. Every article will be silk and of the latest style and pattern." In the analysis of the *Yellowstone Journal,* George was masculine and stoic, while the depiction of his wife emphasized her appearance and perceived sexual appetites.[34] Prosecutor T.J. Porter used his opening statement to Regina Geddes' jury to assert that "the beauty of the fair defendant who is on trial for her life is to her what a royal robe would be to a demon queen."[35]

The sensationalism of the *Yellowstone Journal* was put to shame by the *Billings Gazette* when Judge Loud moved Regina Geddes' trial to Yellowstone

[34] *Yellowstone Journal,* May 12, 1898, 3; McRae, "Regina Geddes," 34-35; "Sexual Function Loss Tied to Alcohol Abuse," Public Health Reports 95:5 (Sep.- Oct. 1980):497-98.

[35] Affidavits for Change of Venue by the Defense, Mar. 1898; Affidavits for Change of Venue by the State, Jun. 1898, *State v. Regina Geddes.* "Welch on Trial," *Yellowstone Journal,* Jan. 27, 1898, 1; "Geddes and Wife," *Yellowstone Journal,* Jan. 13, 1898, 1; "A Fair Demon," *Helena Independent Record,* Apr.15, 1898, 2.

County. The paper became consumed with the spectacle of an attractive young mother on trial for murder. Only the declaration of war against Spain kept the trial off the front page. Readers of the *Gazette* were nonetheless bombarded by colorful headlines and sub-headlines such as "She is a Fine Looker," "Mrs. Geddes is Nervy," and "Fair Female on Trial."[36] The actual reporting was equally focused on her appearance and allure:

> *When court opened yesterday morning Mrs. Geddes, faultlessly attired, occupied a seat just inside the railing, with her back to the spectators. She is prepossessing in appearance, albeit what might be termed handsome. Thus far, she has maintained a calm and dignified demeanor, showing hardly a trace of nervousness. She is a woman who would attract attention in most any gathering and in most any place. Her big, coal black eyes, shaded by long lashes, are a distinguishing feature of her physiognomy. Unlike the prisoner however, they are restless. As black as a jet, they seem to look through and through a person.*[37]

ON TRIAL FOR HER LIFE

Murder Case of the State Against Mrs. Geddes Began in the District Court.

SHE IS A FINE LOOKER

Work of Securing a Jury Nearly Completed—Taking of Evidence to Begin Thursday.

This headline greeted page three readers of the *Billings Gazette* in its April 12, 1898, edition. This image and caption were not included in the original *MMWH* article.

The press coverage characterized Regina as either the conniving harlot defending her illusory virtue or the beautiful white Andromeda facing daunting odds. Reporters swooned over her beauty, demeanor, dress, children, and sisters. Her personal biography was almost entirely ignored, except for some western Montana papers that noted her family's history in Lewis and Clark County. Likewise, George Geddes and Tom Welch were always described in masculine terms, even the decidedly negative ones. However, their

[36] "This Means War," *Billings Weekly Gazette*, Apr. 15, 1898, 1; "Fair Female on Trial," *Billings Weekly Gazette*, Apr. 15, 1898, "On Trial for Her Life," *Billings Gazette*, Apr. 12, 1898; "Fair Female on Trial," *Billings Weekly Gazette*, Apr. 15, 1898, 5; "A Black Fiend's Crime," *Billings Weekly Gazette*, Apr. 12, 1898, 3.

[37] "On Trial for Her Life," *Billings Gazette*, Apr. 12, 1898, 3.

looks and physiognomy were scarcely commented on, and then only to bring attention to Tom Welch's Native American descent.[38]

To absolve the attractive white mother, the *Billings Gazette* needed a target and quickly found it in racist stereotypes of Richard Dixon. The paper described the admitted shooter in blatantly racist terms and highlighted inconsistencies in his testimony: "The state's star witness [Richard Dixon], the black fiend incarnate who sent the soul of poor Winnie Brown unbidden into eternity to save his own miserable, worthless neck, has given his testimony and made way for other witnesses for the prosecution." The *Gazette* continued its use of racist slurs in describing Dixon, stating, "In appearance, he is vicious and absolutely repulsive . . . the grinning Senegambian became greatly enraged at times and fairly shouted forth some of his answers."[39]

George and Regina Geddes' parental responsibilities evoked gendered treatment in the newspapers as well. During his trial, coverage of George never included descriptions of him being a father to three young children. Only after his conviction and sentencing was this fact relevant to the *Billings Gazette,* but solely to draw attention to Regina Geddes' newly imposed plight as a young mother. "The woman who is the center of attraction in this important trial is the mother of three small and beautiful children, the youngest a babe in arms," the *Gazette* reported. "They are being cared for by the prisoner's sister

[38] Regina's mother, Mary Goetz Johnston, divorced her husband when Mary was fifteen, based on abandonment. A few years later, Mary married Patrick Powers, the sheriff of Lewis and Clark County. The couple had three daughters and one son before Patrick died from a short illness. Throughout most of her adolescent years, Regina Johnston used the surname "Powers." Some western Montana newspapers were quick to deny Sheriff Powers' parentage of Regina Geddes. Powers' lack of parentage and the fact that Regina grew up near Helena is the only biographical information that some newspapers saw fit to print. For press denying Regina's father was Powers, see *Anaconda Standard,* Jul. 2, 1898, 6. For Powers' family, see *Tenth Census of the United States, 1880. Unionville, Lewis and Clark County, Montana;* Roll: 742; Page 309A; Enumeration District: 019 (NARA microfilm publication T9, 1,454 rolls), Records of the Bureau of Census, RG 29, National Archives, Washington, D.C. On Powers' death, see "Jottings About Town," *Helena Independent-Record,* Oct. 22, 1892, 6; On Powers' marriage to Mary Johnston, see *Helena Weekly Herald,* Nov. 23, 1873, 8. "Welch on Trial," *Yellowstone Journal,* Jan. 27, 1898, 1; Quoting the article: "The hair would indicate a strain of the Negro, but this the features belie, which are more suggestive of the Indian of the southern rather than the northern continent. The eyes, well apart and restless, but of goodly size are also indicative of the Indian. The *Journal's* analysis of Welch's physical form is an amateurish application of scientific racism, which was popular at the time. For race in the courtroom, see Peggy Pascoe, *What Comes Naturally: Miscegenation Law and the Making of Race in America* (New York: Oxford Univ. Press, 2009) 109-30.

[39] "A Black Fiend's Crime," *Billings Weekly Gazette,* Apr. 19, 1898, 3. Dixon was born in Iowa, so the "Senegambian" reference is clearly a racist slur. "Dixon, Richard" in Montana state prison records, "Descriptive list of Prisoners Received at the State Prison During the Fiscal Year Dec. 1896-1904," Jul. 15, 1898, Montana State Archives, SMF 36, MHS.

in the absence of their father, who is serving a sentence of ninety-nine years." Regina's motherhood presented a problem for the all-male jury. "The case looks very black for the accused, but the fact that the prisoner is a woman with three small children will doubtless have weight with the jury," the *Yellowstone Journal* speculated. "Though her husband was given a life sentence on evidence less conclusive of conspiracy and this despite the fact he was in Chicago when the crime was committed."[40]

Billings citizens openly questioned the jury's ability to convict Regina. Witness Fannie McGurk swore in an affidavit that "the jury which did try her was what they called an acquittal jury . . . no jury there would convict simply because she was a woman and a mother." On May 3, 1898, the Regina Geddes jury hung, with only one juror considering a murder charge. "After the jury had been discharged, the ten men who had voted for acquittal on every ballot gave vent to their feelings and roasted to a finish the man who had been the cause of the disagreement," the *Billings Gazette* reported. "It appears that [the contrary juror] offered to compromise on a verdict of murder in the second degree with the minimum penalty—ten years. The others, however, wouldn't entertain any such proposition."[41]

Contrast this with the *Yellowstone Journal's* jury interview for the George Geddes trial in Miles City. "The first ballot was unanimous on the question of the defendant's guilt. A second ballot was then taken as to the degree of the crime. This resulted in one vote for murder in the first degree and 11 for murder in the second degree," the *Journal* reported. "Several more ballots followed, all with the same result. The jury then asked for further instructions, which were received and again retired and more balloting followed until the final ballot when the man who so long had held to his opinion surrendered, and a verdict was reached."[42]

The Tom Welch jury struggled to obtain its verdict, taking fifty-four hours to a compromise that was similarly lopsided. "The statement is made authoritatively that on the first ballot, the vote stood two for acquittal and ten for conviction," the *Yellowstone Journal* reported. "One of the men who voted in favor of the defendant changed front on the second vote and after that the vote stood

[40] "On Trial for Her Life," *Billings Gazette,*" Apr. 12, 1898, 3; "Mrs. Geddes Trial," *Yellowstone Journal,* Apr. 28, 1898, 3

[41] Affidavits for Change of Venue by the State, Jun. 1898, *State v. Regina Geddes.* "One Man Hangs Eleven," *Billings Weekly Gazette,* May 3, 1898, 3.

[42] "Found Him Guilty," *Yellowstone Journal*, Feb. 10, 1898, 3.

eleven to one until the last ballot when he gave in and a verdict was reached." While there were subtle differences in each trial, each had the same fundamental structure. None of the three conspirators had shot Brown. Much of the evidence of their involvement in a conspiracy was Dixon's testimony, and he had the motivation to lighten his sentence through cooperation with the prosecutors.[43]

The trial location alone cannot explain the differing verdicts, which brings forth questions of race and gender. Community and juror bias is plausible. Detailed news accounts of the first two trials were published throughout Montana, so intense publicity was not limited to Custer County. It seems unlikely that proximity would explain how the three juries came to such different conculsions regarding the veracity of Dixon's testimony. Jurors from both communities evaluated Richard Dixon, so the impact of Dixon's race in the deliberations of the all-white juries would not seem to be the deciding factor, given that Miles City and Billings were both moderately sized frontier communities less than 150 miles apart. Miles City juries convicted the two male conspiracists in two separate trials. Male juries decided all three *Geddes* trials. Montana did not allow women to serve as jurors until 1924, despite receiving the right to vote in 1914. It seems unlikely that some characteristic unique to either city made these divergent verdicts possible. It is not only the verdict themselves that were contrary, but even the first ballots of all three juries reflect strongly divergent opinions. George Geddes was unanimously guilty, Welch was ten to two guilty, while Regina Geddes was eleven to one for acquittal. These are not difference in shade; they are difference in kind.[44]

[43] "Tom Welch Convicted," *Yellowstone Journal*, Feb. 10, 1898, 3.

[44] Juries in Miles City were known for avoiding convictions. Later, in 1910, after Ray Tarbell was released following two separate trials that failed to convict him of murdering George Mitchell, the *Miles City Independent* lamented, "There was not a Miles City man on the jury, contrary to the general belief, which asserted that Miles City people have turned loose every man from the county charged with a crime." "Tarbell Goes Free," *Miles City Independent*, Jun. 15, 1910, 8. T.A. Larson, "Montana Women and the Battle for the Ballot," *Montana* 23:1 (Winter 1973): 24-41. As Christina Rodriguez has explained, in the nineteenth century to serve on juries was not as intertwined with the right to vote as is currently held. Christina M. Rodriguez, "Clearing the Smoke-Filled Room: Women Jurors and the Disruption of an Old-Boys' Network in Nineteenth-Century America," *Yale Law Journal* 108:7 (May 1999): 1805–44. Rodriguez's review illustrates the short-lived experience with mixed-gendered juries in two western states in the nineteenth century: Wyoming and Washington. The first mixed jury in America occurred in March 1870 in Laramie, Wyoming, where the trope that female jurors could not "relate" to capital murder crimes was quickly dispelled. In the case of Andrew Howie, a six-man and six-woman jury returned a verdict of first-degree manslaughter. During that term of court, the district judge found that defense attorneys soon began using their peremptory challenge to strike female jurors because they were too "law-and-order." However, women's presence on juries quickly fell into widespread disfavor in Wyoming Territory and was discontinued after 1871. However, frontier women jurors were more than capable of handling any of the three Geddes trials on the merits. Nancy Marder, "Gender Dynamics and Jury Deliberations," *Yale Law Journal* 96:3 (Jan. 1987): 593-612.

After Judge Loud denied the prosecution's change of venue request for Regina Geddes' retrial, county attorney Porter was faced with a conundrum. He would have to conduct a new trial in what he viewed as a hostile environment with severely strained finances. The *Geddes* trials had drained Custer County's funds to the point of collapse. Because of this, he declined to retry Regina Geddes. By June 1898, she was a free woman. Porter's woes did not end there. In March 1899, the Montana Supreme Court reversed the convictions of both George Geddes and Tom Welch, ordering new trials. The basis for the reversal was an overreliance on the testimony of conspirator Richard Dixon in violation of Montana's penal code. The court criticized the prosecution's conduct, particularly in the Welch case. Custer County's depleted finances again caused Porter's office to decline further prosecution.[45]

County attorney Thomas J. Porter was the prosecutor for the three murder trials and secured the confession and testimony of Richard Dixon. However, the Geddes trials brought Porter more trouble than he bargained for, as the prosecutorial costs nearly bankrupted Custer County. When the Montana Supreme Court overturned the convictions of George Geddes and Tom Welch, Porter declined to retry them. Despite prosecuting Regina, Porter later served as her attorney in proceedings against George Geddes. PHOTOGRAPH COURTESY OF THE RANGE RIDERS MUSEUM, MILES CITY.

The supreme court's opinion revealed the State's extensive reliance on the testimony of Richard Dixon. It is worth noting that in the racialized frontier West, it is suprising that

[45] The *Little Whirlwind* cases also contributed to the strained county finances. "She's a Free Woman," *Billings Weekly Gazette,* Jun. 21, 1898, 1. Quoting the Montana Supreme Court opinion in the Geddes case: "Section 2089 of the Penal Code provides as follows: 'A conviction cannot be had on the testimony of an accomplice, unless he is corroborated by other evidence, which in itself and without the aid of the testimony of the accomplice, tends to connect the defendant with the commission of the offense; and the corroboration is not sufficient if it merely shows the commission of the offense or the circumstances thereof." *State v. George Geddes; State v. Welch.* Quoting the Montana Supreme Court in the Welch case: "We are indeed compelled to believe that the attorneys prosecuting, in their strong zeal to convict, were unconsciously disposed to regard as inadmissible much evidence which it was clearly the right of the defendant to lay before the jury." *State v. Welch.* "Cases Dismissed," *Billings Weekly Gazette,* Mar. 10, 1899, 1.

testimony from a Black man and an admitted killer convinced the prosecutor's office, two juries, mulitple newspaper reporters, and large swaths of the public to believe in the elaborate murder conspiracy led by an upper-class white man with a wife and three young children. The confessed killer, identified by the victim's dying statement, had every motivation to mitigate his position by deflecting responsibility. One defense witness testified that Dixon himself was violently upset at Brown's rumor-mongering, suggesting a more straightforward motivation for the killer. George Geddes' character seems pivotal, too. There are no trial witnesses or newspaper accounts representing George Geddes as a good neighbor or a particularly honorable man. His supposed wealth was the only positive quality that is described in any detail.[46]

Race impacted this case in ways other than press coverage. The killer viewed his circumstances fatalistically and seemed resigned to his powerlessness once he fully confessed. The prosecution manipulated this to some degree. Historically, Montana has been home to smaller numbers of African Americans compared to other states. Miles City had one of the smaller Black populations in the state. Trial testimony suggests that Dixon's initial confession may have been motivated by fear of being lynched by a mob. Tom Welch himself expressed racial animosity toward Dixon, stating, "I can't say that I have any particular hostilities to [African Americans], but I'm rather prejudiced, I believe. I have known some good [African Americans], and some bad." There is little evidence that Regina or George Geddes themselves had much racial animosity. Despite his bluster, George Geddes was loathe to get his own hands dirty when it came to the murder. Because of the whipping, George knew he would be suspected in Winnie Brown's killing. To counter this, Geddes drew on a Black man and a mixed-race man to target Brown in at least two attempts. The use of non-white but trustworthy agents to perform the deed may have been a deliberate ploy

[46] Examples of racialization in the Geddes cases include the press treatment of Dixon and Welch, George Geddes' use of Dixon and Welch for his dirty work, and Regina Geddes' alleged sexual habits. For discussions of race in the frontier West, see Anthony Wood, *Black Montana: Settler Colonialism and the Erosion of the Racial Frontier, 1877–1930* (Lincoln: Univ. of Nebraska Press, 2021), 69-135; and Willam Loren Katz, *The Black West* (Garden City, NY: Doubleday Books, 1971), 281-304. Regarding racialism and legal history in the West, see Katrina Jagodinsky and Pablo Mitchell, eds., *Beyond Borders of the Law: Critical Legal Histories of the North American West* (Lawrence: Univ. of Kansas Press, 2018), 1-40. *State v. Welch*. In one instance, Dixon himself defended George against the charge of being drunk and quarrelsome. Describing an earlier Christmas dinner where Mrs. D'Arcy (Regina's sister) made such an accusation, Dixon testified, "I says that wasn't if people would let him alone." *State v. Welch*.

by George and Regina to obfuscate their obvious motivation in the subsequent investigation.[47]

Richard Dixon pleaded guilty to second-degree murder and received a thirty-year prison sentence. He was paroled in 1911. After his release in 1899, Thomas Welch found work at the Anaconda smelter. When he died soon after in 1901, the *Anaconda Standard* marked his passing: "The death of Welch has brought to public notice the fact that there is a possibility of [George] Geddes being tried again." According to the *Standard,* George had reason for concern: "It is stated upon pretty reliable authority that Geddes' wife has turned against him and would be willing to tell all she knew about one of the blackest crimes that ever disgraced Eastern Montana.[48]

By that time, George Geddes had deserted his family and fled to the British colony of New Zealand. Before he left, he pressured Regina "to sign a deed conveying a valuable piece of ranch property. She had brought suit to have this conveyance set aside and will probably sue her husband for separate maintenance and support," the *Anaconda Standard* reported. "At any rate, she is credited with making a number of sensational disclosures that, if substantiated in court, would go hard with her husband regardless of the law in regard to a woman testifying against her husband." Regina Geddes' attorney for these new actions against her soon-to-be ex-husband was none other than T.J. Porter, the man who prosecuted her four years before. George had apparently "inherited a large fortune from his godfather, George Smith, banker at Edinborough, Scotland." Difficulties extraditing Geddes

[47] Dixon was well aware of the possibility that he might be hung, by official or unofficial means. "My neck is my own," he told prosecutors when he told his full story. *State v. George Geddes*. Wood, *Black Montana,* 35. Wood identifies the African American population of Miles City in 1910 at sixty. He also states that the entire African American population in Montana in 1890 was 1,490 individuals. *State v. Welch.* Welch's racial animosity was also specifically applied to Dixon: "I would like to civilize that [African American] by kicking his shins and knocking him around." Both quotes can be found in *State v. Welch.* The part-Indian Welch's self-described antipathy to African Americans was not unheard of. Peggy Pascoe describes anti-miscegenation laws targeting those of African descent in the Indian Territory by the Cherokees and the Chickasaw Nation. See Pascoe, *What Comes Naturally,* 20-21. Available evidence suggests quite the contrary, even outside of Regina's alleged relationship with Dixon. The trial testimony contains numerous references to Elizabeth Young Kelly, an older African American woman who married a white man and lived in Miles City at the time. The Geddeses often stayed at the Kelly residence while in Miles City. Custer County historian Johnnie Lockett Thomas, herself African American, stated in a 2008 history forum blog post that Elizabeth Kelly was a known friend to the Geddeses and may have even initially adopted the Geddes children after the trials. milescity.com (History and Genealogy/the 92nd/For Johnnie). There is evidence of George occasionally, but not exclusively, using the racist nickname Richard Dixon was known by.

[48] "Got Thirty Years," *Billings Weekly Gazette,* Jul. 12, 1898, 1. "Dixon, Richard" entry index card, Montana state prison records, SMF 36, MHS; "Recalls an Almost Forgotten Tragedy," *Anaconda Standard,* May 30, 1901, 11.

and obtaining witnesses, some who had died or moved out of Montana, scuttled any possible retrial of the Brown murder. George Geddes remarried for a short time in Australia. He deserted his second wife in 1910, returning to the United States. He is listed in the 1910 census as living with his father in New York. George died of unknown causes in California in 1912.[49]

Following these sensational trials, the legend of the Geddes murder conspiracy grew. The coulee where Richard Dixon waited for the Brown boys has been unofficially known by a racist slur ever since. In 1986, Wally McRae, Montana's popular cowboy poet, published a poem condemning Regina Geddes and her associates. The three trials, *State vs. George Geddes, State vs. Tom Welch,* and *State vs. Regina Geddes,* demonstrate the impact that ideologies of gender and race held in jury trials and the criminal justice system in the frontier American West. The Black killer, who turned state's evidence and confessed, served the longest prison sentence. A jury exonerated the white mother, who, according to Dixon, directed him to murder Brown and then hid the evidence. Separate juries convicted the other two male members of the conspiracy, neither of whom served out their sentences due to the court's reversal of their convictions. Over time, the actual circumstances of the crime mixed with that of other tales, becoming blurred into a self-congratulatory morality tale, if it was remembered at all. The truth, in this case, was even stranger than the fiction.[50]

The saddest part of this extraordinary tale belongs to Winnie Brown and his family. Winnie Brown certainly did not deserve to be whipped, nor die from a painful gut shot. He was a poor twenty-one-year-old who was spreading rumors, and neither class nor gossip justifies torture or murder. His family went through the debacle of testifying in three trials only to see the lone man who took any responsibility pay for his crime. The Geddeses believed they were entitled to their lifestyle, and it is telling that they held the life of lower-class Winnie Brown in such low regard. Winnie was eventually buried in a small plot along today's Lay Creek/

[49] "Recalls an Almost Forgotten Tragedy," *Anaconda Standard,* May 30, 1901, 11. With regard to George Smith's estate, see Alice E. Smith, *George Smith's Money: A Scottish Investor in America* (Madison: The State Historical Society of Wisconsin, 1966), 169, 171. There is no evidence that George Geddes himself inherited anything from George Smith. His father, Peter Geddes, was the recipient of $100,000 from Smith's estate. Given Peter Geddes' previously existing fortune, it is possible that Peter promised his son a portion of Smith's legacy. *New South Wales Police Gazette* (Sydney, Australia), Aug. 10, 1910. *Thirteenth Census of the United States,* 1910 (NARA microfilm publication T624, 1,178 rolls), Records of the Bureau of the Census, RG 29, NARA, Washington, D.C.; California, U.S. Death Index 1905-1939, Surnames E-L, Ancestry.com.

[50] Patty Kluver, "History of Rosebud County," *They Came and They Stayed: Rosebud County History* (Bilings: Western Printing and Lithography, 1977), v-vi; McRae, "Regina Geddes," 34-35.

After his death, Winnie Brown was buried in Custer County. Winnie's death was a tragedy; a poor young man killed to soothe the wounded ego of a remittance man with a brutal streak. Only one of the conspirators served any meaningful prison time, the admitted killer. Winnie's brother, Clarence Brown, who was with Winnie at the time of Dixon's attack and his death, was eventually buried alongside his brother, and they were later joined by their mother. The small burial ground is locally known as the Brown Cemetery. PHOTOGRAPH BY SHANE DUNNING.

Greenleaf Road. He was joined by his brother Clarence and his mother. Today, the Brown cemetery contains only those three graves with no individual markers.

NOTES ON CHAPTER 32:

- This article was published in the Winter 2022 edition of *Montana, the Magazine of Western History.* A related sidebar article (Chapter 34 in this collection) was also published in that edition.

- There was an error in Footnote 38 that was published in the original *MMWH* article and is corrected here. The original note stated that "Mary Goetz Johnson, divorced her husband when Regina was fifteen, based on abandonment." The corrected version states an uglier truth about Regina's upbringing: that her mother divorced her husband when *Mary* (not Regina) was fifteen. Regina would have been an infant when her father abandoned her mother.

"The Geddes Murder Trials" won the 2024 Wrangler Award for Outstanding Magazine Article from the National Cowboy Hall of Fame and Western Heritage Museum. This image shows author Shane Dunning holding his award in April 2024. This image and caption were not included in the original *MMWH* article. PHOTOGRAPH BY JERRY HYMER.

An elevated view of Forsyth, 1904. Regina's infamy followed her after the murder trials ended. Divorced and left destitute, she relinquished custody of her children. Her attempts at a new lease on life landed her in Forsyth, Montana, where she started a brothel and attempted to stay out of the public spotlight. PHOTOGRAPH BY BY L.A. HUFFMAN, COURTESY OF THE MONTANA HISTORICAL SOCIETY, 981-796.

34

Whose Twenty Is This?
The Final Bow of Regina Geddes

Abandoned by her husband, Regina released parental rights to all three of her children. Her name returned to the papers again in 1901, this time in Forsyth while operating a brothel. Regina had been left destitute when George fled to the antipodes to avoid a retrial and spend his new inheritance unhindered by family obligations. Forsyth was the seat of the newly formed Rosebud County. The new county seat was serviced by a single newspaper, the *Forsyth Times,* until 1901. Ira Cole, the paper's longtime editor and publisher, was a zealous Republican and welcomed the first batch of predominantly Republican county officials. As Forsyth grew, the *Times* soon had competition. Beginning in February 1901, the *Rosebud County News* began countering the partisanship of

its competitor with editorials and articles. The contrast between the two papers was never clearer than when Undersheriff W.H. Lyndes tried to shake down Regina Geddes.[1]

On September 12, 1901, the *Rosebud County News* emblazoned the headline "Courts to be Eliminated" across its front page.

> *Sometime early in August Mrs. Geddes received a visit from Undersheriff W.H. Lyndes and was apprised of the fact that she was expected to pay a fine. No papers were served, no returns made to any court—no costs included, but in exchange for the twenty dollars she was given the following receipt:*
>
> > *Forsyth, Mont., August 2, 1901.*
> > *Received for Mrs. G. Geddes, et al., Twenty Dollars as fine for herself and two girls for the month of August 1901.*
> >
> > *W.H. Lyndes, Deputy Sheriff. $20.*[2]

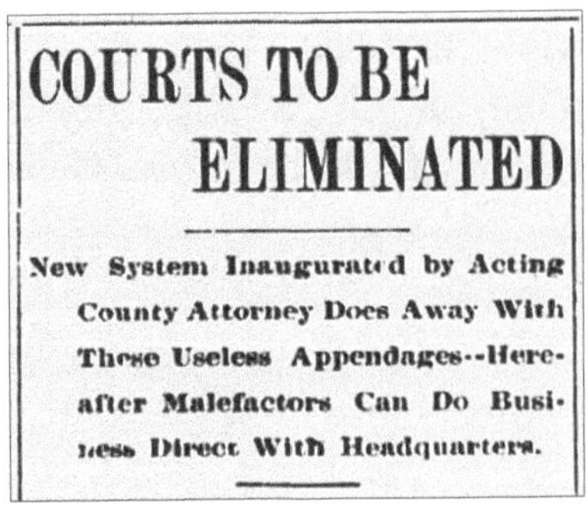
COURTS TO BE ELIMINATED

New System Inaugurated by Acting County Attorney Does Away With These Useless Appendages--Hereafter Malefactors Can Do Business Direct With Headquarters.

Right: With this page one headline, the *Rosebud County News* began a sarcasm-filled series of articles and editorials that lambasted the corruption of the newly elected Rosebud County justice officials. From the September 12, 1901, edition of the *Rosebud County News.* This image and caption were not included in the original *MMWH* article.

---

1 "One of the recent 'industries' acquired by Forsyth with the past year is a house of ill-repute owned by one Regina Geddes, a woman widely known in this end of the state. Mrs. Geddes' maison du joie is located north of Marcey's warehouse and immediately under the eyes of the county attorney's and sheriff's offices." "Courts to be Eliminated," *Rosebud County News* (Forsyth), Sep. 12, 1901, 1; "Geddes Case Again," *Rosebud County News,* Jun. 6, 1901, 4; Rosebud County Bicentennial Committee, "Publishing in Rosebud County," *They Came and They Stayed: Rosebud County History* (Billings: Western Printing and Lithography, 1977), 365-66. *Rosebud County News,* Feb. 28, 1901, 4. In its initial editorial, the *Rosebud County News* claimed to be non-partisan. "Believing that a non-partisan paper that will direct its efforts to the general good of the community rather than wielding the cudgel for any political clique or clan will meet with the united support and approval of the people of Rosebud county, the News will endeavor to steer clear of any entangling political alliances and whatever criticisms it may make editorially will be done in a spirit of fairness and impartiality." In the federal elections of 1902 and 1904, the *Rosebud County News* advocated voting a straight Democratic ticket. *Rosebud County News,* Oct. 30, 1902, 1; Oct. 27, 1904, 1; Coincidentally, Undersheriff W. H. Lyndes was one of the jurors in the Tom Welch case in Miles City. *State v. Welch.*

2 "Courts to be Eliminated," *Rosebud County News,* Sep. 12, 1901, 1.

The enterprising deputy had not selected his shakedown victim with sufficient care, as Regina Geddes demanded a receipt for this extraordinary transaction. She began voicing her displeasure at this extortion and displayed the evidence. Under Montana's 1895 penal codes, running a house of prostitution was a misdemeanor, but rarely enforced. Extortion was also a misdemeanor; however, enforcing this law against a corrupt sheriff's deputy was unlikely.[3]

Further detailing the incompetence and corruption of the deputy, the receipt was apparently in the handwriting of the acting county attorney, J.C. Lyndes, the deputy's brother. After several weeks, the undersheriff finally turned the money over to the county treasurer. An ill-timed effort was then made to put the matter on the docket of Rosebud County's court system. Justice of the Peace Cassius Gates was in poor health and could not supervise the clerical work of his court. Under the direction of acting county attorney Lyndes, the order charging Geddes with operating a house of ill-fame, Geddes' guilty plea, the fine of $20, and payment were finally recorded, along with supposed court costs of an additional $2.50. This irregularity was so glaring that Judge Gates denied receiving any court costs and refused to sign the order. Gates resigned a few days later and died within the month.[4]

For several weeks, the *Rosebud County News* torched the sheriff's department, the county attorney's office, and the court for their grift and incompetence. The paper relished embarrassing the Republican officeholders. In contrast, the *Forsyth Times* did not print a single word regarding the money throughout the controversy. The only officeholder the *Rosebud County News* deemed sympathetic was the county treasurer, Thomas W. Longley. His plight was yet another reason to eviscerate the sheriff's office. The upstart paper reached its sarcastic peak with a screed titled "Whose Twenty is This?"

> *County Treasurer Longley has a twenty-dollar bill with a history and is wondering who owns it. The rightful owner can, on proving his or her claim, recover the same. The twenty came to his office in the routine of business and although the county has no claim whatever on it, he was obliged*

[3] Quoting the article: "And what is more to the point, no entries were made on any docket until after the news was noised about by Mrs. Geddes herself that she had paid a fine. The receipt, which appears to be in the handwriting of J.C. Lyndes, acting county attorney, places the responsibility for the transaction." "Courts to be Eliminated," *Rosebud County News*, Sep. 12, 1901, 1; Wilbur Fisk Sanders, ed., *The Complete Codes and Statutes of the State of Montana* (Jul. 1, 1895), IV:§566-57; IV:§914-23

[4] "Courts to be Eliminated," *Rosebud County News*, Sep. 12, 1901, 1; "Cass Gates is Dead" *Rosebud County News*, Sep. 26, 1901, 1.

to accept it and receipt therefore. It is the same twenty that was collected from Mrs. Geddes by a deputy sheriff at the instance of the county attorney. The twenty in question reposed peacefully in the pockets of one of these gentlemen for over a month and might have been there yet but for the indiscretion of the former owner who told of it later. The money was then turned over to the treasurer as "fine collected" and that's the way it stands now. As no case has ever been instituted against Mrs. Geddes and no fines of this nature ever imposed on her, it is evident that the officers had no right to collect this money. But having collected it they were equally anxious to be rid of it and so unloaded it on the treasurer. And now it is cluttering up the books of the county treasurer—a maverick twenty with no one to father it. It threatens to be as homeless and friendless a waif as the thirty thousand turned in by Fred Whiteside during the Clark-Daly feud.[5]

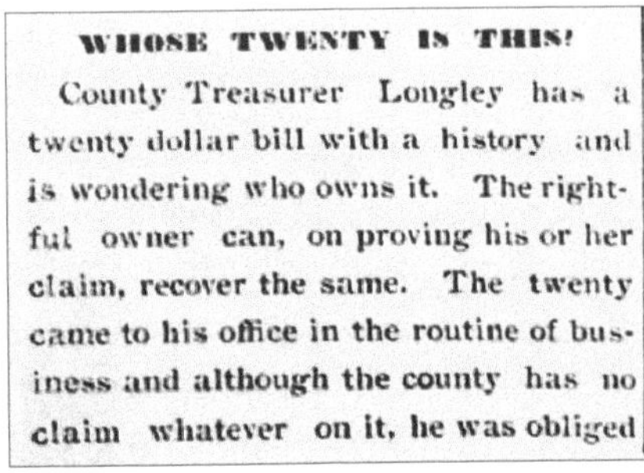
WHOSE TWENTY IS THIS!

County Treasurer Longley has a twenty dollar bill with a history and is wondering who owns it. The rightful owner can, on proving his or her claim, recover the same. The twenty came to his office in the routine of business and although the county has no claim whatever on it, he was obliged

The *Rosebud County News* editorial headline for its October 17, 1901, edition asked the question spawning this article's title. This image and caption were not included in the original *MMWH* article.

A week after this editorial, the *Rosebud County News* finally let the matter die. Within five years, Forsyth again became a one-paper town when Ira Cole bought and closed his competitor.[6]

This later career of Regina Geddes blended with recollections of the Brown murder trial in the minds of the local populace, but also highlights how she struggled after her acquittal. Multiple renditions of her story exist with distortions traceable to either of these incidents. Most of these morality tales claim that Regina operated a "sporting house" in Miles City, and that Winnie Brown's rumor-mongering related to her profession. In Regina Geddes' Forsyth escapades, she again shows a remarkable determination to survive her circumstances. Her reputation, one of the main motives of the Brown murder, had been permanently

5 "Whose Twenty is This?" *Rosebud County News*, Oct. 17, 1901, 4.

6 "Without solicitation of its contemporary up the line [*Forsyth Times*] the NEWS takes this means of serving notice on the *Times* that it has 'ceased firing' in order that 'Uncle' Hiram's boys may let the Lyndes out of the cage and 'make clear' through their medium, that 'twenty dollar deal.'" *Rosebud County News*, Oct. 31, 1901, 4. *Rosebud County News*, Mar. 15, 1906, 4

shattered during the trials. In 1899, the Montana Supreme Court ordered her husband released. That same year, George's wealthy godfather died. By all accounts, 1899 should have seen Regina's triumph. Instead, George abandoned her and their children, leaving her destitute. Following this incident, however, Regina disappeared from the spotlight. She remained in Forsyth until at least 1903, relocated and ran a boardinghouse in Boise, Idaho, around 1908, and followed her children through to adulthood as they eventually moved to the Portland, Oregon, area. She married Charles Griffiths and died in 1957 at the age of eighty-two. Regina outlived all her enemies and died in blessed obscurity, far away from the memory of Winnie Brown.[7]

NOTES ON CHAPTER 34:

→ This was a short "sidebar" for the main Geddes articles (hence the "two-and-a-half" articles referenced in this book's introduction). It was published in the same Winter 2022 edition of *Montana, the Magazine of Western History.* ←

[7] Arch Kelly, "Old Trails Retraveled: Part Two, in *Faded Hoofprints, Bygone Dreams,* ed. Maude Beach (Broadus, MT: Powder River Historical Society, 1989), 170-171. Kluver, "History of Rosebud County," v-vi. George Geddes was not the first of Regina's husbands to abandon her. Regina's first husband was John F. Burke, whom she married in 1890. Burke abandoned Regina less than a year later. "Wants a Divorce," *Helena Independent-Record,* Apr. 10, 1892, 5. The divorce was granted based on desertion in September 1892. "Burke vs Burke," *Helena Independent-Record,* Sep. 4, 1892, 5. Within three weeks of the divorce, she married George Geddes. *Helena Independent-Record,* Sept. 23, 1892, 5. The last indication of Regina Geddes in Forsyth (1903) was when she charged a man with assault. Mrs. Geddes' alleged assailant was arrested by Undersheriff Lyndes. The incident was documented in "Forsyth Notes," *Butte Miner,* May 3, 1903, 3. For Regina Geddes in Boise, Idaho, see "Chinese Laundryman Gets into Trouble," *Idaho Daily Statesman* (Boise), Mar. 28, 1908, 5. The referenced laundryman did not adequately perform paid laundry services for one of Mrs. Geddes' boarders. Regina complained and the laundryman's subsequent interactions with the local police were not well received. For Regina (Geddes) Griffths' obituary, see "Resident of County Dies," *The Columbian* (Vancouver, WA), May 28, 1957. The date of her marriage to Charles M. Griffiths is unknown, but she is listed as his wife in the 1930 Census. *Fifteenth Census of the United States,* 1930 (T626, 2,667 rolls), Records of the U.S. Bureau of the Census, NARA, Washington, D.C. Charles Griffths died in 1938. Ancestry.com, *Washington, U.S., Death Records,* 1883-1960 [database online] (Provo, UT: Ancestry.com Operations Inc., 2008); original data: various county death registers [microfilm], Washington State Archives, Olympia, Washington.

An artist's rendering of what the Moorhead Dam may have looked like had it been built. The view is looking generally south, with the main valley of the Powder River stretching off on the upper right.
THE IMAGE IS TAKEN FROM THE DEFINITIVE PLAN REPORT (VOLUME I) MOORHEAD UNIT—MONTANA, BY THE U.S. BUREAU OF RECLAMATION.

35

MOORHEAD: A DIVIDED MONTANA LOSES

In two previous columns, I described the unsuccessful effort to build a dam on the Powder River three miles south of Moorhead during the 1940s. My first column outlined the general history of the project as the Reclamation Bureau prepared for the structure's construction. An initial congressional appropriation of $900,000 (in 1947) included the creation of a base camp for engineers and workers. My second column described how the opposition, based primarily in Wyoming, organized themselves and utilized the political power of Senator John C. O'Mahoney to scuttle the project. Key to this opposition were the actions of the Kendrick Cattle Company and its President, Manville Kendrick. This third column will detail how division among Montana interests prevented the creation of a united effort necessary to counter, if not overcome, Wyoming's opposition to the Moorhead Dam.

Support for Moorhead north of the Wyoming border was relatively easy to find. Early advocates like Broadus Mayor Ashton Jones testified before several congressional committees. Broadus resident A.O. Pemberton organized "Ranchers for Moorhead" and constantly communicated with Montana's congressional delegation regarding the project. Economic development advocates such as the Chamber of Commerce in Broadus and Miles City publicly expressed support.

It is essential to understand that the initial purpose of the Moorhead Dam was flood control. Indeed, its initial $900,000 appropriation was part of an overall effort of the Truman Administration to reduce flooding across the entire Missouri River drainage. Broadus had been victimized by a catastrophic flood of the Powder River in 1923 and several more minor floods in other years. Dramatic flooding in Truman's home state of Missouri the previous year (1947) gave the Reclamation Bureau a great deal of political momentum during the first phase of the Moorhead debate. One of the opposition's most useful criticisms painted the Reclamation Bureau as a bunch of undemocratic idealists hell-bent on constructing their engineering ambitions over the local populace. Wyoming's unity and political heft in opposition were initially deployed to counter the Reclamation Bureau's bureaucratic momentum. The commissioner of the Bureau later recalled:

> *Wyoming citizens, including Manville Kendrick, present heir and head of the Kendrick Land and Cattle Company, founded by his father, the late United States Senator Kendrick of Wyoming, stormed into the senate appropriations committee when under my commissionership, a budget for the Moorhead construction was presented and blasted the project asserting it would flood their best Powder River Wyoming bottom lands for benefits only reaped downstream in Montana.*
>
> *Fascinated listeners included Senator Joseph O'Mahoney of Wyoming, then acting chairman of the appropriation subcommittee. The senator came to Washington originally as a protege of the late Senator Kendrick, labored in Senator Kendrick's office, and naturally is not indifferent to Wyoming and Kendrick views.*

Wyoming's disproportional political influence was successfully able to stall the Bureau's momentum. Dams and reservoirs, however, are not the product of a single year's effort. If Moorhead supporters could mount a similarly effective advocacy effort, it was thought, the project conceivably could still move forward.

To facilitate such advocacy, the Reclamation Bureau made the fateful decision to make significant changes to the Moorhead project. It tripled its requested budget, and what was a 300,000-acre-feet structure built for flood control suddenly became a 1.1 million-acre-feet irrigation dam costing over $20 million. Adding irrigation to the dam's function tripled the reservoir's size, as this change was deemed necessary to provide water to potential customers above and below the dam site. This new proposal quickly backfired by creating significant and vocal opposition along the Powder River in Montana. Specifically, many Powder River residents balked at creating an irrigation district limiting them to 160 acres, considerably less than many of their existing ranches.

Moorhead advocates claimed that they could get the 160-acre limit waived, but the damage had been done. Further analysis showed that the vast majority of the irrigation would benefit Montana, which only intensified Wyoming's opposition. The Reclamation Bureau's credibility was now openly questioned, weakening the pro-Moorhead ability to convince fence-sitters about the viability of such a controversial project.

Montana's congressional delegation during this initial period included Senators James E. Murray (D) and Zales Ecton (R), along with Congressmen Mike Mansfield (D) and Wesley D'Ewart (R). While all these politicians supported the construction of the Moorhead Dam, they could not match the vehement opposition from the Wyoming delegation. Complicating matters for these Montana politicians was the behavior of some of their constituents. The amount of correspondence from Montana in opposition to the project was considerable and often blunt.

A portrait of Montana Senator James E. Murray, courtesy of the Truman Presidential Library. Murray was a Montana Senator from 1934 to 1961.

One Moorhead couple questioned the Reclamation Bureau's priorities in a letter to Senator Murray, throwing in a patriotic plea regarding the new war in Korea:

> *Can't we control the Reclamation Bureau? Have they gained such power as to spend $20,000,000 on their dream projects when the government says atomic bombs are too costly to spend in Korea? If we need tanks, bombs, and guns to save our boys in war, we are asked to buy bonds, pay higher taxes and send our sons to war, is it too much to ask the Reclamation Bureau to lend the $20,000,000 to help? May God help us if we allow the Reclamation Bureau to spend one cent that will help save one boy's life for the future.*

Wyoming Senator O'Mahoney successfully blocked any movement on the project by including an amendment explicitly prohibiting Moorhead Dam funds in the Bureau's yearly appropriation bills. By 1949, the Reclamation Bureau threw in the towel. "The Bureau of Reclamation has no desire nor intention of building Moorhead Dam, or any project for that matter if it appears to be contrary to the desires of the majority of the people whose lives and properties will be affected," wrote Commissioner Michael Strauss to Senator Murray.

To counter the Bureau's pessimism regarding popular support for the project, Broadus Mayor Ashton Jones presented a series of four petitions to Senator Murray and others. These separate petitions included ones by Powder River residents subject to the irrigation, another from landowners who previously opposed the dam but now supported it, a third from Broadus residents supporting the dam for flood control, and a final petition from Powder River County residents not living in the affected valley but supportive of the dam. The effort was not enough to convince lawmakers.

The last semi-serious attempt to construct Moorhead came in 1955 when the Reclamation Bureau under the Eisenhower Administration floated a new plan for the Moorhead Dam, which now included a power plant at the spillway's base. The estimated cost of this structure was over $35 million. Michael Strauss, Reclamation Bureau Commissioner during the Truman Administration, advised Senator Murray that:

> *While I believe that, like whisky, all reclamation is good and some is better, nobody believes the Moorhead project is the best, or that it has much chance of survival in existent climates. If consulted, I would suggest the Montana delegation and Senior Senator let a good head of steam build up in the state for Moorhead (and it has not built up yet) before leaping into the leadership for this project, which is, at best marginal.*

NOTES ON CHAPTER 35:

— This column first appeared in the *Powder River Examiner's* February 6, 2023, edition.

ABOUT THE AUTHOR

PHOTOGRAPH BY MIRANDA MINOW OF MGM IMAGES IN BROADUS, MT.

Shane Dunning writes local history for the *Powder River Examiner* in Broadus, Montana, and for his personal website, www.redshalereflections.com. After a long career in healthcare administration, he now specializes in the history of northeast Wyoming and southeast Montana. In 2022, the Western Writers of America awarded Shane the Spur Award for Best Short Non-Fiction for "The Right Man to Do a Wrong Thing: Charlie Thex, the Bear Creek Sheep Raid and the Primacy of Fear." The National Cowboy Hall of Fame and Western Heritage Museum awarded him the 2024 Wrangler Award for Best Magazine Article for "The Geddes Murder Trials: Race, Gender and Murder-for-Hire in Eastern Montana's Criminal Justice System." Both of these articles were published in *Montana, the Magazine of Western History*, the official journal of the Montana Historical Society. Shane has earned degrees from the University of Wyoming and the University of Oklahoma and currently resides in Birney, Montana.